Lady Gaga
and the Remaking
of Celebrity Culture

Lady Gaga
and the Remaking of Celebrity Culture

Amber L. Davisson

McFarland & Company, Inc., Publishers

Jefferson, North Carolina, and London

Library of Congress Cataloguing-in-Publication Data

Davisson, Amber L.
   Lady Gaga and the remaking of celebrity culture / Amber L.
Davisson.
      p.   cm.
   Includes bibliographical references and index.

   ISBN 978-0-7864-7475-2
   softcover : acid free paper ∞

   1. Lady Gaga — Criticism and interpretation.   2. Celebrities.
I. Title.
ML420.L185D38 2013
782.42164092 — dc23   2013023674

British Library cataloguing data are available

On the cover: Lady Gaga at the MTV Video Music AID Japan on
June 25, 2011 (Associated Press/Itsuo Inouye).

Manufactured in the United States of America

*McFarland & Company, Inc., Publishers
   Box 611, Jefferson, North Carolina 28640
   www.mcfarlandpub.com*

Table of Contents

Acknowledgments

Over the course of this project, I have been fortunate to have numerous friends and colleagues offer both insight and encouragement. The project has benefited greatly from a supportive network of associates at universities across the country. I would like to express my very great appreciation to Hillary Jones. She was the first person to realize that what I thought was an article was actually a book. I am grateful for the number of times she told me I had to finish my book because she wanted to read it. Also, I would like to offer a special thanks to Shira Chess, who has been an incredible source of support, keeping me on top of things and productive throughout this process. I would like to acknowledge the help of friends who had been through the publishing process and helped me navigate the completion of my first project. Paul Booth and David Karpf have both been generous in sharing their experiences.

This work was made possible by the incredibly supportive community of scholars I work with at Willamette University. I owe a debt of gratitude to all my colleagues in the Rhetoric & Media Studies Department at Willamette University: Robert Trapp, Catherine Collins, Jeanne Clark, Cindy Koenig-Richards, Courtney Dillard, Christopher Swift, and Alexandra Nutter-Smith. You have all listened to me tell many stories about Lady Gaga over the past two years. Thank you for being so supportive of my one-track mind. I want to express a special thanks to my colleague Una Kimokeo-Goes, who directed me to the Lady Gaga interview that started me down this path. Her direction, support, and friendship made this project possible. Outside of my department, I wish to acknowledge the support of my Willamette colleagues David Gutterman and Stanislav Vysotsky. I appreciate how generous both of you have been with your time and your words of encouragement.

As a professor, I have been fortunate to have many opportunities to share the ideas for this project with my classes. My students have continually been a great source of feedback and moral support. A special thanks to students in my Gender & Communication and Rhetorical Criticism courses. These classes asked great questions and pushed me to think about my subject in new ways. In particular, I owe a debt of gratitude to my students Alex Lopez, Tiara Christopher, Stephen Yamada, and Eoin Sinclair for their humor and encouragement. I wish to acknowledge the opportunities provided by Adam Torgerson through his wonderful program: Willamette U Think. Adam, I appreciate the space you provide for Willamette professors to take their ideas out of the classroom and into the Salem community. Additional thanks go out to the Willamette Institute for Continued Learning. I am grateful for the chance to present my ideas, and the insights that came out of that experience. I owe a special thanks to two of my former students. Angela Leone has provided invaluable commentary and feedback at every stage of this project. Thank you for continually pushing me to be a better writer and a better scholar. Kayla Cothrun stepped in during the final weeks of completing the manuscript to help me format citations and finish preparing the manuscript. Kayla, I am grateful for both your time and enthusiasm during the completion of the book.

I owe many thanks to friends and family for their interest and support as I completed this research. My mom has been a constant source of encouragement. I am grateful to my cousin Crystal Bogart for her enthusiasm for my scholarly interests. I am very fortunate to have a grandmother who is an author. Watching her write and publish books has taught me a lot about the craft of writing. Thank you to my friends Katie Booth and Anthony Jones. You have both been quick with a smile, willing to listen and offer ideas.

This book would not have been possible without the support of my two constant companions. Macey's continued presence, reminding me to take breaks and go outside, makes the work I do all the more enjoyable. My deepest thanks go to my loving and supportive partner, Chris Wood. Thank you for your comments, your edits, the many times you have been a sounding board, and, more important, for cheering me through this entire process. All of my work is more fun with the two of you in my life.

Introduction

I had new material and I had on this amazing outfit. So I sat down, cleared my throat and waited for everyone to go quiet. It was a bunch of frat kids from the West Village and I couldn't get them to shut up. I didn't want to start singing while they were talking, so I got undressed. There I was, sitting at the piano in my underwear. So they shut up. That's when I made a real decision about the kind of pop artist that I wanted to be. Because it was a performance art moment, there and then. You see, you can write about it now and it will sound ridiculous. But the truth is that unless you were in the audience in that very spontaneous moment, it doesn't mean anything. It's, like, she took her clothes off, so sex sells, right? But in the context of that moment, in that neighborhood, in front of that audience, I was doing something radical.[1]

This description of the birth of the Lady Gaga persona, in a Greenwich Village club called The Bitter End, gets at many of the elements that have given Stefani Germanotta her staying power as a performer. There is plenty to be said about Germanotta's musical career as Lady Gaga. Her first two albums sold a combined 8 million copies in the U.S. alone, and she's one of only two artists to have their first five singles reach number one on the *Billboard* pop song charts.[2] Still, the music alone does not explain the spectacle of Lady Gaga. In her description of this early moment, Germanotta hints at two other key elements: her relationship with the audience and her ability to recognize the way context impacts the meaning of a performance. Throughout her career as Lady Gaga, Germanotta has demonstrated a keen awareness of the way context changes communication: in concerts, online, in interviews, and in television performances. In all these spaces, she finds a way to quiet the noise and be heard. It is because of this talent that she has been crowned the Mother Monster and taken on the role of leader for a legion of fans, whom she affectionately dubs her little monsters. Just as Germanotta taking her clothes off at The Bitter End was a radical act used to capitalize on an opportune moment, her use of the monster image has been a call to revolution within the context of modern media and celebrity culture. The Lady Gaga persona allows Germanotta an outlet through which she can break boundaries as an artist. The character of Gaga creates an opportunity for a performance art project that takes on the role of monsters and celebrities in today's society and uses them to encourage fans to rethink the relationship between what the media deifies and what is vilifies.

She may have been born Stefani Joanne Angelina Germanotta, but after several years of living a 24/7 performance art piece it seems safe to say she has been thoroughly reborn as Lady Gaga. At the core of Lady Gaga's unique performance of stardom is an intimate connection with her fan community. Gaga has developed a reputation for being removed from the typical celebrity party culture. She has built her celebrity status not from associating with other celebrities but by connecting with the fan base that supports her records and shows. Her strongest public relationships are with her little monsters. Biographer Maureen Callahan has commented that unlike other young stars her age—Nicole Richie, Paris Hilton, and Lindsay Lohan, for instance—Lady Gaga has been careful to control images of her partying and her social life. She is never photographed drunkenly stumbling out of clubs.[3] This is because, as Gaga has said, she doesn't "really have a tremendous connection to the celebrity world.... My friendships are really with my fans, and that's how I really communicate. My vision is through them and through music."[4] Lady Gaga's vision is not one of separation and power dynamics but one of acceptance. In her music, her concerts, and her daily performance of self, she has articulated a message about questioning the social hierarchies and power structures that so often lead to discrimination, bullying, and self-hatred. Gaga calls on her fans to accept themselves as they are and create a space where others can feel accepted. When Oprah asked Lady Gaga what she really wanted for her fans, she said, "I want them to free themselves, and I want them to be proud of who they are.... I want them to celebrate all the things they don't like about themselves the way that I did, and to be truly happy from the inside."[5] It is in the spirit of this mission that she has continually cultivated a relationship with her fan community, to the point where she often describes them as her family: "Seeing the beautiful faces of my fans each night in the crowd is all I need. The inspiration they provide is limitless. Everything I do is for them, and as long as we have each other, nothing else matters."[6] Developing an intimate relationship with millions of fans is an ambitious project that is not easily accomplished. This book explores that mission: the ways in which Gaga has made innovations in bridging the gap between a star and their fan base, and the implications her successes have for understanding celebrity culture in a digital age.

The Social Function of Celebrities and Monsters

While mass media is responsible for greatly expanding the power and notoriety of celebrities, the existence of celebrity as a cultural phenomenon predates the vast majority of the media outlets we are familiar with today. P. David Marshall contrasts modern celebrity with its historical roots. In a mass media world, he argues, "it has become a term that announces a vulgar sense of notoriety. In English culture, it may have articulated the separation of old wealth and new wealth.... Celebrity can be thought of as a label that works to differentiate layers of the bourgeoisie."[7] Assigning someone celebrity status used to mark them as a kind of interloper in high society. It was assumed that they did not come from money but had achieved their position of power and influence by some other means. Celebrities, then just as now, were common people who had reached some level of repute that moved them up the ranks of the social order. At that time, if celebrities were famous it was a kind of local fame where everyone in a community, maybe even a larger area, had heard of them. The role of local celebrity still exists, but today true celebrity tends to require a much larger audience. David Giles explains modern celebrity "is a phenomenon associated with mass communication, specifically television and print media. All celebrities are famous."[8] A genuine celebrity, by contemporary standards, has realized fame at a level "beyond what can be achieved through mere popularity, and so it requires either a specific deed or achievement to generate publicity, or a vehicle for the spread of news."[9] The modern criterion for celebrity is media attention, which moves someone from being popular in a relatively small community to being known on a global scale.

Celebrities are traditionally the individuals who a society believes are worthy of celebration. They are people who are held up by the media as examples of what everyone should strive for; "the celebrity, in this sense, is not distant but attainable — touchable by the multitude. The greatness of the celebrity is something that can be shared and, in essence, celebrated loudly and with a touch of vulgar pride. It is the ideal representation of the triumph of the masses."[10] Richard Dyer defines a star as a member of "an elite, privileged group who yet on the one hand do not excite envy or resentment (because anyone may become one) and on the other hand have no access to real political power."[11] The narrative of the star or celebrity is that of a person who is plucked out of obscurity by some talent that makes them worthy of grand notoriety. The rise from humble beginnings often makes them loved, and accessible, because they are examples of what anyone can supposedly achieve. David Marshall describes Horkheimer and Adorno's theory of the manipulative power of celebrity culture: "The star is meant to epitomize the potential of everyone in American society. We are psychically drawn to identify with stars as ourselves. This, however, is only appearance. The dialectical reality is that the star is part of a system of false promise in the system of capital, which offers the reward of star-dom to a random few in order to perpetuate the myth of potential univer-sal success."[12] In this myth, "the mass audience is central in the definitions of individual value and worth. The celebrity embodies the ideal type of hero that emerges from the mass audience."[13] Although they lack access to real political power and are used to deceptively maintain economic inequality, stars themselves do not lack ideological significance. Dyer argues that we should not mistake celebrities' inability to make political decisions for them being ineffectual.[14] Celebrities are people "whose insti-tutional power is very limited or non-existent, but whose doings and way of life arouse a considerable and sometimes even maximum degree of interest."[15] The way a celebrity lives, and how they explain the choices they are making, demonstrates an advertised path, even if a false one, to wealth and to a better life. Media viewers and fans may take the advice seriously and be compelled to imitate the examples of people they believe have achieved something desirable. So, celebrities occupy a unique space in society. They achieve notoriety but not necessarily direct access to polit-ical power. Their power lies in the promise they hold that others can follow their path to success. A celebrity is proof that it is possible to suddenly climb the economic ranks and rise up out of obscurity. Their fame as heroes is an outlet for impacting behavior and directing the choices of others. Lady Gaga has embraced a life of what might be termed extreme celebrity, in that she chooses to live in a very public way. This has allowed her to maximize the power that comes with celebrity and use that power to articulate her own philosophy of fame.

Lady Gaga's rise to celebrity came at a unique time in celebrity culture. She entered the media spotlight after the birth of the reality star. In a 2009 interview with the *LA Times*, Janice Min, a former editor for *Us Weekly*, commented on the rise of the reality star in celebrity culture. According to Min, "Thanks to cable television, reality TV and the Internet, the whole power structure of celebrity has shifted. It's not just that Kim Kardashian is a celebrity and nobody knows why. It's her sister, her mother. Young women in particular have forged a connection with the stars of reality TV."[16] Reality television takes people into the daily lives of the glamorous and obscure, making the narrative of the path to the good life even more visible and transparent. Min argues that reality TV has generated a desire by fans to see even more of the day-to-day life of traditional celebrities. Popular media has begun to pick up on that desire and make it marketable. *Us Weekly*, for instance, includes a popular weekly segment called "Stars— They're Just Like Us," which features images of celebrities renting movies, buying groceries, and shopping for pet food.[17] According to Min, as a result of these types of images from the celebrity news media, "the whole relationship dynamic between the general population and celebrity has morphed into a belief that there's very little separating you from being like them."[18] Lady Gaga has played off this belief in a very interesting way. She chooses to live her life in a spectacular way— never being seen out of character— but she does so with the message that the way she lives could be real life. When observed outside of performances, she is still wearing the same over-the-top costumes and makeup. Whether on or offstage, Gaga is always performing and she is always aware of her audience. She embraces the way a near-constant viewership can be used to her advantage, and in this way her version of celebrity is defiant of the polarized celebrity narrative that has emerged from reality TV.

From the beginning of her career, Lady Gaga has seemed very aware of the type of power celebrities have over the public. She is consistently using her daily life and choices to make an argument. One of the most powerful aspects of this argument comes from her willingness to forgo a traditional private life and live her decisions publicly:

I believe as an artist, being private in public is at the core of the aesthetic, the message. However, I profusely lie about my personal relationships in an effort to protect that aesthetic and that message. Today people are distracted by unimportant things—like what my diet is, or who I'm fucking.... I do sometimes feel that I'm on a stage all the time, and I do feel that life is a stage for my art. When I'm dancing, singing, making breakfast. But there is a moment of freedom, when the stage disappears: when I cry. On stage, off stage, alone or with someone. There's something very honest about that. It has nothing to do with taking off a wig or smearing my lipstick.[19]

The way Lady Gaga articulates public and private here is critical to her larger argument. Privacy is no longer about the moments when no one is watching. As a celebrity and an artist, Gaga owns the fact that the public is almost always watching. Thus, sometimes her private life takes place publicly and her public performance continues even when no one is watching. Lady Gaga is the consummate celebrity, and she is very aware of the power in that performance.

Lady Gaga's day-to-day public performance of celebrity is an embodiment of her philosophy of fame and her message to her fans. One of the first tenets of this philosophy is that celebrity and fame are not things that happen just when the media and paparazzi are paying attention. Lady Gaga argues that a celebrity is something you just *are*, even when no one is looking. She embodies this belief by maintaining her spectacular celebrity wardrobe and appearance 24 hours a day, 7 days a week. It is common to open up a magazine and see both photos of celebrities at events and photos of celebrities "in real life." Celebrities model the move from normal person to star by switching back and forth between designer wardrobes for staged photo shoots and candid shots in a less than flattering wardrobe. The message behind these kinds of images is that celebrity life and real life are two separate things. Viewers are led to believe that, offscreen, celebrities are inelegant and live similarly to their audiences. However, Lady Gaga does not live that way. Reporters often comment, after meeting Gaga, that she is the same person in her day-to-day life as she is at any media event. According to Lizzy Goodman, a writer for *New York Magazine*, Lady Gaga "goes to the grocery store in McQueen platforms. She spends her downtime on the road practicing her new material in a silk dressing gown on the all-white piano she requests for her hotel room. She goes for a drink in a fetish policewoman's outfit. She's not playing Gaga; she is Gaga ... at least that's the concept."[20] Maureen Callahan has maintained that in the early parts of her career Gaga dressed like most young women when traveling or on a day off: jeans, T-shirt, no makeup. It was only after the British tabloids started really hounding her in 2008 that Germanotta started to perform Gaga 24/7. According to Callahan, the commitment was born out of a relationship with the media.[21] However, Gaga's propensity for outrageous fashion choices, such as wearing nothing but a leotard in public, seems to have started much earlier. Gaga is quoted in 2007, before the release of her first album, as saying that "I just feel freer without pants."[22] During her first trip to Britain in 2008, Gaga was photographed out and about in "a green leotard and not a lot more. Then she was pictured in sparkly pants, a flesh-colored top and fishnets, and to cap it all off, there was the PVC corset, fishnets, and open-toed sandals on a music television show."[23] In New York City, she has been seen buying groceries in a Stop & Shop wearing a see-through bodysuit, with just a bra and G-string underneath.[24] In 2009, in LA, she was threatened by the police for not wearing pants in public.[25] This type of behavior would be typical for a star at an awards show, a concert, or some other media event where the goal is to generate attention in the midst of a spectacle. Gaga treats media events and daily life as one and the same. As she puts it: "I am a show with no intermission."[26]

From an early age, Lady Gaga was surrounded by people who had been raised in the celebrity culture. She went to high school at Convent of the Sacred Heart on the Upper East Side. Years before she attended, Caroline Kennedy went to school there, as did Paris and Nicky Hilton. Though Gaga's time at Sacred Heart did not overlap with that of any of these big names, she has said that the school normalized a lot of upper-class conventions. The school has become a legend in New York's social scene. It is the setting for the film *Nick and Nora's Infinite Playlist*, and it is rumored that the school in *Gossip Girl* was based on this high school.[27] Lady Gaga has said of her time there: "I've always been Gaga.... It's just that all the years of schooling and being in a Catholic environment and living in a place where we were kind of told what was the right way to be, I suppressed all those eccentricities about myself so I could fit in. Once I was free, I was able to be myself. I pulled her out of me, and I found all of those things about myself that I so desperately tried to suppress for so many years."[28] Her time at Sacred Heart planted the seeds for Lady Gaga to rebel not just against the strict Catholic rules the school enforced but also against the larger social norms that came from being immersed in the upper class.

The typical celebrity narrative created by the media focuses on the average person thrust into a spectacular life. Lady Gaga treats even the average parts of her life as spectacular, creating some disruption in this narrative. Lisa Robinson, a *Vanity Fair* reporter, has interviewed Lady Gaga multiple times. During the second interview, Gaga invited Robinson to her parents' home in New York City and the performer cooked the whole meal herself. According to Robinson, Gaga looked at home — dressed in "a black lace Chanel dress, extra-high Louboutin stiletto heels, glass earrings, full makeup, and a Daphne Guinness–inspired black-and-white wig" — in her parents' kitchen, chopping a salad and making spaghetti sauce from scratch.[29] Writing about her evening in the Germanotta home, Robinson commented that "all the slicing and dicing while wearing a Chanel dress seems perfectly natural in the Gaga world. People always ask me what she's really like. This is what she's really like." The idea that Gaga wears Chanel and wigs at home does not seem that far off. She has told reporters there is "absolutely no way I would give up my wigs and hats for anything" and that she "would rather die than have my fans not see me in a pair of high heels."[30] For Gaga, these clothing choices are not arbitrary: "I'm a performance artist and use my clothing as a huge form of expression. Each piece is delicately selected to tell a story, create a feeling, fulfill a vision."[31] The Lady Gaga who shows up at awards shows wearing a fur coat made out of Kermit the Frog is the same Lady Gaga who makes dinner at home for her family wearing a black-and-white wig.

Lady Gaga uses the consistency of her image to point out the omnipresence of modern media. Gaga told a reporter in 2009, when asked about her extreme appearance, that "this isn't my 'look,' this is my life. I dress like this all the time, you're never gonna catch me at the grocery store in flip-flops."[32] The phrasing here — "catch me" — points to the fact that she was already very aware of media scrutiny and attention. Lady Gaga has commented that the constant media surveillance is not exclusive to celebrities. In an interview on *60 Minutes* with Anderson Cooper, she said that "right now, we're in a bar, right? And there's a camera right there and a camera right there.... But if I were to be sitting in this bar, and we didn't have a scheduled interview, there would still be a camera over there and over there and over there. I'm always on camera."[33] When Gaga was talking about the first set of cameras, she pointed at the television crew that was there for the interview. When she talked about the second set of cameras, she began pointing at people in the bar with cell phones. The indication is that even if she were not a recognized celebrity, the cameras would still be there all the time. Elizabeth Kate Switaj argues that with statements like this, Gaga's "theatrical actions reveal the performativity of the everyday actions of celebrities and, by extension, would-be celebrities posting apparently casual images and videos to Facebook and YouTube."[34] Where celebrity is typically something granted to a select few, Gaga's pointing to the consistency of mediation begs the question: Who chooses the few?

Lady Gaga's constant performance of celebrity has caused many reporters to raise questions about the authenticity of her identity. In 2010, she did a photo shoot for *Q Magazine* and appeared on the cover topless, cupping her breasts with her hands. This is one of several photo shoots Lady Gaga has done nude or semi-nude. She has said that photographers are constantly requesting to see her naked, under the belief that if you strip away all the makeup, ridiculously high heels, and couture clothing you will get the *real* Gaga. Lady Gaga laments that "photographers say this to me all the ... 'I want to photograph the real you.' I'm, like, 'What the hell are you looking for? I'm right here. You've seen me with no makeup. You've asked me about my drug history, my parents, my bank account.' I mean, how much more real could I be? ... This is what I'm really like. This is exactly what I'm really like."[35] In a moment of anger, she told *Q Magazine*, "you don't really wanna get to know me or photograph my soul, you want to do some version of what you already think I am and then expose something that you believe is hidden. When the truth is, me and my big fucking dick are all out there for you. But I'm not angry, I'm laughing. The joke is not on me, it's on you."[36] Gaga is derisive about media outlets' constant attempts to uncover the "real person" behind the celebrity. For Gaga, the celebrity *is* who she is. In an interview with Andrew Murfett, reporter for the *Sydney Morning Herald*, she said that "the biggest misconception about me is I'm a character or a persona.... That when the lights and cameras turn off, I turn into a pumpkin. It's simply not true. I make music and art and design all day long. Yes, I wash my face and go to sleep but when I wake up, I am always Lady Gaga."[37] This defies the typical image in the magazine where people are shown celebrities doing fabulous things—attending awards shows and taking lavish vacations—

next to images of celebrities acting "just like us." Those two sets of images together are meant to maintain the difference between a celebrity life and "real life"—the life the audience could possibly have and the life most of us are restricted to. Gaga maintains that the celebrity is not something she has been transformed into, it is the true nature of her identity.

Conversations about Gaga's relationship to the media and her true identity always seem to return to her physical appearance. Does a certain costume make her Lady Gaga? Does putting on makeup for a photo shoot transform her into a celebrity? In a lot of interviews, reporters talk about the costumes and the makeup as if they are what Gaga consists of, the implication being that without them the performance stops and she would be just herself. The focus on material symbols of wealth plays into the celebrity narrative of the everyday person transformed. Lady Gaga flips the narrative by adopting those symbols in everyday life and performing a vulnerability and naturalness in moments that would typically be understood as spectacular. In a 2011 *Harper's Bazaar* interview, Gaga commented on this: "I don't really view it as 'natural,' ... I think that artifice is the new reality. It's more about just being honest and sincere to the core of what you do. Whether I'm wearing lots of makeup or no makeup, I'm always the same person inside."[38] Lady Gaga blurs the lines between the performed self and the authentic self. She argues that the performed self is a series of choices that at first may seem like a lie but are ultimately the most authentic truths. As she later explained in an article she wrote for *V Magazine*: "I have said before that I am a master of escapism, which many attribute to my wigs, performances, and my natural inclination to be grand, but perhaps that is also a lie. Maybe I am not escaping. Maybe I am just being. Being myself."[39] In the photo shoot for *Harper's Bazaar* she was posing with minimal styling to show the "natural Gaga." She said that "there's this idea that it's all natural, but everything's been staged to look natural. It is also an invention. It's just that my inventions are different."[40] Even the natural is created and directed, and even the overdone can be a representation of self. Owning these facts gives Lady Gaga a degree of honesty that may be lacking elsewhere in media attention.

Celebrities are symbols of what is possible and they are focal points for all that is desirable. They are supposed to have a dual identity as people who are the embodiment of all that is to be desired and people who are non-performative. Society expects celebrities to fill their function on the screen and come off the screen to be *real people*: "Because stars have an existence in the world independent of their screen/'fiction' appearances, it is possible to believe ... that as people they are more real than characters in stories. This means that they serve to disguise the fact that they are just as much produced images, constructed personalities as 'characters' are."[41] As real people, they make it seem like it is possible to look perfect and airbrushed all the time. Lady Gaga has taken that performance to a new extreme; she vows to never be photographed out of her celebrity character, because she *is* her celebrity character. This makes paparazzi photos of Gaga an integral part of her performance. Marilyn Manson has commented on these photos of Gaga that he "thought they looked the way that rock stars should look, as exciting as something that Warhol or Dali would do. And I don't consider her to be similar to her contemporaries—the other girls that do pop music—simply because she knows exactly what she's doing. She's very smart, she's not selling out, she's a great musician."[42] The photos of Gaga's "real life" maintain the illusion of celebrity on and off the screen.

Gaga's narrative about truth and performance creates a sometimes uneasy relationship between the performer and the mainstream media. This is because Gaga's narrative runs counter to the typical media narrative of celebrity. As P. David Marshall explains, "in all cases, celebrities are the production locale for an elaborate discourse on the individual and individuality that is organized around the will to uncover a hidden truth" or the true person.[43] Because celebrities represent the common person transformed into one who has achieved fame, the media has a vested interest in revealing both their commonness and the characteristics that make them worthy of fame. The media presents itself as performing a public good when it tracks down the "truth" behind a celebrity performance, as if they are writing an exposé and enlightening the public to exclusive knowledge. Gaga makes this excessively difficult, because there seems to be no getting behind the performance: "[T]he excesses of her performance make apparent that she is always performing and thus always actively participating in the social constructions that allow her to purchase fame with these performances of her body."[44] Ann Powers, reporter for the *LA Times*, argues that this is part of a larger change in the relationship between individuals and the media. In the age of social media, "the split between 'real' and 'fake' seems to have closed. This isn't because the quest for authenticity has been abandoned. It's because, for artists like Gaga, fake has become what feels most real."[45] When Peter Robinson, a reporter for British entertainment magazine *NME*, did an interview with Lady Gaga and her publicist, her publicist said he gets request every day from media who want to show the world "the 'real' Lady Gaga." Gaga added, "What are they looking for?" Peter Robinson explained: "People want proof that you are a fake, we say, because if you are fake it backs up traditional ideas of what divides a plastic, manufactured pop star from an authentic alt.rocker." Robinson said in the article, after meeting Lady Gaga, "The point does stand: If you like to put your musicians into little boxes, Gaga must be deeply troubling."[46] Indeed, for no matter how close one looks, Lady Gaga's performance seems to be surprisingly consistent. The troubling aspects of Gaga's performance have evolved over time into a larger discussion about monstrosity.

Typically, monsters play on the familiar, taking things we know and making them into things we fear. Edward Ingebretsen argues that the image of the monster serves a civic function — it tells people where the boundaries are in a society and warns of the consequences for crossing those boundaries. This function makes it uniquely important that one approach the monster critically, with an eye towards what they are attempting to teach.[47] Monsters invoke terror by their very action and existence, and the violence that follows the monstrous warns viewers to keep back. What is more, the hideous appearance of monsters is meant to make people afraid to imitate them; the mutated body of monsters is taken as a consequence of their behavior.[48] Because Lady Gaga performs celebrity constantly and to such extremes, her version of celebrity often starts to look monstrous. Take, for instance, the video for "Born This Way," where Gaga performs an entire dance sequence painted with skeleton tattoos all over her body. Richard Gray II argues that in images such as this "Gaga transforms the dead body signifying the unknown, the hopeless, lifelessness, and death itself into an object of beauty. Through the zombie dance sequence, Gaga shows us that poignancy, pathos and pain ultimately lead to the discovery of the beauty found within our agonizing life experiences."[49] Lady Gaga uses a variety of techniques and performances to combine images of beauty with images of the monstrous, in order to comment on celebrity culture and also change the way one typically interprets the monster narrative.

Celebrities are held up as heroes and examples of what is possible, while monsters are cast as villains and warnings of what happens if one follows the wrong path. Lady Gaga's public performance combines the celebrity and monster, the hero and villain, to create a new message about both. Ingebretsen tells us that in addition to being warnings, monsters "are also guardians ... protecting human boundaries against those who think to test them by crossing out. Monsters warn by example: they are themselves terrible consequences."[50] When Lady Gaga appears as physically both the celebrity and the monster, she seems to be warning society of what happens when celebrity is achieved while also questioning the terrible consequences of becoming a monster. As previously discussed, Lady Gaga dresses everywhere she goes as if it is a major media event or red carpet. However, in all these appearances there is something "off" in her performance of celebrity. As Mathieu Deflum argues, "nearly every time that she wears certain clothing or makes a stylistic choice that might otherwise have been sexy, indeed, she does it in a way that is grotesque, even repulsive."[51] One example of this is Lady Gaga's ever present high heels. She often chooses heels that are so high they are awkward or make it physically impossible to walk. While high heels are typically cast as sexy and feminine, her heels may force her to stand or walk in a way that is awkward or masculine and draws attention to the unnaturalness of the shoes. Elizabeth Kate Switaj elaborates that "to the extent that Gaga's decorativeness meets the demands of normative beauty, the performative aspect of her grotesque costumes becomes more apparent. It becomes clear that she puts on the grotesque rather than being inherently grotesque."[52] Another classic example is the meat dress that Gaga wore to the MTV music awards and the meat bikini she was later photographed in for *Vogue Hommes Japan*. In both cases, the clothing was crafted to resemble a typically sexy or provocative look, while the meat made the outfit hideous to many viewers. In this case, "the meat dress thus makes the repulsive desirable and the desired object also horrifying."[53] In response to these fashion choices, biographer Maureen Callahan compares Gaga to Leigh Bowery, an eighties club promoter who often styled himself in a way that was difficult for viewers to take in.[54] Lady Gaga is not necessarily trying to look like the height of celebrity; sometimes she is intentionally embracing the bottom. As a celebrity, who is typically supposed to be held up as the goal for the average person, Gaga has constructed an image that the average person may fear.

These fashion choices are not simply faux pas made by a young star unsure how to navigate high-pressure social events. The styles that Lady Gaga wears are often described as incredibly expensive works of art. The look that Gaga portrays is both monstrous and strangely beautiful. Typically, with a monster, the collapse of social boundaries is emphasized in a way that hides the humanity behind the collapse.[55] Gaga's monstrosity flaunts the loss of our humanity. This book explores the various ways she straddles that line in her public appearances. According to David Annandale, through fashion Lady Gaga's body is repeatedly broken and pieced back together in new forms.[56] The violence and beauty represented in Gaga's public performance conflate the monster and the celebrity. Much of this gets back to the question of celebrities' public and private lives. Monsters are often portrayed as having something to hide, and they need boundaries because they are doing something unseemly that they do not want seen. Beneath the horror is something that is unacceptable and worthy of being hidden. The fear is that what celebrities hide will also be something that negates their hero status. Lady Gaga is the monster and the celebrity publicly—forcing viewers to confront their relationship to both figures.

Chapter Overviews

In recent years, several biographies of Lady Gaga have emerged that attempt to tell the truth behind the celebrity. The present work takes a slightly different approach. It is partly biographical, in that it covers many of the events of Gaga's rise to fame and her life as a celebrity. However, rather than trying to get at some kind of authentic Lady Gaga, the chapters that follow explore what can be learned from the Gaga performance. As Lady Gaga has already said, "everyone knows what my breasts look like, who I'm sleeping with, what my real hair looks like, and when I'm wearing wigs— all the information is out there.... But somehow there's an ambiguity that hovers."[57] Looking closer at the ambiguity, the relationship between her espoused philosophy and her day-to-day choices provides key insights into the way celebrity is changing in digital media environments. Much of that change relates to Gaga's use of the notion of monsters.

One of the earliest and most important narratives of Lady Gaga's career is that of the fame and the fame monster. Chapter 1 outlines these narratives and discusses how they led to the introduction of the titles "Mother Monster" and "little monsters." The chapter explores Gaga's notion of fame as shared, not belonging solely to herself. Lady Gaga has said repeatedly that being famous has nothing to do with how other people see you. It is about how you see yourself. She preaches fame as a way of life that is accessible to all. As the Mother Monster puts it, "it's a sharable fame: I want to invite you all to the party, I want people to feel a part of this lifestyle."[58] This does not mean that everyone should seek celebrity status from the media. Instead, Gaga wants "people to walk around delusional about how great they can be, and then to fight so hard for it every day that the lie becomes the truth."[59] From the early stages of her career, Gaga has modeled this philosophy, like most mothers, as someone hoping her little monsters will follow in her footsteps. Gaga's fame is about embracing the celebrity lifestyle, and it is truly monstrous, insofar as "a monster is a beast of excess, and monster stories are tales of excess."[60] To gain the type of fame Gaga is talking about, one must first battle the fame monster. The fame monster is the mainstream media's story about what is good and what is bad. It is an amalgam of all the things people are taught to fear, the cautionary tales that keeps people from claiming their own individual fame.

Gaga's use of the word "monster" has not been entirely consistent; the fame monster is a bad monster and little monsters are good monsters. Even more tangled, little monsters are Lady Gaga followers who have embraced the fame. Much of the relationship between the concepts links back to the traditional relationship between monsters and audiences: "The monster is never just an isolated individual, although certainly the rhetoric suggests, and intends, such an effect. To the contrary, the person singled out as monstrous is, already, a collusion, a prejudice, a ritual and community effort. Monsters are nominated by popular, not singular, acclaim. They only play to crowds."[61] It is in the relationship between Gaga and her fans that the distinction between good and bad monsters becomes clear. This relationship also makes the monsters numerous, and harder to destroy. Typically, "the monster story works because of the totalizing energy it releases. Locating evil in one site makes its eventual elimination that much simpler."[62] Gaga is building an army of little monsters who are everywhere and therefore much more resilient to elimination. Although

monstrosity is conceptually complex within the realm of Gaga's performance, taking on many different roles and personas, looking at the way she
has talked about the relationship between monstrosity and celebrity over
the first four years of her career allows one to disentangle some of these
relationships.

Lady Gaga's discussion of monstrosity is often a tool as well, used to
tackle other social issues. Chapter 2 looks at the way this image translates
when applied to questions of gender and drag. In particular, the chapter
examines how Gaga has used the idea of the monster to tackle sexual identities that are typically treated as deviant. In the mainstream media, "the
monster is that which inspires disgust, anxiety, and even nausea. The marginalized are the monstrous and the monstrous is marginalized. The monster, more than our fears, also represents our hatreds. Whatever makes us
lose our lunch, whether natural or supernatural, can be defined as a monster. The monster is the sickening Other."[63] Monstrosity is often associated
with drag and homosexual lifestyles, to communicate social distaste for
people who act outside the "norms" of sexual behavior. Lady Gaga has
used her own relationship to the gay community and her performance of
drag to question these norms and bring alternative gender identities into
more general public discourse. The disingenuous or ambiguous nature of
Gaga's gender performance has been a running theme since she first
received national attention in 2008. Heather Duerre Humann argues that
Gaga's many alter egos suggest an "ambiguity with respect to gender and
an arbitrary, rather than pre-assigned, nature to gender choices."[64] This
is made all the more troubling by the highly sexualized nature of her performance. She consistently combines exaggerated feminine and masculine performances with the monster metaphor to illustrate the disturbing
aspects of the overly erotic celebrity spectacle. As Gaga has explained: "I'm
not trying to make your dick hard the way other girls are. I'm trying to
teach your dick to get hard when it looks at other things. I love Grace
Jones and David Bowie because they played with gender, with what 'sexy'
means."[65] In the development of Lady Gaga's public identity, multiple
forms of drag have been used to argue for an ambivalent relationship
between physical sex and erotic attraction. This chapter explores Gaga's
performance of drag during the first three years of her career—following
the release of *Fame* in 2008 through her 2011 appearance on MTV's Video
Music Awards as her alter ego Jo Calderone.

In 2009, the same year that Gaga hit *Billboard* charts with *The Fame* and *The Fame Monster*, Christina Aguilera made headlines for commenting, in regards to Gaga: "I don't know if it [*sic*] is a man or a woman." The statement foreshadowed what would become an ongoing narrative about the sex, gender, and sexual preference of Lady Gaga. Over the course of her career, both male and female drag have played prominent roles in Lady Gaga's public performance. In the early stages of her career, Gaga's work in the burlesque and drag community influenced her appearance as a drag queen. This faux queen performance generated public speculation that Gaga was either a man or a hermaphrodite. The performer used the opportunity generated by these rumors to comment on the position of women in the music industry and cultural assumptions regarding feminism. In 2011, Lady Gaga fed the speculation by introducing two new alter egos: Jo Calderone and Yüyi the mermaid. Lady Gaga's public performance of both these personas has been largely erotic in nature. Male and asexual drag has provided Gaga a space to comment on her own performance of femininity and the complicated nature of desire within the transgender community.

Since the beginning of her career, Gaga has maintained that her work is more accurately categorized as performance art. Chapter 3 looks at this claim and talks about what it means for the creation and interpretation of Lady Gaga's performances. In many ways, Gaga is not so much a pop star as she is a modern Frankenstein of pop culture references. As she explained in her column for *V Magazine*: "Glam culture is ultimately rooted in obsession, and those of us who are truly devoted and loyal to the lifestyle of glamour are masters of its history. Or, to put it more elegantly, we are librarians."[66] Gaga's work is a vast library of allusions to pop culture's past. Monsters are often reminders of history and the way that past transgressions can haunt a community. The monster is connected human failure; "the monster reifies very real incidents, true horrors, true monsters. This is why they are always complicated and inherently sophisticated."[67] This chapter looks at the role of parody, allusion, and referencing in Gaga's work. Lady Gaga uses the constant referencing of other people's work to separate viewers into different audiences. For Gaga fans, the hints at different pop culture moments are a provocation to track down the meaning behind her work. For non-fans, the constant referencing produces allegations of plagiarism. The struggle between these two perspectives often boils down to questions of whether Gaga is authentic or inauthentic, whether she is truly original or just another in a long line of Madonna wannabes. Social media has played an important role in Gaga's attempts to construct her fan community as a collection of media-literate individuals dedicated to critically interpreting popular culture as art. This chapter argues that Gaga's relationship with her fans and her construction of the fame are necessary components of her parodic performance.

Lady Gaga uses new media to interact directly with her fans and works with them to communicate and translate the meaning of her sometimes obscure references. Typically, the mainstream media has a tremendous influence over how one reads a monster or a celebrity. Images of celebrities are presented with captions to tell the audience what they should think about how the person is dressed, how they are behaving, or what they have said. Monsters are even more silenced, and language often turns them into something beyond human. This begins with the word "monster" itself; "the history of the word signals abnormality and deviancy, but, in addition, it conveys a sense of wonder. The word itself is monstrous—noun, verb, sometimes adjective. It transgresses linguistic and social boundaries, collapsing categories of biology, sociology, ethics and aesthetics, theology and philosophy. Its exclusionary force has been applied to individuals, races, genders, even culture and society."[68] As non-human, monsters are often considered without a voice; "describing dastardly events and villainous persons as beyond human speech implicitly places them beyond moral evaluation, even while the language is intended, ostensibly to reach ethical conclusion."[69] As both a monster and a celebrity, Lady Gaga's use of social media is an empowering way to claim and craft her identity. Rather than relying on mainstream media to identity her references or translate her ideas, she goes to her fans directly. In addition, the social network she has built for her fans—Littlemonsters.com—provides them a space to develop their own media identities. The way she actively involves and engages her little monsters in these conversations reinforces her message about the possibilities of fame being accessible.

Many of the chapters in this book explore ways that Lady Gaga has worked to develop an identity that responds to typical celebrity culture. Chapter 4 considers the ways Gaga has used the economic and legal aspects of the established media industry to her advantage. As the alter ego of Stefani Joanne Angelina Germanotta, Lady Gaga is a piece of intellectual property worth a lot of money. While Gaga may claim to operate outside the standard celebrity factory structure, she still relies on many standard economic and legal practices to retain control over her work and her identity. This chapter argues that the way she negotiates these systems reveals a lot about the authenticity of her philosophy of fame. To get at these issues, the chapter looks at Gaga's 360-degree deal with Interscope Records and the many copyright and trademark lawsuits she has been involved in over the past four years. Of particular interest is Lady Gaga's attitude towards copyright law.

Over the last ten years digital media technology has raised a host of new issues for copyright law. Torrents allow users to illegally access and distribute copyrighted material without paying for it. On YouTube, users routinely repurpose copyrighted material in the creation of recording new work. Several recording artists have chosen to fight copyright violations of their work, and some have gone on the record to say that these new violations will be the end of the music industry. Then there is Lady Gaga. Lady Gaga routinely distributes her music for free, and through social media such as Twitter and Facebook she distributes the work of fans who violate the copyright on her work. Beyond this, Gaga has herself been the subject of copyright lawsuits for illegally posting videos of her appearances on television shows and allegedly using other people's work in her music. Gaga defies long-standing media standards by freely distributing her music and publicly praising fans who violate copyright to use her work in creative ways. What the performer does file lawsuits over is trademark violation. Gaga seems to care very little if fans use her music, but she consistently sues commercial institutions that try to use her name. Through these actions, Lady Gaga maintains an argument that her music is not what she is selling. What she is selling is herself.

Monsters and celebrities perform many educational functions in a society, but it seems that the media draws the most lessons from their deaths. Chapter 5 looks at the repeated deaths of Lady Gaga. In June 2012, at a concert in Melbourne, Australia, Lady Gaga premiered her newest song: "Princess Die." The lyrics ask the audience to "leave the coffin open when I go" and describe Gaga's desire to look spectacular even as she passes away. The sentiment in the lyrics echoes something Lady Gaga said in her *60 Minutes* interview with Anderson Cooper:

That's what everyone wants to know, right? "What's she gonna look like when she dies? What's she gonna look like when she's overdosed?" on whatever they think I'm overdosing on? Everybody wants to see the decay of the superstar.... They wanna see me fail, they wanna see me fall on stage, they wanna see me vomiting out of a nightclub. I mean, isn't that the age that we live in? That we wanna see people who have it all, lose it all? I mean, it's dramatic.[70]

There is a great obsession with the death of celebrities and monsters. Things that are so spectacular and excessive have difficulty sustaining themselves. The concluding chapter discusses the sustainability of Lady Gaga's various narratives. Throughout the Monster Ball Tour Gaga died repeatedly onstage, and in the *Born This Way* tour she performs giving birth to herself. This book concludes by arguing that in the new celebrity model, much like the old celebrity model, the monster still dies, but there is always space for rebirth and reinvention.

A New Celebrity Culture

Years after her appearance at The Bitter End, Lady Gaga told Joshua David Stein and Noah Michelson, reporters for *Out Magazine,* that in taking off her clothes and revealing herself to her audience she "felt a spontaneity and nerve in myself that had been in a coffin for a very long time."[71] When Stefani Germanotta made the transition into her new life as Lady Gaga, she embraced that nerve and spontaneity as critical parts of her personality. To some, the notion of living an identity publicly and constantly might sound exhausting but not particularly heroic. A brief study of Lady Gaga reveals that, in the face of 24-hour news media, this is a noteworthy accomplishment. The performer laments that "nobody knows the fucking bravery it took for me to be me with this fucking media. All of these interviews. All of these questions. I could have just woken up one day and put out my music in T-Shirt and jeans and I never did that once."[72] Instead, Gaga has daily committed to taking her art beyond just the music she releases to encompass her concerts, her videos, and even her trips to the grocery store. This commitment is a necessary part of Gaga's overall argument.

Lady Gaga has said she wants to change the way her fans understand fame and that she hopes a new understanding of fame will change the way they understand themselves. At the core of these arguments are critical questions about media, identity, and agency. The mainstream media works to frame and define celebrities and monsters for the general public. As Gaga has told reporters: "This isn't the Lady Gaga newscast.... Nobody gives a shit what is really going on — everyone wants me to tell them a story. Art is a lie, and every day I kill to make it true."[73] Lady Gaga has worked through multiple outlets to maintain her ability to define herself: "If you look at every single interview, every single television appearance, every single performance of my life, it's been devoted to who I am. Devoted to my identity, devoted to my craft. And if that isn't fucking art I don't know what is."[74] She wants her fans to claim the same kind of ownership over their sense of self. Claiming that kind of agency often means little monsters must ignore the people in the mainstream media, or in their own lives, who say they are weird, different, monstrous freaks. Gaga challenges her little monsters to embrace the thing that makes them monstrous as the thing that also makes them amazing. Lady Gaga models this self-acceptance for her fans and offers them an image of a new way to interact with the media.

At various points in her career, Lady Gaga has been called crazy, a freak, or simply a media whore — desperate for public attention. She embraces these attacks: "I think what has been lovely about my relationship with the public is that they expect something unexpected from me."[75] And she does not fight any of these titles; instead she says: "I've always been delusionally ambitious to the point where people don't understand me."[76] In the examination that follows, one should see that Gaga is a lot of things, but she is not delusional. As reporter Peter Robinson concluded, "the closer you get to Gaga, the more genuinely she starts to make sense."[77] A closer examination of Gaga seems to reveal that the monsters are no longer hiding under the bed. They are coming out in broad daylight, and under the leadership of Lady Gaga they have a whole new set of lessons to teach.

Chapter 1
Monstrous Celebrity

Monsters exist in the shadows of society. They are brought to the light in horror movies or on the nightly news to serve as object lessons and morality plays. Media depictions of monsters are not unlike those of criminals; the fictional narrative of the man who becomes a wolf once a month, losing all control of his urges, has much in common with the pseudo-nonfiction narrative of the ashamed homosexual who kills his lovers to hide his inability to resist sexual urges. Edward Ingebretsen, in his work on monsters, comes to the conclusion that "every society needs a person ... who live(s) at the boundaries of social maps. Aliens on the social landscape, they can be pointed to as living beyond the social pact.... Persons on the margins of civil life, whose only safety is hiding in social crevices, are important largely because they demonstrate the symbolic nature of the pact itself."[1] The narrative of the monster figure teaches us about the boundaries of a civilized society by illuminating where such boundaries lie and functioning as an example of what happens when they are crossed. Celebrity and monstrosity are similar in this way, each existing outside the realm of the common class. Monsters and celebrities have even more in common when examined in their roles as teachers to the general public. The role of celebrity exists above the role of the civil life, in a place of exaltation and popularity. Depictions of celebrity decadence offer up the dream of a good life to which all citizens can aspire. The monster is the converse — a cautionary tale of what happens when wants and indulgences go to the extreme. In short, celebrities demonstrate what is to be desired and monstrosity shows us the consequences of taking that desire too far. In her first two albums, Lady Gaga constructed an image that combined these two roles. She simultaneously became a Mother Monster and a modern celebrity. By bringing the two together, she was able to highlight

23

the ways these personas are used by the media to create and enforce a moral code. Gaga makes the code transparent and encourages her fans to take on the roles of celebrity and monster to rewrite the morals of the stories the media is telling.

Lady Gaga's public performance brings together the roles of celebrity, mother, and monster to alter the very definitions of fame and horror. Where traditionally the role of monster is used to warn people of the dangers of excess, Gaga claims the title to juxtapose the things we dread with the things we exalt. Fans call Lady Gaga the Mother Monster and she affectionately refers to her loyal followers as her little monsters. As a mother figure, Gaga is an image of nurturing love and understanding. She tells her fans: "When you are lonely, I'll be lonely too."[2] While a monster, Gaga embodies the grotesque. She publicly performs her bloody death, wears clothing that distorts her body, and often intentionally makes herself difficult to look at. Lady Gaga's celebrity status is gained not only through the fame she has acquired as a pop superstar but also in the ways she relates to her fans and claims them as her children. Through the familial relationship, Gaga is able to define her behavior as something to be emulated and herself as a mother modeling a lifestyle. Like most mothers, she is hoping her little monsters follow in her footsteps. She builds on unspoken parental values and the traditional hope that one's children will be more than their parents. Mothers are often depicted as willing to fight battles for the possibility that their offspring will have new options. Lady Gaga's public performance of fame and motherhood creates the necessary conditions for her fans to challenge the traditional celebrity spectacle. Gaga's excess and monstrosity transgresses boundaries to make it easier for the little monsters to cross those same lines.

Lady Gaga did not begin her music career playing the persona of the Mother Monster; it is a role she grew into as her relationship with her fans developed. The role of mother evolved out of Gaga's early statements about her philosophy of celebrity and fame. This chapter looks at the symbolism of the Mother Monster in two parts: *The Fame* and *The Fame Monster* and the emergence of the Mother Monster as a body in transition. For Lady Gaga, *The Fame* was not just a catchy title for her first album; it was also an introduction to her own personal philosophy of celebrity culture. On the album, and in the interviews promoting it, Lady Gaga articulates her belief that fame is not something that one is granted, but rather it is an identity and a way of performing self. Most people's fears and insecurities prevent them from embracing this notion of fame — that it is something they have access to, if they choose to take risks. It is out of her discussion of this fear that Gaga developed her arguments about monstrosity. Typically, labeling something a monster is a straightforward way to signal it as a grotesque mutation or aberration. Monsters are freakish mistakes, and society is saved by killing them. In Lady Gaga's philosophy, monsters are still rooted in the things we fear, but she furthers the argument by pointing out that not everything we fear is bad. Gaga's fame provides a lens for determining the difference between good monsters and bad monsters, or that which we should use fear as cause to avoid and that for which we should overcome our fear. Through the album *The Fame Monster* and the Monster Ball Tour, Gaga was able to delineate between the monsters that should be fought and the ones that should be embraced. In concerts, albums, and interviews, Lady Gaga has tried to embody these distinctions and this philosophy. Acting as a figurehead for that process eventually made Gaga the mother of a movement. With the release of the music video for the single "Born This Way," she openly proclaimed herself as the mother of "a race within the race of humanity. A race that bears no prejudice, no judgment, but boundless freedom." In the music video, Lady Gaga plays "the eternal mother." The representation could be interpreted as a goddess or an alien from another universe. In this form, Gaga gives birth to two things: a legion of little monsters and a thing that is the very substance of evil. She says that each requires the other to exist. The task for the little monsters is to take what nurturing and guidance Gaga has given them and fight for their own fame.

The Fame *and* The Fame Monster

Lady Gaga preaches fame as a choice and a way of being — accessible through personal decisions and separate from the status that comes from mainstream media attention. As she puts it, "it's a sharable fame: I want to invite you all to the party, I want people to feel a part of this lifestyle."[3] This does not mean that everyone should seek celebrity status from the media, although that has been traditionally held as the main way to acquire celebrity in American culture. In fact, Gaga's notion of celebrity denies the media's jurisdiction over deciding who is famous and who is not. It also questions the way money and possessions are used by the media as status symbols:

> Fame is not pretending to be rich, it's carrying yourself in a way that exudes confidence and passion for music or art or fishing or whatever the hell it is that you're passionate about, and projecting yourself in a way that people say, "Who the fuck is that?" It has nothing to do with money. I can wear a $2 pair of pants and a T-shirt and a pair of sunglasses for two bucks on the street, but I can make it look like I'm Paris Hilton. You gotta have the fame, you gotta exude that thing. You gotta make people care, you gotta know and believe how important you are. You gotta have conviction in your ideas.[4]

Traditionally, celebrities have fed consumer culture by convincing people that material goods were necessary status symbols. These ideas of celebrity being rooted in wealth and possessions rely on something external to validate one's sense of self. For Gaga, fame is an internal process. She invites her fans "to walk around delusional about how great they can be, and then to fight so hard for it every day that the lie becomes the truth."[5] The delusion includes eschewing the trappings of consumer culture in favor of developing a sense of self. This way of discussing fame echoes Mikhail Bakhtin's arguments about carnival.

In his writings on François Rabelais, a French Renaissance satirist known for bawdy jokes and grotesque humor, Mikhail Bakhtin places the origins of carnival at a medieval festival known as the Feast of Fools.[6] According to Bakhtin, this was a space where the social norms of a society were turned upside down. In Europe, during medieval times, the church and the government exercised an extreme amount of power over people's daily lives. This, combined with harsh economic conditions, made citizens restless. The Feast of Fools offered a brief, albeit church-sanctioned, revolution. Citizens were given license to express all the dissent and unrest they normally suppressed — including mocking the sexual habits of priest and parodying the behavior of bishops. Typical communication practices were cast aside to create a level of familiarity in language that would not have been seen in traditional conversation.[7] Unlike other festivals or public performances, "carnival is not a spectacle seen by the people; they live in it, and everyone participates because its very idea embraces all the people."[8] This festival was a place of escapism and a release valve for pent-up frustrations.

Gaga's fame embraces the spirit of escapism and the subversion of social norms: "The "notion" of escapism may be a lie, but for some of us this lie is our truth. You must desire the reality of fantasy so profusely that it becomes necessity, not accessory."[9] This lie forms the basis for Gaga's relationship with her fans, the little monsters. At the start of each concert on the Monster Ball Tour, Gaga read the *Monster Manifesto*, which stated: "It is in the theory of perception that we have established our bond, or the lie I should say, for which we kill. We are nothing without our image, without our projection; without the spiritual hologram of who we perceive ourselves to be or rather to become, in the future."[10] The fame Gaga advocates is a modern Feast of Fools. It is a space to ignore the rigid social hierarchies established by the media and create a new reality.

During the medieval Feast of Fools, the traditional audience–speaker power relationship was forgone in favor of an almost abrasive casualness that pulled the audience into dialogue with the speaker.[11] Performers would shout profanities at viewers until the audience was forced to give up their role as passive watchers and return the abuse. Bakhtin points to footlights as a primary element that differentiated carnival from other types of public performances at the time.[12] In the theaters of that era, footlights were lamps traditionally placed at the base of the stage, with their light shining on the thing perceived as deserving of attention. The lights created a distinction: On one side of the footlight would be the audience sitting in darkness and on the other side is the performance, illuminated, for everyone to see. In carnival there is no footlight. There is no audience. There is no performer. The whole of the festival was part of the show. Today the mass media often functions like a footlight; it shines a light on celebrities, so it is clear who is the audience and who is the performer. Gaga is arguing for a new carnival-like atmosphere. One where everyone should ignore that footlight and embrace a world where they are no longer audience but celebrity.

While the notion of a sharable fame might sound harmless—just a bunch of teenage girls strutting around their high school declaring themselves celebrities— it contains the possibility of a much larger disruption of authority. Typically, the media controls the major outlets of popular expression, deciding who is worthy of public attention and who is granted fame. Gaga's message raises questions about where fame comes from: "What I want to deliver, as a message about fame, is that anyone can have it. My fame lives in my friendships, in my convictions about the power of art and love."[13] That attitude creates a space similar to the one Bakhtin described. Within this environment, "whatever the authority of a discourse, those who are seeing it as an image, as a mask that has been revealed to be a mask, now have the capacity to judge whether it represents their own condition."[14] Carnival communication has an informal quality; "when two persons establish friendly relations, the form of their verbal intercourse also changes abruptly; they address each other informally, abusive words are used affectionately, and mutual mockery is permitted."[15] The carnival assumes this friendly relationship between the speaker and the audience. Profanity or abuse could be taken as spectacular within commonplace entertainment, but within the familiarity and intimacy of carnival communication they take on an "ambivalence."[16] Lady Gaga speaks to her fans with familiarity, calling them her "little monsters." She attributes her success to their dedication as much as her own and holds them in the regard of family. After she won two Grammys for her first album, *The Fame*, she got little monsters tattooed on the arm that she holds her microphone with, and she named the second album *The Fame Monster* as an expression of affection for her fans.[17] These moments of blurring the power relationship between celebrity and spectator integrate into the notion of sharable fame as the motivation behind the carnivalesque style. Robert Hariman describes this as one of the functions of the carnival performance, pulling the rhetoric down and "casting that image before the most democratic, undisciplined, and irreverent conception of a public audience."[18] Carnival does not mimic lived experience exactly; it places the absurd in the context of lived experience.

Gaga's rhetorical choice not to move back and forth between real life and stage life constructs her performance as an immersive experience. This move is part of her overall concept of *the* fame, which she distinguishes as something apart from the typical mainstream media notion of fame. Gaga explains that the "fame, which I'm experiencing now, is very different from *the fame*. The fame is when nobody knows who you are but everybody wants to know who you are. I still experience a lot of that."[19] The fame is treated not as a status, or a line that is crossed, but as a daily choice. Generally, fame is about celebrity status and media recognition: "That kind of fame, to me, is the kind of fame that everybody knows about, and the kind of fame that I write about is a very special kind of fame that I think is really positive and can affect people's lives in a really, really amazing way."[20] A big part of what separates the two notions of fame is personal agency. One is about doing something that gets other people to recognize you as important, and the other is about recognizing that quality in yourself and embracing it. Gaga's conception of fame sets up a very different kind of power relationship between the performer and her fans. Rather than inviting them to mimic her, she is inviting them to find something great in themselves.

All of Gaga's work shows a unique relationship to the spectator. Her use of the carnivalesque style changes the nature of her public discourse. She still often wears the mask of spectacle, but she performs the mask in such a way that it alters its nature. With Gaga, the face behind the mask turns out to be the mask. As she puts it, "persona is the first word people think of when they're trying to figure out how to describe what it is that I do.... Gaga is not a character.... Everything you see is an extension of me. It's not a character that I play on television."[21] This shift in expectation effectively changes the overall environment of the conversation she is having with her fans. As she puts it, "it's the context of what I'm doing that makes people concerned."[22] This same behavior through a more traditional media outlet, separated from the user-generated content, would function to reinforce the footlights. When Lady Gaga performs it constantly and publicly it ceases to look like a mask and starts to look like the truth.

Lady Gaga has said that her ultimate goal is to live an identity that encourages fans to rethink how they express their own identities. In an interview with Barbara Walters, Gaga professed: "I aspire to try to be a teacher to my young fans ... who feel just like I felt when I was younger.... I felt like a freak, I guess, what I'm trying to say is, I want to liberate them, I want to free them of their fears and make them feel ... that they can create their own space in the world."[23] Part of that liberation is a sense of fame that is personal and close: "I want to give people the self-confidence and the sense of inner fame that I feel without being pummeled by the paparazzi as I walk down the street."[24] When Gaga talks about fame, she draws some important distinctions between fame and modern celebrity culture. As mentioned before, traditional fame and celebrity are often attributed to those who possess characteristics that society considers worth glorifying. According to traditional standards, fame is defined by outside attention. Someone knows they are famous when the paparazzi are trying to catch their every move and media is scrutinizing those moves to decide if they live up to celebrity standards. Gaga is advocating a sense of fame that exists without outside validation. This sort of fame is liberating, because it is not predicated on trying to be worthy of media attention.

Often when Gaga articulates the meaning behind the fame, she uses metaphors of space and discusses it as an interaction with her fan community. By situating fame in the direct interaction between Gaga and her fans, she removes the mainstream media as the center of celebrity and refocuses the conversation in a way that changes the agency of both herself and her audience. Commenting on her album *The Fame*, Gaga said that "it's fame in the Warholian Studio 54 kind of way, not the stereotypical fame that people read about in tabloids and is considered very poisonous."[25] She uses the metaphor of the famed Studio 54 to delineate between her notion of fame and fame that comes from the media. That communal notion of fame, based on directly interacting with fans, requires an extreme openness and authenticity. Lady Gaga argues that there are ways for celebrities to be open with their fans, develop a community, without giving up a sense of self: "Part of my mastering of the art of fame, part of it is getting people to pay attention to what you want them to pay attention to. And not pay attention to the things you don't want them to pay attention to."[26] This attitude definitely raises questions about the authenticity of Gaga's honesty with her fans. As she has explained, "My philosophy is that if I am open with them about everything, and yet I art direct every moment of my life, I can maintain a sort of privacy in a way. I maintain a certain soulfulness that I have yet to give."[27] The argument she is making is that the performance of total honesty allows her to hold something back so she always has more to give. She manages to hold back while always appearing to give everything to her fans. Perhaps this is the lie of celebrity that Gaga so often talks about in interviews.

Inner fame comes without the specter of losing the "it" factor. Gaga's fans have embraced this philosophy. In an American *Vogue* interview with Jonathan Van Meter, Lady Gaga commented on the evolution of the nature of her fans: "Every show there's a little more eyeliner, a little more freedom, and a little more 'I don't give a fuck about the bullies at my school.'"[28] Despite Gaga's movement into mainstream popular culture, "for some reason the fans didn't become more Top 40. They've become even more of this cult following."[29] Ann T. Torrusio points out that "Gaga's fans always perceive her adoration for them as genuine, and it is possible that they may well be correct. However, it cannot be ignored that her well-cultivated relationship ... has lured her 'Little Monsters' into the margins of culture."[30] In her shows, Gaga constantly pushes to develop a relationship to the fans; "I am not going to saunter around the stage doing pelvic thrust and lip-synching.... I want to be your cool older sister who you feel really connected with, who you feel understands you and refuses to judge anything about you because she's been there."[31] Being a Lady Gaga fan is not about embracing a trend; it is more about joining a community who actively declare themselves as living on the fringes of society.

The paparazzi is a critical part of the culture surrounding modern celebrities, and as part of her commitment to spreading fame Gaga enjoys playing paparazzi for her fans. After signing a major promotional deal with Polaroid, Lady Gaga began carrying around a camera and taking pictures of her fans everywhere she went.[32] In 2012, Lady Gaga had more than 26 million followers on Twitter. So, when she plays paparazzi and posts a picture of her fans online that photo has almost as many viewers as a major magazine. Gaga's fans help to make her famous and she returns the favor. She does not stop at Twitter. In 2010, *V Magazine* did an issue that was dedicated to the "new." As part of the issue, Gaga nominated the little monsters as the "new fan." The issue included collages and full-page photos assembled by Gaga, featuring fans posing in their various homages to the star.[33] Gaga is promoting her fans through mainstream media outlets, and she is sharing the spotlight with them. Even in small ways, the Mother Monster likes to act as a fan of her fans. Lady Gaga told a reporter that at a concert in Japan "I brought my favorite pocketbook and I wanted all my Japanese fans to sign it, so I could always have you with me." Just like fans hound Gaga for autographs, she goes after them. Lady Gaga was upset because her Birkin bag was unrelatable, "[s]o how do I create and it into something that they [her fans] will love and adore, and turn it into a performance-art piece in itself? My fans are more iconic than this purse. I love fashion, but I don't love it more than my fans. And that's what this bag is all about." The bag was covered in fan art from her tour in Japan and Taiwan.[34] In September of 2012, Lady Gaga made a post to her YouTube account labeled "Oh! You Pretty Things," which is the title of the David Bowie song that provides the sound track for the video. The video was a series of short clips of fans, members of the Haus of the Gaga, and paparazzi that Gaga had recorded while she was out on tour for *Born This Way*. Within only two days it had more than 62,000 views, and that number was continuing to grow. The behavior of playing paparazzi and getting fan autographs offers tangible reinforcement for Gaga's philosophy of fame. In her interactions with her fans, Lady Gaga mimics the way fans treat celebrities. This works to break down typical communication patterns in celebrity culture.

Lady Gaga combines the performance of the 24/7, "always on," celebrity with an intimate communication style to demonstrate that fame can be normalized. A major factor in this performance is a sense of honesty that goes past the traditional confessional celebrity moments. During an interview with Anderson Cooper on *60 Minutes*, Gaga said: "When you asked me about the sociology of fame and what artists do wrong, what artists do wrong is they lie. And I don't lie. I'm not a liar. I built good will with my fans. They know who I am. And I'm just like them in so many ways."[35] As discussed in chapter 1, Gaga has lived her fame very publicly and treated her quest for celebrity as something she shares with her fans. For that to work, the interactions have to lose their staged confessional quality and become about real intimacy. The celebrity status that Gaga advocates is about a lifestyle: "I believe in living a glamorous life and I believe in a glamorous lifestyle.... What that means is not money or fame or prestige. It's a sense of vanity and glamour and subculture that is rooted in a sense of self. I am completely 100,000% devoted to a life of glamour."[36] As she said after releasing *The Fame Monster*, it is all about "the dream of wanting to make something of yourself."[37] The fame is about a sense of self and agency that cannot be granted or taken away by any media outlet.

This way of talking about fame is not wholly new. In fact, most people have experiences of interacting with small-scale fame and local celebrity in their day-to-day lives. There are two things that make Gaga's discussion of fame noteworthy. First, given her position in celebrity culture, it is interesting that she attempts to separate fame from media attention and economic status. Chris Hedges comments that with the influence of the media "real life, our own life, is viewed next to the lives of celebrities as inadequate or inauthentic. Celebrities are portrayed as idealized forms of ourselves. It is we, in perverse irony, who are never fully actualized, never fully real in celebrity culture."[38] The media translates celebrities into an ideal and the audience is continually pushing for that ideal. Gaga says ignore the media ideal and be your own ideal. Still, the notion of average people as famous is not new to the world. Psychologist David Giles points out that there are multiple forms of fame.[39] There is the fame that is attributed by mainstream media consensus that a person is worthy of the attention of a large audience, and then there is a more localized fame that happens with small communities and interest groups. In every high school there are a small number of students who seem to receive more attention than the others. In local sports leagues there are players whom everyone seems to watch. In this sense, Giles points out, fame is "best regarded as the process by which people become well-known."[40] What Gaga is talking about goes beyond even this kind of fame. Even Giles's notion of fame requires some outside verification. Gaga argues for fame as wholly internal.

Gaga's first album, *The Fame*, builds upon her experiences becoming a celebrity and sets the stage for claims she would later make about "the fame." It provides a first look at fame as a lifestyle full of decadence. One the first singles from the album — "Beautiful, Dirty, Rich" — talks about the blind indulgence of party culture. The lyrics provide a glimpse of kids living a glamorous, drug-filled life while being broke and borrowing money from their parents. The video that accompanied the single showed a group of twenty-somethings destroying an expensive home, partying, and smoking money. Further reinforcing the message, the song was used for the opening credits of *Dirty Sexy Money*: an ABC prime-time drama about a lawyer handling the affairs of the richest family in Manhattan. The song portrays people acting famously, even if they do not have the resources to back it up. Songs like "Just Dance" and "Disco Heaven" advocate for individuals ignoring life conditions — problems with relationships, economic status, et cetera — and focusing on indulgently partying. As Gaga has said in interviews, "I don't equate money with style, nor do I equate it with happiness. I'm often content hiding in the back of places like Claire's, schlooping costume jewelry into a basket."[41] With the release of the second album — *The Fame Monster* — Gaga starts to explore a darker side of fame. The lyrics and video for the song "Bad Romance" become Gaga's metaphor for "how the entertainment industry simulates human trafficking, the woman as the commodity."[42] At the end of the video, Gaga reacts violently towards her capture and blows up the man who has just purchased her for a million rubles. The message is clear: Trying to buy, sell, and control Lady Gaga is a dangerous business. There is a remarkable difference between the excessive party life of *The Fame*, with invitations to "Just Dance" and play a "Lovegame," and the ominous feel of *The Fame Monster*, with "Bad Romance" and stalker-like threats of the "Paparazzi." After the release of *The Fame Monster*, Gaga began the Monster Ball Tour in support of the album. It was during this tour that Gaga began to explore a new element within her performance: the vision of monstrosity.

Pop concerts have never been small events, and over the years acts like Queen, Prince, and Madonna have elevated them to a spectacle and an art. Lady Gaga's shows follow strongly in this tradition, moving past a simple musical performance to a full theatrical experience. One of the major narratives of the concerts on the Monster Ball Tour was Gaga's epic battle with the fame monster. The stage would go dark, with just a spotlight on Gaga, and the audience could hear her scream that she was afraid of the darkness. Then a monster that looked like a cross between a giant anglerfish and a many-tentacled alien would appear, looming above the performer's head. Gaga has said, of her inspiration for this moment in the concert, "I guess one of my favorite monsters is the Angler Fish — a real monster from my childhood."[43] While singing the song "Paparazzi," Lady Gaga does battle with the giant fame monster. Halfway through the song, she says to the audience, "Ok, I need your help. I can't kill him all by myself. So, get out your cameras and take his picture."[44] The obvious argument here is that the fame monster cannot survive audience scrutiny. However, "beyond the spectacle, it is worth underscoring the performative, ritual role the audience undertakes here, becoming part of a mini-narrative unfolding on the stage."[45] Lady Gaga is tying audience actions to her larger philosophy of performing fame. The mainstream media, a massive fame monster, consumes celebrities and starlets. However, it is only able to do this if the audience is not paying attention. At this point in the battle, the fame monster begins stripping Gaga out of her clothes and she calls for the audience to help her. In the end, it is with their aid and Gaga's own Roman-candle bra that the monster is ultimately defeated. She tells the audience, "[M]onsters, as we stand together, we can achieve anything, we can do anything."[46]

Much of Lady Gaga's discussion of monsters seems to be about negotiating the difference between good monsters and bad monsters. Many of the monsters she wants to banish are related to fear. After writing *The Fame Monster*, Gaga said, "I realized that I had written each song about a particular fear that I had come across on my journey promoting the fame."[47] The songs are about how things like the fear of death, fear of love, and fear of sex become monsters that ruin lives. She encourages her fans to embrace the aspects of themselves that others might see as monstrous, but she also pushes them to fight the monsters that keep them from accepting who they are. In that way, her tour was a sort of catharsis: "the Monster Ball Tour is in essence an exorcism for my fans and for myself where we sort of put everything out on the table and reject it."[48] During the Monster Ball Tour, Gaga often spoke encouraging words to her fans between songs: "Tonight I want you to let go of all of your insecurities. I want you to reject anyone or anything that ever made you feel that you don't belong. Free yourself of these things tonight! Yeah!!!"[49] Long since the Monster Ball Tour ended, Gaga has continued to point to the link between mainstream media messages and the fears her audience experiences every day. In a memo to *V Magazine*, Gaga accused journalists of "instilling fear in the hopes and dreams of young inventors in order to establish an echelon of tastemakers. There is a difference between getting a B — in Biology with a series of poignant red marks from your teacher and being given a spanking with a ruler by an old nun. The former we can learn from, while the latter is just painful."[50] The pain instilled by the media tells people what to fear and what to be insecure about. Gaga labels fear as the ultimate monster. Fighting fear, like the angler of her nightmares, allows Gaga to transform herself into a monster powerful enough to defeat the monstrosity of mainstream media control.

The Mother Monster

Historically, monster tales have not been kind to mothers. Mothers occupy a critical space in the image of the American dream: "[B]odies of mothers and children jointly support the favorite American self-narrative, being a haven for domestic virtue."[51] As time has moved on, the haven has proven unsustainable and the role of motherhood has become corrupted. The image of the bad mother as monster works to reinforce the social boundaries of the domestic unit. Scott Poole points to the way conservative rhetoric in the 1970s and 1980s focused on the dangers of the sexually empowered woman who acted on her own agency. The new monster was a female monster, supernaturally productive of a brood of monstrous offspring. Conservatives feared that the family home had become a haunted mansion of female desire run amok, of monstrous reproduction free of patriarchal constraints. The untethering of reproduction from sexual experience transformed the American mother into an American monster.[52]

The image of female sexuality as no longer constrained by motherhood but still the site of reproduction violated the established American narrative. Gaga cites the inspiration for her monster as just before the violation of this narrative: "I've become really fascinated with fantasy and monster movies and naïveté of the '50s. Somehow I feel, socially, after a war or after something really bad happens there's a rebirth of naïveté.... That's where the fame monster is born."[53] Gaga has certainly drawn on images of the 1950s housewife — apron on, in the kitchen, always smiling and ready to serve the family — with appearances, such as her 2011 Thanksgiving special. In taking on an identity somewhere between sexual vixen and doting mother, she has become a "paradox, Lady Gaga constantly dazzles and disgusts a fixated public. In this sense she is a monstrosity; she is a text that embodies our biggest anxieties and desires."[54] Lady Gaga's monster brings together the extreme excess of the devoted mother and the sexually liberated woman. Her performance demonstrates the violence involved when these two images come together.

While Gaga has been talking about the fame from the beginning, the monster was a later addition to her work. The term "monster" first started showing up when Gaga was working on her second album, *The Fame Monster.* In July 2009, the *Sun* reporter Jennifer O'Brien quoted Lady Gaga calling her fans little monsters during a concert. Around the same time, Lady Gaga posted on Twitter: "Obsessing over my new muses. Miss you girls ... you little monsters, be home soon xx." These are the first times Lady Gaga goes from using the term "monster" in reference to her music to "monster" in reference to her fans.[55] In an October 2009 *Vogue UK* interview, she referred to her look as "Monster Fashion."[56]The earliest press reference to Lady Gaga as "Mother Monster" is from April 1, 2010, in an *Advertiser* article about Gaga's birthday.[57] It is worth noting that, in this article, the term is used casually and with no explanation. So, the writers must have felt that it was a recognized part of the vernacular. Lady

Gaga was not using the phrase much before that, first referencing herself as Mother Monster on March 28, 2010, in a Twitter post, signed: "Love, Mother Monster X." There do not seem to be references to the term, at least online, before this tweet. The role of Gaga as mother was not part of the original discussion of fame or monstrosity. This is a role that Gaga evolved into over time. Elizabeth Switaj has argued that Gaga's use of the term "mother" stems from her understanding of creativity and her relationship to her audience: "Her version of motherhood is entangled in her alternative generativity, her production of an art which emphasizes her own monstrosity. In this way, her use of motherhood reclaims childbirth metaphors for creativity from male artists, but in a way that emphasizes relationships and connections over personal power and which literally embodies aspects of motherhood, such as the shifting body, that male artists have typically ignored."[58] With images of the feminine ideal there is often an attempt to fix the body in a particular moment and space. Female celebrities are not allowed to age, gain weight, or generally move past the space of spectacular beauty. Male celebrities go through phases and evolve, where female celebrities are often cited as "reinventing" themselves, as if they arrive entirely formed. Gaga presents a body that is constantly shifting, a body in chaos, and her continuing role as mother works to draw attention to that body.

Gaga's performance constantly places her body on display. Bakhtin argued that one of the primary elements of the carnival environment was an attention to the lower strata of the body. In spectacle or the sublime the body is portrayed as larger than life, but in the carnival the body is brought down to the very elements of life. In this communication environment the "bodily element is deeply positive. It is presented not in a private, egotistic form, severed from all other spheres of life, but as something universal, representing all the people.... This is why all that is bodily becomes grandiose, exaggerated, immeasurable."[59] Sex, food, defecation, illness—all the elements of physical life that are seen as private are brought forward in a way that pulls the identity down to a level of the body. Bakhtin referred to this as the grotesque body, or the body in its least spectacular forms. In Lady Gaga's music videos, the grotesque body interrupts the spectacle of the performance in a way that shifts the audience's perspective on the body. For example, in the "Born This Way" video there are several shots of rows of partially formed Lady Gaga heads. Presumably, these are the little monsters to which Gaga has just given birth. Each of the heads is unformed and mutated in some way. Spectacular bodies are presented at their height, but the grotesque body is caught mid-transformation, in "metamorphosis, giving a constant sense of 'ambivalence.'"[60] The unformed Gaga heads are not beautiful in the traditional sense. As a result, "the grotesque images preserve their peculiar nature, entirely different from ready-made, completed being. They remain ambivalent and contradictory."[61] That ambivalence impacts the spectators' ability to view Gaga's body. When one is faced with grotesque images, it is hard to maintain the illusion that the height of Gaga's beauty is natural and it becomes easier to see the façade. It functions as a reminder that behind the spectacular body is a "real" body, and this makes the spectacular body one that can be accessed by the viewer.

Gaga's portrayals of motherhood, monstrosity, and the celebrity body all work to reinforce notions of fame. As celebrity Gaga presents a body that is larger than life and spectacular. However, as monster and mother she also shows the body transitioning to its spectacular state. These moments of transition are called liminal moments. "Liminal," coming from the Latin root word *līmen*, or "threshold," refers to something caught in the middle of a change. Often, media depictions focus on one end of the spectrum or the other. Audiences are shown celebrities in their spectacular, polished form or they are shown "in real life" as grotesque. Articles about celebrities without makeup are a ubiquitous trope in modern media and function as part of the "just like us" mentality. When all that is seen is one end of the spectrum or the other, it is difficult to understand how anyone might cross the line from real life to celebrity. Gaga is advocating fame not as a matter of crossing boundaries but as a lived daily experience. To make that experience more real, she presents her body in multiple forms—the grotesque, the liminal, and the spectacular.

Some of the strongest examples of the grotesque body can be seen in Gaga's "Paparazzi" video. Within the video, images of sex and death, disability, and disproportionate costuming bring the message down to the level of the body. In an interview with *Vanity Fair*, Gaga commented on the video: "I thought watching the celebrity fall apart is so fascinating to everybody, why don't I fall apart for seven minutes and see what happens."[62] The opening scenes of the video show Lady Gaga making out with her lover. He takes her out to a balcony and, unbeknownst to her, positions the two of them so that a photographer captures their activities. This results in a struggle, and the lover throws Gaga off the balcony.[63] Gaga is shown slowly falling backwards while posing seductively — sucking on her finger and licking her lips. The message here is clear: Even when starlets fall to their doom their bodies are sexualized. There is no sound when Gaga lands on the ground — no moment of crunching bones or splattering blood. Instead, we see her body posed at an unnatural angle that could be equally perceived as reflecting either a broken limb or a couture photo shoot. As we watch her lying on the ground, injured, the paparazzi begin to swarm around her snapping photos. Over the sound of the cameras, there is a voice reminiscent of a sleazy photographer at a modeling shoot, saying: "Beautiful, beautiful, right here, beau-ti-ful!" These opening scenes lay the groundwork for the relationship between sex, injury, and death that is a theme for the rest of the video. Throughout the video, there are images of overly made-up, sexy, couture-esque women in various death scenes. Bringing together these elements of sex and death distorts the notion of sexuality traditionally seen in the spectacle of music videos. Sex in music videos is normally shown as fantasy, allowing the viewer to move past the awkward bodily elements of real-life sex and move into the fantastic images. In "Paparazzi," the bodies are all simultaneously violent and sensual. The violence in the opening sex scene stops the viewer short of fantasy, breaking the illusion of grandeur, bringing sex back down to the body.

Throughout the video, moments of fantasy are juxtaposed with violence to remind the viewer of the physicality of the body. In one scene, Gaga is shown on a couch kissing and touching two men. This, once again, brings up one of the obvious sexual fantasies that are typically invoked in popular music videos. The scene then shifts to the image of a woman's eyes, which at first appears hooded and sensual, especially when placed in context with the previous scene. The camera flashes to different parts of the woman's beautifully made-up face, then pulls back to reveal just her legs, dangling, hanging limply in the air. It is this last image that tells the audience that the beautiful woman is dead. The fantasy of Gaga making out on the couch, and the fantasy of this beautiful woman's face, is stopped short by the realization of death. The grotesque body in this case works to turn the sexuality in the video into a parody of traditional music video sensuality. By placing the traditional sexuality next to the image of the death, the limits of the body are exposed and reinforced; "the powerful is shown to be vulnerable, the unchangeable contingent, the enchanting dangerous. Parody works in part by exceeding the tacit limits on expression — the appropriate, the rational — but it does so to reveal the limitations that others would want to keep hidden."[64] All of these bodily limits are further reinforced at the end of the video when Gaga is shown, in an almost cartoon-style scene, killing the lover who pushed her off the balcony in the beginning.[65]

This is just one of many violent moments in Gaga's performances, in video and onstage. During Gaga's performance of "Paparazzi" at the 2009 MTV Video Music Awards, she pantomimed stabbing herself onstage and then finished the number hanging limply from a rope.[66] According to biographer Lizzy Goodman, onstage the performer has "been torched, bloodied, bruised, crippled, drowned, poisoned, and hung, but she's always lived to fight another day."[67] As Poole points out, a critical point in the American monster myth is that the monster must die.[68] However, Gaga lives on — continually toying with her audiences by combining and conflating roles of sexual celebrity and absurd monstrosity. As she stated shortly after the "Paparazzi" video release: "I have an obsession with death and sex. Those two things are the nexus of horror films.... If you notice in those films, there's always a juxtaposition of sex with death, that's what makes it so scary. Body and mind are primed for orgasm and instead, somebody gets killed; that's the sort of sick, twisted psychological circumstance" that a Lady Gaga video is trying to invoke.[69] The obsession with sex and violence can be seen in other videos as well. This juxtaposition is a key element in parody for highlighting things that might otherwise be ignored. In "Bad Romance," Gaga wears a pair of sunglasses made of razor blades as a throwback to women she knew in high school who carried razor blades in their cheeks.[70] At the end of "Bad Romance," she lights her lover in the video on fire. All of this, while perhaps constructing death as spectacular, disrupts the sensuality of the performance and prevents the viewer from indulging in the body in its spectacular state.

Disability is introduced in a second set of bodily images that Gaga plays with in the "Paparazzi" video. In the scenes after she is pushed off the balcony, Gaga is shown first in a wheelchair, stripping, then dancing with the aid of a set of crutches. The stripping and the skimpy metallic outfit that the performer wears seem to be attempts to sexualize Gaga, playing into fantasy tropes that are typical to music videos. This time when the fantasy is stopped, it is by images of disability. The awkward movements with the crutches and the limited mobility of Gaga in the wheelchair both serve as reminders of the very physical limitations the performer is suffering from after being injured. This is made all the more poignant by the fact she was injured by her lover. Sex, rather than being fantastic or spectacle, is linked to a body that is also portraying its limitations. In the video for "Bad Romance," Gaga's body is again seen in a transformative moment. At the beginning of the video she is shown emerging from a coffin labeled "monster," and as the video progresses she dances with her hands contorted and face covered to symbolize her body as mutant. The image of Gaga as monstrous was expanded on with the release of the album *Born This Way*; on the cover of the album Gaga is shown with spiked protrusions coming out of her face and shoulders. The physical representation of herself as a monster plays off her constant references to her fans as little monsters. Once again, she is reinforcing the interchangeability of their identities. In the same way that sex and death come together to give both a sense of dark reality, fame and the monster are combined to give the spectacular performance a sense of gritty reality. Just as Gaga performs the real as spectacular, the spectacular is halted by the reality of the body.

Bodies are at their most vulnerable in moments of transition, and Gaga repeatedly uses this element of liminality to make the realities of the body visible. The "Paparazzi" video images of Gaga in the wheelchair, then with crutches, then fully healed, play off of Bakhtin's discussion of bodies in transition. The spectacular body is represented at its height. It is in moments of transition that the body is made grotesque and real, a reminder of its full limitations. In this way, "[t]he grotesque body is ... unfinished, outgrows itself, transgresses its own limits."[71] Gaga juxtaposes these images of transition and sexuality, playing the fantasy element at a moment when the body is at its most imperfect. Don Waisanen talks about something similar, with parody, in terms of "contextual clash" bringing together multiple disparate elements to allow them to comment on one another; "in doing so, they playfully help us see political and media discourses in more ways than one."[72] Even though the overall video may be highly fantastical or even potentially absurd, the disparate elements encourage the audience to rethink the traditional fantasy immersion. This juxtaposition was translated into Gaga's MTV Video Awards performance;

the singer performed hobbling on one crutch while one of her dancers performed in a wheelchair.[73] Once again, it is the consistency of the message from one format to the next that gives Gaga such overall rhetorical force.

The grotesque and the spectacular body work together in Lady Gaga's performance in a way that is very much in line with Bakhtin's notion of the body within carnival. In this communication sphere, "the material body present in grotesque realism is offered in its all-popular festive and utopian aspect. The cosmic, social, and bodily elements are given here as an indivisible whole."[74] The craziness of the environment where Gaga places the grotesque body allows for a different relationship to that body. The grotesque body stops the audience from simply entering the fantasy; they are forced into a realistic awareness of bodily limitations even in the context of the sexual imaginary. Perhaps the strongest use of the liminal body comes in Lady Gaga's video for the song "Born This Way." The voice-over at the start of the video announces that this is the "Manifesto of Mother Monster." The opening shot reveals two Lady Gagas, back-to-back, attached to each other. The creature formed by the dual Gagas is the Mother Monster. Over the image of the mother in labor, Gaga proclaims that the birth "was not finite, it was in-finite." Meaning that what we are watching is not an isolated incident but an ongoing process of little monsters entering the world. The voice-over tells the story of the day a new "race within the race of humanity" was born; this new race "bears no prejudice, no judgment, but boundless freedom."[75] In the video, the Mother Monster is rather graphically giving birth to this new race. On the same day, the voice explains, evil was born. The birth of evil splits the Mother Monster in half, and the other Mother is shown giving birth to a machine gun. Bakhtin talks about images of birth and pregnancy within the carnival atmosphere as "ugly, monstrous, hideous from the point of view of 'classic' aesthetics,' ... they are contrary to the images of the finished, completed man, cleansed, as it were, of all the scoriae of birth and development."[76] The video portrays birth with a good amount of viscous material and mucus-like sacs, which produces a rather visceral reaction. Good and evil are not born complete; they are shown in the liminal moments of development and birth. At the end of the prologue, Gaga asks the question "How can I protect something so perfect, without evil?" Lady Gaga is the Mother Monster that Scott Poole said society feared in 1970s. She is the sexually empowered women, shown free from patriarchy and giving birth to a legion of monsters.

The images of Gaga giving birth to her brood of monsters continued as she performed "Born This Way" live. On *Saturday Night Live*, Gaga danced to the song wearing a black leather belly that made her tiny frame look extremely pregnant. Her backup dancers placed Gaga in metal stirrups, and while her black leather pants seemed to be blocking the birth canal, an ooze of viscous material and glitter still seemed to pour out of her. Two of the male backup dancers even rubbed their hands in the ooze and licked it off their fingers. While these images may seem graphic, they pale in comparison to the Born This Way Ball. In concert, the song starts with what looks like Gaga lying down with her legs open to the audience, in the throes of childbirth. Her actual legs and belly have been replaced by a seven-foot belly with a zipper down the middle where one would typically expect to see Gaga's vagina. As Gaga mimes the pushing and grunting of childbirth, her actual torso and head are seen sitting up behind the oversized womb. An image of a face is projected onto the belly and it seems to be moving around while Gaga labors. Towards the end of her labor, Gaga screams to the audience, "I am not a prisoner."[77] Then she leans back to give the final push, and soon she begins emerging from her own birth canal. In this performance Lady Gaga gives birth to her own monstrosity.

Many of the images associated with "Born This Way" imply that Gaga has given birth to herself. This has a lot of important implications for both her role as a monster and her role as a celebrity. In concert, Gaga walks out of her own womb. In the music video, thousands of heads are shown in what look like eggs. Each of them appears to be a pre- or unformed version of Lady Gaga's head. The ultimately formed monsters, dancing in the video, look very different from Gaga. However, at the beginning stages she seems to understand them as versions of herself. When Gaga gives birth to herself as a monster, she takes credit for her own monstrosity. Typically, the media declares people as monsters and "individuals nominated as monsters become textually undone, victim of metonymy and metaphor, prey to sloppy habits of public thinking, linguistic failure, and a narrative rush to closure that is tantamount to an act of direct prejudice."[78] Gaga does not allow any such fate to befall her. In the same way that she owns her own fame, she owns her own monstrosity. Alternatively, this can be interpreted in light of Gaga's discussion of celebrity, which is built around the notion of excess. Eventually, she so thoroughly outgrows her body that she is forced to give birth to herself. Gaga seems to be sending a message: The media could not have conceived a monster or a celebrity like her because she found her fame outside their official channels.

Just beneath the role of mother, images of birthing the self, and proclamations that she is not a prisoner, one can still see an impish and childlike side of Lady Gaga. In the "Born This Way" video, Gaga dances with Rico, a performance artist who is covered head to toe in a tattoo of his skeleton. For these scenes, Gaga was painted with tattoos that mirrored Rico's. At one point, during the video production, Gaga said she asked Rico why he had the tattoos and he responded simply: "Bazooka gum." This interaction inspired her side ponytail and bubble gum popping in the final music video. In an article in *V Magazine*, she explained:

> My fans needed to see me in that juvenile way in order to understand the intention behind why I wrote "Born This Way." Accompanied with a side ponytail, it took me back to moments when I was just a little baby monster. When my mother would perch a pony high on my hair and we would dance so hard to the tape deck that the perfectly perched pony she fashioned would fall to the side. I had to take an uncomfortable journey back into high school, where my youth represented tears. Wishing I had a mask. Hoping that I could artistically hide the wounds buried deep from years of being bullied. I have since reckoned with this psychology in my performance art. But this time, the revelation was clear: I still want to wear a mask, but now I wear it proud, and with the same effervescence and innocence I had when I was 6, dancing with my mom.[79]

Gaga presents herself as always in transition and continually giving birth to new versions of herself. The transition she portrays physically mimics the way she describes her overall philosophy. She does not want her fans to see her solely as a leader or a mother. Gaga wants them to also see her as a child, someone who is developing and growing along with them.

These are the images that Gaga holds up as a part of her performance of motherhood and as a general example for her little monsters. As we interpret Gaga's grotesque, sometimes mutated, and monstrous body, it is important to remember how it relates to the longer history of monsters that lurk in our culture. It is not just herself that she defines as a monster; "Gaga avoids systematic structuration by smashing the distinction between performer and audience, forcing both to coexist in an escapist monsterdom."[80] Her relationship to her fans links them to her monstrosity. Scott Poole warns that we risk grave misunderstanding when we reduce monsters to metaphors or symbols: "[T]he monsters walk among us, leaving a trail of gore and ichor in their wake.... There are victims of our monsters. Not victims screaming on the screen or within the pages of paperback horror fiction but historical victims, sacrificed to the nation-state and its sometimes bloodthirsty folk culture."[81] Monsters have a history of committing violence and justifying violence against those on the fringe of society. When Gaga claims the role of monster and gives birth to a brood of monsters, she is tapping into a very bloody history. Ingebretsen reminds us that a hallmark of monster legends is that evil cannot possess without some human invitation.[82] Gaga invites society to understand her and her offspring as something other than human and in accepting that invitation there is the potential for very real consequences. When the Mother Monster and the little monsters are accepted, they are given permission to enter and change the world they live in.

A Legion of Little Monsters

As the Mother Monster, Lady Gaga has developed a unique relationship with her fans, her little monsters. During the Monster Ball Tour she often read her "Monster Manifesto" as explanation of that relationship:

> There is something heroic about the way my fans operate their cameras. So precisely, so intricately and so proudly. Like Kings writing the history of their people, it is their prolific nature that both creates and procures what will later be perceived as the kingdom. So the real truth about Lady Gaga fans, my little monsters, lies in this sentiment: They are the Kings. They are the Queens. They write the history of the kingdom and I am something of a devoted Jester.[83]

The little monsters are rulers of Lady Gaga land. Where more traditional elements of modern society might shun them as alien, in the world that Gaga has created they are the Kings and Queens. This is a drastic shift from the way monsters are traditionally perceived. Typically, they are held up by the media as examples for citizens of what is inappropriate and to be avoided, for the most part; the mediation ensures that this lesson can be learned from a safe distance. Citizenry can gawk and stare at monster without ever having to deal with the humanity behind the monstrosity. Whether one is sitting in a movie theater watching a horror film or positioned at home on the couch watching the nightly news, with the monster story the "narrative structure positions the reader less as witness to suffering than as voyeur, keeping her or him at a distance safely away from untoward emotional distress."[84] As voyeurs, witnesses are allowed both a physical and emotional distance from the monster and the victim. Audiences are not encouraged to empathize with the distress inherent to the morality play unfolding in front of them. Instead, the rush of adrenaline comes from the safety of the distanced position. Audiences are asked to simply wait and see how it turns out. In these shows, "the performance of deviancy confirms the privilege of the nondeviant, who can be involved without fear of consequent shame or arrest."[85] Put another way, "a civic order distances itself in various ways from those whom it perceives to be carriers of its destruction. The distance, however, extends in two directions. Monstrous rhetorics simultaneously establish who the monster is, while insuring that its depredations are, nonetheless, out of reach of any human energy."[86] In Lady Gaga's performance, these norms are violated. Rather than allowing the viewer to passively observe monstrosity, she invites fans to confront their demons and embrace their monsters. Her concerts involve monster pits where groups gather to revel in their outsider status and she has established a social networking site online where people sign up to *be* little monsters. In 2010, teens in China started replacing "Oh my God" with "Oh my Lady Gaga."[87] In a variety of ways she is designing an immersive experience of monstrosity. Furthermore, rather than treating the media as a safe boundary between the monsters and the viewers, she is using it to recruit and engage. The resulting little monsters are still an object lesson for the rest of society; Gaga has just changed the moral of the story. What's more, Gaga's little monsters do not inoculate society from impropriety. They are contagious.

When Gaga calls her fans monsters, this may seem like a metaphor. However, assuming the title "monster" is simply a figure of speech ignores the history of the monster myth. Scott Poole points out that the monster myth in American history is more than metaphor, "because they have a history coincident with a national history."[88] Ingebretsen argues that in many cases the use of the term "monster" "acts metonymically rather than metaphorically, proposing association rather than direct comparison."[89]

Metaphor implies a parallel between two things, and comparing the two works to emphasize a characteristic. With metonymy one word is substituted for another with the same meaning. It is the difference between saying fans and celebrities are like monsters and saying fans and celebrities are monsters. To say that someone *is* a monster is to emphasize that they are outside the constructs of humanity — as either inhuman or more than human. This creates a tricky language problem: the term "monster" is meant to imply that the thing is unhuman or other. Yet most often the thing we call monster is decidedly human and shares more of our characteristics than we are comfortable admitting.[90] The term removes the monster from society, while the reality is that the monster is very much one of us. Society's uneasy relationship with the monster might explain the history of violent reactions monsters have prompted.

Even before Gaga unleashed a horde of little monsters, the label "monster" was thrown around by mainstream media to remind viewers of the dangers that surrounded them in everyday life. However, the monsters of the mainstream media were different from Lady Gaga's monsters. Those standard "monsters serve as exemplars of a social inadequacy.... Speechless and unspeakable, they can only provoke dramatic and spectacular commentary about — never dialogue with, or, God forbid, speech by. Endlessly spoken about, they lose their voice for the good of those who might have to listen to them explain."[91] Lady Gaga's monsters may be examples of social inadequacy, but they are certainly not speechless. In 2010, on *Larry King Live*, Larry King asked Lady Gaga why she called her fans little monsters. She said that when she was on the Monster Ball Tour her fans "were rabid. They couldn't wait for me to sing my new songs, and they just behaved like monsters.... So I just started calling them my little monsters. And before I knew it, they were all holding their hands up like this in the audience [holds her hand up as claws]. And then this became the symbol for the little monster."[92] The symbol is not about fans saying they are like monsters; instead they are identifying themselves as monsters.

Lady Gaga has fully taken on the role of the monster and has made it acceptable for her fans to adopt the identity. Maureen Callahan points out that from the beginning of Gaga's career the narrative has been the same: "She was and is a freak, a misfit, a lost soul in search of her fellow travelers."[93] This statement echoes the assessment of *Rolling Stone* in June 2009, which dubbed Gaga a "pop star for misfits."[94] Even in the early stages of the Monster Ball Tour, fans seem to physically embody Gaga's mission. One viewer described a group of concertgoers this way: "Nearly all the girls—who outnumber the boys about three to one—are dressed like their heroine.... They're trotting and trembling on five-inch spike heels, dressed in Day-Glo colors, and have forgone pants in favor of long tops and tights; they've donned wigs and sunglasses and applied drag-queenish heavy makeup."[95] These are the little monsters, and "her fans, pledging allegiance to Gagaland, are a nation unto themselves."[96]

Traditionally, fans of popular culture have been portrayed as ravenous consumers. Superfans become obsessed with something and there is a need to know everything that can be known about it. They collect information, paraphernalia, anything that brings them closer to the object of their affection. Paul Booth argues that traditional fan studies have been based on a market narrative of consumption and studies of digital fandom need to shift to a narrative of production.[97] Fans in a digital culture draw from a variety of texts, but they also produce texts of their own. In this way, fandom becomes a part of identity: "Whatever we are fans of, we base part of our identity on our appreciation of that fandom ... being a fan means identifying with a media text."[98] Richard Dyer expands on this notion, pointing out the difference between imitation and projection in fan behavior. With imitation the star acts as a role model for the fan. Projection goes much further, to the point where fans begin asking themselves how the star would live their life in a given moment. These questions lead to a merging of celebrity world and fan world.[99] Both Lady Gaga and her fan community are products of the new wave of digital fandom. While Gaga fans may obsess about the star, they also draw from the many texts she has created to construct narratives of their own. They broadcast their own narratives, often in the same places as Gaga: Facebook, Twitter, YouTube, et cetera. David Annandale elaborates, "Gaga and her fans, then, do not construct a monologic narrative together, but rather a polyphonic fantasy of meanings that speak to the specific needs of the individuals."[100] In a monologic celebrity-fan relationship, the fans imitate and construct themselves in the image of the celebrity until the two become enmeshed. In the polyphonic fan-celebrity relationship, the fan and celebrity are in dialogue. This requires serious recognition on both sides of the personhood of all those involved. Gaga wants her fans to have a voice of their own and she does things to promote the voices of her fans.

The maintenance of the polyphonic relationship also requires that Gaga respect the opinions and attitudes of her fans. Take for instance the 2012 controversy over Gaga wearing a Hermès fur coat. After Gaga was photographed wearing the coat, PETA and several members of the press pushed the star to say whether or not the fur was real and shamed her for wearing fur. Gaga refused to answer whether the coat was real and instead responded on littlemonsters.com, her personal social networking site: "For those press and such who are writing about whether or not my fur is actually real, please don't forget to credit the designer HERMES. Thank You!"[101] In Dan Matthews's, PETA's VP's, public statement, he recalled a statement Gaga had made on *The Ellen DeGeneres Show* in 2010: "I hate fur and I don't wear fur."[102] In the letter, Matthews called Gaga a "turncoat" and linked the violent treatment of animals with the suppression of gay rights.[103] Aside from the question of Gaga contradicting herself, which she does often, the letter she penned in response to the controversy shows a real attempt to respect her fans' beliefs while maintaining her own individuality. In a memo titled "Furgate," posted to littlemonsters.com, Gaga said: "I am choosing not to comment on whether or not the furs I purchase are faux fur-pile or real because I would think it hypercritical not to acknowledge the python, ostrich, cow hide, leather, lamb, alligator, 'Kermit' and not to mention meat, that I have already worn. This should already put me in a category as one who appreciates and adores the beauty of animals in fashion, but am not a strict vegan."[104] In these statements, Gaga does not apologize for her behavior or her previous actions; instead she attempts to paint herself as someone with nuanced beliefs involving fashion and animal cruelty. All this is particularly interesting given that the "Kermit" dress she references was originally articulated as a commentary on fur in fashion. Gaga goes on to defend her choices, while applauding the choices of her fans, stating: "You see a carcass, I see a museum pièce de résistance. But I am truly sorry to fans who are upset by this, it's a fair and applaudable feeling about the health and safety of animals. I respect your views, please respect mine."[105] Gaga delineates clear boundaries between her beliefs and the beliefs of her little monsters. Her statements indicate that she does not believe that the beliefs need to come into alignment. The little monsters are not meant to be imitators but a diverse group of individuals with causes of their own.

Superfandom is often associated with imitation of an idol and the cataloguing of information. There is definitely a lot of that in the little monster community. However, in Gaga's interactions with her fans she often seems to be pushing them to go beyond imitation and develop opinions separate from hers. For instance, Gaga was asked in a *Harper's Bazaar* interview if the body modifications she has done might encourage her fans to hurt themselves to emulate her. She said:

> And how many models and actresses do you see on magazine covers who have brand-new faces and have had plastic surgery, while I myself have never had any plastic surgery? I am an artist, and I have the ability and the free will to choose the way the world will envision me.... Trust me, I know that. I think a lot of people love to convolute what everyone else does in order to disempower women. But my fans know me. They would never hurt themselves. And if they have hurt themselves, they come to me and say "Gaga, I want to stop, and your music helps me want to stop. Your music makes me want to love myself." I am in no way promoting sadomasochism or masochism.[106]

Lady Gaga is articulating here a difference between her fans looking up to her or seeking out her help and her fans imitating her behavior. Part of this has to do with the way she distinguishes between the physical extremes of her performance and the message of her work. She sees her fans as part of a community that is invested in the message behind the work as much as they are invested in the image put forth in her performance.

All this makes for a difficult relationship between Lady Gaga and her fans—as a celebrity she is beholden to them, but she encourages them to find their own identity. The narrative of Lady Gaga is wrapped up in the narrative of her fans, and "for the fantasy to be accessible and universal as possible, its avatar needs to be in a state of perpetual transformation."[107] Rather than Gaga pushing fans to adopt a specific identity, the narrative of the little monster is about embracing their own identity. This works with the mutability of digital culture. Being a Lady Gaga superfan is partly about identifying with Gaga, but it is also about identifying with yourself. It is about identifying yourself as your own particular brand of monster. Calling this a metaphor or mistaking it for consumption ignores some of the very real consequences for following the path Gaga proposes. As Scott Poole points out, when discussing historical monster narratives, "it is not enough to call these beliefs metaphors when they shape actual historical behavior or act as anxious reminders of inhuman historical acts, a cultural memory of slaughter. How limp and pallid to use the term metaphor for cultural structures that can burn the innocent to death, lynch them, imprison them, or bomb them. The monster has helped to make all these things possible in American history."[108] To become a Gaga fan, to embrace being a little monster, is to align oneself with the character in the narrative that most often dies.

Summary and Concluding Thoughts

Lady Gaga's role as the Mother Monster both evolved out of her larger philosophy of fame and helped to transform that philosophy into something more. As will be discussed in the next chapter, Gaga has built on these ideas in her work with Don't Ask, Don't Tell, a piece of legislation she fought to have overturned, which prevented individuals in the military from being openly gay, and the development of the Born This Way Foundation. Her philosophy of fame and monstrosity has yielded tangible results for her fans. So much so that Gaga received a letter from the White House commending her work in helping to abolish Don't Ask, Don't Tell.[109] In interviews, Lady Gaga has often said that she reaches out to society's misfits and monsters because that is how she saw herself growing up. All of this builds off the cult of personality that Gaga has developed, which "is undeniable and not a little shocking, not least because Lady Gaga, as smart and shrewd and witty as she is, seems to buy into it."[110] People who meet her describe her as "gracious and touchingly polite."[111] It is continually commented that she is as kind in person as she appears in performances and campaigns. In a 2012 interview on Oprah Winfrey's show *Next Chapter*, Lady Gaga described being bullied in middle school. She told Oprah she was walking home one day when a group of boys who were hanging out with the popular girls picked her up and put her in a trash can. The whole group laughed and pointed, causing Lady Gaga to run away crying. That experience, and many others, helped to form the monster Gaga would become as an adult. The Mother Monster told an interviewer for *Q Magazine*: "I felt like a freak when I was growing up. I was teased a lot because my personality didn't fit in. And I feel like there's lots of kids out there that feel the way I used to feel. I used to use the word 'misfit,' but that's derogatory. I think my fans are like me. They feel the same way I feel. So I try to create a musical, cultural and live space for them to live."[112] The live space created by Gaga on tour and online has proven attractive to millions of fans who see something of themselves in the experiences that she is describing. Embracing inner fame, even when society would define it as monstrous, is Gaga's larger strategy for fighting the pervasive problem of bullying faced every day by her little monsters.

The Mother Monster has taken the lessons she learned as a little monster and used them to develop a new foundation under the title Born This Way. The foundation was formed in 2011 under the leadership of Lady Gaga and her mother, Cynthia Germanotta. Their mission statement proclaims: "We believe that everyone has the right to feel safe, to be empowered and to make a difference in the world. Together, we will move towards acceptance, bravery and love."[113] With this foundation, Gaga is translating the philosophy of fame she developed in her first album into a concrete set of actions geared towards improving the lives of her little monsters. While the Born This Way Foundation is still in its infancy, it hints at the continued forward momentum of Gaga's philosophy.

Lady Gaga is rethinking what it means to be a monster, and in the process she is inviting her audience to rethink what it means to be a citizen or a member of society. Part of how we create our notion of citizenship, our sense of self as a people, is by defining boundaries that necessarily create an "other" category. The term "monster" becomes a means for marking the "other" as not just outside the norms but as dangerous.[114] For a long time, monster movies and the monsters on the news have been part of a narrative that "produced what might be called the normalized citizen, but it also made possible the monstrous, secret alien."[115]Those monsters and aliens are often bullied and silent — chased out of town by mobs with pitchforks. During the Born This Way Tour, when Gaga recited the Monster Manifesto there was a screen flashing a variety of images. All the pictures showed people wearing masks that gagged them or somehow coved their mouths, preventing them from speaking out. The larger theme of the fame is about removing the mask and monsters finding their voices.

So, what is the role of the Mother Monster in all of this? Lady Gaga's statements about fame and the media do not specify an outcome or a result so much as they point to a new set of circumstances. In the manifesto, she calls herself a jester, and "the jester, a member of the court identifiable by ridiculous behavior and flamboyant costuming, is the only member socially sanctioned to publicly make a mockery of the court."[116] She is the one who models the new communication style of the carnival atmosphere she is promoting. Gaga uses all the force of the mainstream media to mock the system and reveal its behaviors. The goal is to change the way the industry relates to viewers, so that viewers have more agency within the system. As Gaga has explained, "I made an internal pact with myself when I put out 'Born This Way.' This time, when I 'win,' I want it to mean something. How can every 'win' be a force? Not a tiara, a pat on the back, or the cashing of a check, but how can I look out into the sea of fans and know that our 'win' changed the industry and changed each other?"[117] For Gaga the fame is not about winning celebrity in any of the traditional senses— money and media attention — it is about performing celebrity in a way that creates the carnival space where the little monsters can find their own fame.

Chapter 2

Dragging the Monster

In July of 2010, *Vanity Fair* magazine hit the stands featuring a whole new kind of cover girl: Lady Gaga. Photographed intimately, she was wearing only some terribly expensive jewels and a long, flowing blond wig. The headline read: "Naked came the world's no. 1 pop star. Who is she? Why is she? Should you worry?"[1] The photo shoot seemed to be an attempt to capture a more natural Gaga, without the layers of eye shadow and sequins. So, it was surprising to see the comments of popular bloggers, such as Celebitchy, saying "she looks like an angelic drag queen."[2] The assessment that Gaga looks like a drag queen was nothing new. In 2009, Christina Aguilera made headlines for commenting that she was not sure if Lady Gaga was a woman or a man in drag.[3] Most visible evidence seems to indicate that Lady Gaga is physically female, and at least one reporter has followed her into the bathroom to verify that assumption.[4] Still, despite her seeming femaleness, when Lady Gaga performs female something about the performance does not seem genuine. The disingenuous or ambiguous nature of Gaga's gender performance has been a running theme since she first received national attention in 2008. Heather Humann argues that Gaga's many alter egos suggest an "ambiguity with respect to gender and an arbitrary, rather than pre-assigned, nature to gender choices."[5] This is made all the more troubling by the highly sexualized nature of her performance. She consistently combines exaggerated feminine and masculine performances with the title "monster" to emphasize the disturbing aspects of the overly erotic celebrity spectacle. As Gaga has explained: "I'm not trying to make your dick hard the way other girls are. I'm trying to teach your dick to get hard when it looks at other things."[6] This chapter explores Gaga's performance of drag during the first three years of her career—following the release of *The Fame* in 2008 through her 2011 appearance on MTV's Video Music Awards as her male alter ego, Jo Calderone. In the development of Lady Gaga's public identity, multiple forms of drag have been used to argue for an ambivalent relationship between physical sex and erotic attraction.

Lady Gaga's use of drag originated with her attempts to incorporate her experiences in New York City's burlesque community into her main stage performance. Much of its continued development appears to be a response to media commentary about her body. The narrative surrounding Gaga's sex and gender can be broken down into roughly three stages. In the first stage, during early part of her career, Gaga's performance of femininity moved from the typical pop princess image to something more akin to bio-drag. Even her moniker, Lady Gaga, sounds like something one would expect to hear in a drag show. Modern burlesque performances tend to exaggerate femininity to be cheeky and create a humorous take on what is appropriate feminine sexuality. Oftentimes burlesque shows are operating in the same clubs and the same communities as drag shows. In these spaces, extreme feminine sexuality is played up for humor value. The term "bio-drag" refers to performers who, rather than performing across sex, engage a hyperexaggerated performance of their physical sex. Within the drag community, "faux queen" is the title used for a woman who performs as a drag queen. Because drag is culturally associated with crossing sex lines, Gaga's use of the faux queen persona generated media and public discussions about the performer's biological sex. In responding to these public discussions, Gaga's performance of sex as drag entered a new phase. At this second stage, Gaga combined drag with the monster metaphor to create an erotic, sexually ambiguous body. She began using penile prosthetics and playing with rumors that she was potentially a hermaphrodite. This ultimately culminated in the third stage, where Gaga used three alter egos to play with sex and gender dynamics within the context of heteronormativity. There was the already existing alter ego of Gaga herself, and during the release of her single "Yoü+I," she promoted two new alter egos: the sexless mermaid, Yüyi, and Gaga's male lover, Jo Calderone. In this final stage Gaga worked with different forms of drag in order to challenge the notion that desire naturally follows from a given gender performance.

Incorporating various forms of drag into her public performance has ultimately helped boost Gaga's celebrity status and allowed her to introduce alternative gender performances into everyday public conversation.

More than that, though, she has used it as a strategy to control her identity and claim agency in media conversations. As discussed in the preface, celebrities typically become the objects of public conversation. For female celebrities, there is a constant running commentary on weight, clothing choices, aging, and sex appeal. Female celebrities are held up as both objects of desire and reminders that any slight failure in maintaining the body will render a woman undesirable. Lady Gaga has challenged this expectation, managing to shift public conversation about her sexuality: "Slipping effortlessly between female and male drag, between cone-bras and strap-ons, gay male S/M-sex scenes and lesbian make-out sessions in her videos and public appearances, Lady Gaga refuses to be defined by her sexuality—a fate common to most other female pop stars."[7] By refusing to be defined in the typical way, she alters much of the mainstream media's conversation about desirability. At the same time, Gaga introduces new options into the conversation about what is desirable. John M. Sloop points out that "people take on their understanding of their 'selves' and their worlds from available discourses and, once taking on their identities and cultural meanings, can only work change within those meanings."[8] Traditionally, there have been a limited number of options for identities that are desirable or erotic. When non-traditional sexual identities are discussed in the media, it is often in the context of violence or deviance. Gaga is supplying a whole new set of popularly circulating discourse about sex and gender. Her alternative sexual performances are spectacular, fabulous, irreverent, and erotic. With every stage of her development, Gaga demonstrates Judith Butler's argument that, with drag, "part of the pleasure, the giddiness of the performance is in the recognition of a radical contingency in the relation between sex and gender in the face of cultural configurations of casual unities that are regularly assumed to be natural and necessary."[9] By changing how she is talked about, Gaga creates new options for how the little monsters might talk about themselves.

From Burlesque to Drag

Before she became famous as Lady Gaga, Germanotta spent time performing as a go-go dancer with Lady Starlight and doing burlesque shows on New York's Lower East Side. It was here that Gaga proved herself to be an oddity even in the New York club scene. Her act often made use of stuffed animals and heavily referenced the sex culture of furries.[10] Furthermore, she was known for performing to rock 'n' roll music and incorporating pyrotechnics into her act. For Gaga, burlesque "was a performance, a chance to learn how to lose herself, to push through her own comfort level, to see what worked and what didn't and figure out ways to adjust accordingly in the moment. It was, to her, art."[11] In a 2007 interview with *Women's Wear Daily*, shortly after performing her first major concert at Chicago's Lollapalooza, Gaga showed the influence of the cheekiness and irony of burlesque. Gaga performed the concert in her underwear. She told the reporter that she enjoyed combining lacy bras with high-waisted "granny panties" because it's not just about being sexy — "it's got to be funny."[12] As part of this first concert, Gaga did a striptease and lit hair spray on fire.[13] Nandini D'Souza, in *W* magazine, labeled Gaga's first performance at Lollapalooza "burlesque rock."[14] After her first concert, Lady Gaga was described by Beth Wilson, reporter for *Women's Wear Daily*, as performing in "risqué lingerie only" and the magazine made repeated mention of the fact that Gaga bought her outfits in porn shops.[15] Lady Gaga did not look like your typical pop princess, and even when she got closer to looking like one it was clear she was just playing a role.

Generally, one thinks of drag as a man dressing as a woman or a woman dressing as a man. Sue Devitt explains that "traditional notions of drag appear at first glance to be predicated on a sex-based performative cross accomplished through costumes and mannerisms."[16] To make it clear that what you are seeing is a man performing as a woman, or vice versa, the performance is often hypersexualized and exaggerated. Still, drag has less to do with performing gender in opposition to sex and more with making the relationship between sex and gender ambiguous. Judith Butler points to three significant aspects at play in drag — anatomical sex, gender identity, and gender performance.[17] Anatomical sex is the clearest of these categories: It is the genitals the performer had or was assigned at birth. Gender identity has to do with the way someone understands their sense of self in relationship to concepts of masculinity and femininity. Gender performance is the way that identity is portrayed to others. Generally, "if the anatomy is already distinct from the gender of the performer, and both of those are distinct from the gender of the performance, then the performance suggests a dissonance not only between sex and performance, but sex and gender, and gender and performance."[18] What we generally read as drag is an incompatibility between these three characteristics. With certain types of performances, the feeling of incompatibility has less to do with the lack of matchup between sex and gender and more to do with an extreme performance of gender that makes the connection between sex and gender seem unnatural. Debra Ferreday has built off of Butler's discussion of drag in her critique of the modern burlesque movement. She argues that today's burlesque has an awareness of the ironic that influences the performance of femininity.[19] Femininity is played up for its humor value and there is a focus on the tease element of the striptease. Burlesque shows and drag shows are operating out of same spaces and in the same communities. These shows have a strong relationship to the faux queen and bio-drag communities in that all of these presentations are essentially parodying the feminine performance.[20] Gaga's experiences in these clubs encouraged her to understand sex and gender as something that is performed.

During her time as a burlesque dancer, Lady Gaga used her real name: Stefani Joanne Angelina Germanotta. Germanotta's work as a burlesque dancer is evidenced in the development of the Lady Gaga persona. At her first concert, when asked about her real name, Gaga told a reporter: "She's not here anymore.... [S]he's covered in sequins."[21] Chicago did not know what to make of her, and reviews of the performance were not favorable. At that point, Gaga was "this goth-looking chick singing dance music in a black bikini top and working her stripper moves in the sunlight, turning her back to the audience and bending over in her thong. It was confusing."[22] She received a citation for indecent exposure, and many of the reporters mistook her for Amy Winehouse.[23] After leaving Chicago, Gaga began doing her first television appearances. The negative experience of Lollapalooza encouraged her to tone down the burlesque aspects of her show. What resulted was a less subversive and more awkward stage performance. This is, in part, because when she attempted to move small elements of burlesque performance into mainstream spaces she was not decipherable. Ferreday notes that the irony of burlesque and drag by women is often difficult for audiences to read; "while drag is performed by male bodies, and hence potentially from a position of power, a female performer is held to be both complicit with patriarchal power, and herself powerless: the performance thus emanates from a doubly powerless position. Because femininity is imagined as a property of 'women,' to parody femininity is to parody oneself and is hence open to being read as a performance of self-hatred."[24] Ultimately, Gaga would get better at integrating burlesque into her shows. The 2009 Monster Ball Tour has been described as having a "burlesque-inspired female mimicry."[25] Still, these early performances end up being read and received, not as discontinuous gender performances, but as an awkward, immature female seductress, attempting to sell sex.

Over the course of the year following Lollapalooza, after Gaga released *The Fame* and began promoting the album, her broadcast performances developed more of the sophistication of a pop music star, while also displaying a certain level of awkwardness that gave the performance the ironic or parodic feel that foreshadowed her later work. In April of 2008, Lady Gaga released the first single off her first album —"Just Dance"— to "little reaction" from the popular press and mainstream media.[26] It was a link to the video from Perez Hilton's blog in June 2008 that caused the song to "blow up."[27] As promotion for the video, Gaga did television appearances on *So You Think You Can Dance, Jimmy Kimmel Live*, and *The Ellen DeGeneres Show*. For most of the American public, the music video and these television appearances were their first exposure to the performer. On television, Gaga showcased her "disco stick"— referenced in the song — and a pair of video sunglasses. The disco stick, an obvious phallic reference, was an interesting element when it was held by a consistently pantsless Gaga. The video glasses had an LCD scroll that played words, such as "pop music will never be low brow." The look of the LCD glasses and light-up stick, combined with the electronic music, gave the show a mechanical feel. In some ways, Lady Gaga looked like a very typical young female performer. However, certain elements— a variety of long blond wigs for these performances, black lipstick, extreme eye shadow, huge eyelashes, and in one case a very orange tan —continually triggered the sense that something about the performance was unnatural. The mechanical feel and the unnaturalness serve as constant reminders that what was being viewed was a performance.

During these early performances, Lady Gaga developed a fetish for sunglasses, which continually kept her eyes hidden from the audience. During live performances, the glasses contributed to the overall mechanical feel by disconnecting Gaga from her audience. The choice to continually wear glasses is in sharp contrast to the way Gaga uses her gaze in music videos, which is discussed in Chapter 3. In the early parts of her career, the glasses were part of the Lady Gaga mythology and she was rumored to travel with more than 150 pairs of vintage sunglasses.[28] Often these glasses were not practical. For instance, the crystal sunglasses that Lady Gaga wore for live performances of "Just Dance" were designed to light up when used with the disco stick. Because they were covered in crystals, she could not see through them. As a result, she was often blind for the last minute or so of her performances. The performance is an example of Lady Gaga using opaque glasses to juxtapose a body on display and certain emotional boundaries.[29] The simultaneous display of self and disconnection places the viewer in the awkward position of voyeur.

Lady Gaga's costumes during her promotion of "Just Dance" showed the influence of her time as a burlesque dancer. Two signature outfits emerged from these shows—a red bodysuit with a hood and an origami dress with a removable skirt. The red bodysuit resembled costumes that Gaga wore while she did burlesque, and the removable skirt gave the show the striptease moment of the reveal that is critical to burlesque. In addition, costuming for each of the performances had an architectural, geometric feel that reshaped the body in various ways. Bodysuits with large shoulder pads and origami dresses with pronounced bubble skirts, signature looks for Gaga, exaggerated her hips and made her look simultaneously sexy and uncomfortable. This was echoed in the music video for the single, which began with the performer arriving at a party wearing a red coat with incredibly high shoulder pads. The emphasis on the shoulders tended to give a sense of masculinity to Gaga's otherwise slight frame, while the costumes that overemphasized the hips offered a pronounced sense of the femininity of her figure. The complexity of Gaga's gender performance took time to develop. The costumes shaped her body in ways that bordered on sexual but were ultimately awkward. However, none of this was awkward enough to seem deliberate, so it appeared that she just was an uncomfortable performer. All of these elements were reinforced by Gaga's dance style in video and live performances, which emphasized posing and sharp staccato movements. In an interview with a Canadian reporter, Gaga described this dance style as "crunk-vogue."[30] The sometimes awkwardness was compounded by the fact that Gaga is "not unequivocally sexy, and she does not wish to be a classic beauty, especially not in the sense traditionally understood within the world of pop music."[31] All the elements that would ultimately make up the Gaga spectacle are present but not pronounced.

At this point, the oddness of it all made it appear that Gaga was trying to look like everyone else and failing.

Gaga's success on the queer music scene, and its impact on her development, is likely what kept her career moving forward. At the New York release party for *The Fame* in October 2008, the opening acts were two staples of the queer music scene: Cazwell, a well-known LGBT rapper, and Amanda LePore, a transgender model who once appeared in *Playboy*. When asked what drew her to these performers, Gaga commented that it was "the freaking freedom, the joy, the fun and the spirit. There is no fucking spirit in the world like in the gay community."[32] Furthermore, when Interscope Records was promoting Gaga's first album they hired the company FlyLife, which specialized in marketing to the gay community. This, combined with Gaga playing a lot of gay clubs early in her career, created a strong connection between the performer and the gay community. The community encouraged the more transgressive aspects of Gaga's performance and ultimately pushed her to stop doing things halfway. In an interview with Brandon Voss for *HX Magazine*, Gaga said, "When I play at gay clubs, it's like playing for my friends; they get it and understand what I'm trying to say."[33] An *Out Magazine* reporter, in September 2009, noted that "Gaga has always been gay": "[S]he did Ellen before Leno, performed in gay clubs before straight ones, and plugs the gays constantly in interviews, even those with straight publications."[34] For her part, Lady Gaga has consistently acknowledged the role of the gay community in developing her persona: "When I started in the mainstream it was the gays that lifted me up…. I committed myself to them and they committed themselves to me, and because of the gay community I'm where I am today."[35] The queer community has exposure to more extreme gender performances than mainstream audiences. Her interactions with this community pushed the spectacle aspect of her show. The positive reception in that community encouraged Gaga to change her more mainstream stage show.

Prior to the controversy over Gaga's physical sex, there was much speculation about her sexual preference. The performer has admitted to having sexual relationships with both men and women. However, Gaga does not use media attention to fetishize this part of her identity as a celebrity. When asked about it in 2008, she said: "It's actually something I don't really like to talk about anymore. I'm kind of disappointed by it all." She expanded on this in another interview, saying: "Gay culture is not an underground tool for me. It's my whole life."[36] In response to Katy Perry's popular single "I Kissed a Girl," which was released in the same month as "Just Dance," Gaga said: "I don't like to be seen as somebody who is using the gay community to look edgy. I'm a free sexual woman and I like what I like. I don't want people to write that about me because I feel like it looks like I'm saying it because I'm trying to be edgy or underground."[37] This response does not appear to be a criticism of Perry. In one of Gaga's Gagavision videos in 2009, she asked Perry if she could kiss her so that she could say she had "kissed a girl."[38] Instead, it is part of a larger theme for Gaga about sexuality and celebrity. A year later, she told a reporter: "I just have so much respect for my friends who live bisexual lives and who live transgender lives and who every single day have to fight for their identity and have to deal with all the things that come along with sexual orientation."[39] Lady Gaga wanted to avoid falling into the stereotype of using bisexuality to be provocative; "I like to be as open but as diplomatic as I can be in order not to sensationalize bisexuality in pop music. I have no interest in using my sexual orientation to sell records."[40] Both these comments show an awareness of the commercial and celebrity cache that exists for female pop stars expressing a non-traditional sexual preference. As she commented later in 2009, "Being a woman in the pop world, sexuality is half poison and half liberation. What's the line? I don't have a line. I am the most sexually free woman on the planet, and I genuinely am empowered from a very honest place by my sexuality."[41] Even at that honest place, the performer told an interviewer from *Q Magazine* that she recognized how threatening her sexuality could be: "When a guy says, Oh, I fucked all these chicks this week, there's a high-five and giggling.... But when a woman does it and it's published or she's open about her sexuality or she's free, or liberated, it's, Oh, she must have a dick. There's a threat."[42] In interviews, Lady Gaga demonstrates a remarkable control over her sexual identity. She expresses sexual desire freely while pointing out attempts to persuade her to perform popular fantasies and she consistently comments on the reasoning behind those fantasies.

In a 2009 *Entertainment Weekly* interview with Whitney Pastorek, Lady Gaga summarized many of the issues that had come to surround her sexuality early on. By that point, the performer had developed a reputation for public pantlessness. When Pastorek asked her about this fashion choice, she said:

I just don't feel that it's all that sexy. It's weird. And uncomfortable. I look at photos of myself, and I look like such a tranny! It's amazing! I look like Grace Jones, androgynous, robo, future fashion queen. It's not what is sexy. It's graphic, and it's art. But that's what's funny: Well, yeah, I take my pants off, but does it matter if your pants are off if you've got eight-inch shoulder pads on, and a hood, and black lipstick and glasses with rocks on them? I don't know. That's sexy to me. But I don't really think anybody's d — is hard, looking at that. I think they're just confused, and maybe a little scared. It's more Manson to me than it is sexy.[43]

It might be easy for some to dismiss the star, who had almost been arrested in Chicago and Los Angeles for pantlessness, as just another 20-something pop princess who is trying to sell sex.[44] However, this quote points to early attempts to play with that persona of selling sex in a way that disrupts typical public discourses about sex and gender. The reading of Gaga as a drag queen is heavily influenced by all these early elements of her performance — the burlesque influence, the awkward portrayal of a female pop star, her connections to the gay community, and rumors about her sexuality. When society sees someone failing to perform the typical heterosexual identity — in Gaga's case the female pop star as sexual object — the assumption is that the discontinuity must mean that the person has a different sexual identity. There is a disruption in Gaga's presentations of sex and gender that leads to a questioning of her essential self. Generally, this type of disjointedness goes unseen; "the construction of coherence conceals the gender discontinuities that run rampant within heterosexual, bisexual, and gay and lesbian contexts in which gender does not necessarily follow from sex, and desire, or sexuality generally, does not seem to follow from gender."[45] In Gaga's performance, the discontinuity is more pronounced because none of her gender performances seem to naturally align with the essential self. This may explain why Gaga quickly moved from attempting to play the traditional pop star to conceiving herself as a performance artist and embracing the drag performance.

The Monstrous and Excessive Body

Caitlin Moran, a reporter for *The Times UK*, interviewed Lady Gaga after a stage show in Germany in 2010. After the interview, Moran reports that Gaga invited her out to a sex club and at some point in the evening the reporter followed the performer into the bathroom. After seeing Gaga urinate, Moran felt comfortable confirming that Lady Gaga does not have a penis.[46] The very notion that a reporter would follow a celebrity into the bathroom and watch her use the toilet to confirm the status of her genitals highlights both the ridiculousness of media surveillance of celebrities and the level of social panic over hermaphroditism. Ann Torrusio argues that "the historical threat posed by hermaphrodites was the ability to experience too much pleasure. The excess of pleasure threatened the status quo, and the inability to categorize and compartmentalize the human body threatened the very structure of the state."[47] Even now, "the curiosity and debates over Lady Gaga's sexuality and rumors of her hermaphroditism stem from the legacy of the public's desire to restrict or confine the parameters of an individual's sexual activity and that a deviation from those pre-established categories legitimizes labeling one as a monster."[48] The public speculation over Gaga's genitals is closely tied to her expressed excess of sexual freedom and her self-declared role as the Mother Monster.

The appearance of drag in Gaga's performance is not a result of performing gender cross-sex. It has to do with her use of feminine ritual. Gender is not something that reads intuitively; our ability to read it comes from a lifetime of being exposed to a variety of masculine and feminine rituals that allow for the coding of the body.[49] Gender performance is learned through "a regularized and constrained repetition of norms."[50] In the case of Lady Gaga, these rituals have been thoroughly adopted and exaggerated to the point where they appear awkward, perfunctory, and mechanized. This is the moment of gender parody, when ritual behavior becomes so complete and apparent that it turns "an organic moment into something mechanical, and so reveals the mechanization underlying the original."[51] The overt adoption of gender norms makes it clear that these performances do not derive naturally from sex, and this troubles the viewer's ability to read the relationship between sex and gender. Lady Gaga's performance is an example of how "drag fully subverts the distinction between inner and outer psychic space and effectively mocks both the expressive mode of gender and the notion of true gender identity."[52]

Lady Gaga combines drag with the monster metaphor to create a whole new set of visual arguments about sexuality and celebrity. Take, for example, her April 2010 cover for *Q Magazine* in London. One reporter described the magazine photo spread as "true lads' mag style, the image is of a topless blonde, in black leather-like trousers, one gloved hand coyly positioned over her boobs, the other not so coyly rammed against her crotch. Jutted hips, parted lips and vacuous expression tick the remaining boxes that constitute the image of sexy."[53] Based on this description, the photos might sound like many generic sexualized depictions of women. However, a few things made this image different. Gaga wore a prosthetic penis; the appendage was visible through her pants and she was depicted grabbing her crotch in the cover shot.[54] In the shoot, Gaga also donned long black claws, which she used to cover her breast and clutch her crotch. The juxtaposition of claws/breast and claws/penis reframes her anatomy as monstrous. In the accompanying article, Gaga commented that "we all know one of the biggest talking points of the year was that I have a dick, so why not give them what they want? I want to comment on that in a beautiful, artistic way. How I wanna show it. And I want to call this piece Lady Gaga Dies Hard."[55] Sloop argues that alternative performances of gender are often presented as aberrations to allow members of society to engage them without being threatened by the gender trouble they provoke.[56] That aberration sometimes takes the form of the monster: "Monsters have, or seem to have, freedoms we lack. They transgress, cross over, do not stay put where — for the convenience of our categories of sex, race, class or creed — we would like them to stay. Sometimes it is their painful beauty, or untrammeled individuality; other times it is simply the liberties they take ... that so astonish us."[57] Gaga embraces this notion of monstrosity and aberration. The combination of monster and celebrity allows her to straddle the role of insider and outsider — speaking to multiple audiences at the same time. Some see the aberration and use it as a way to disregard her discourse. It is easier to imagine Gaga as a hermaphrodite, and her sex as ambivalent, than to confront the contradictions in her performance. Fans, on the other hand, strongly identify with the arguments about sex and aberration. In this way, "[t]he monster pleasures as well as polices."[58]

Despite the bio-drag extreme version of femininity that Gaga performs, her physical performance of sex is often perceived as male. That disconnect is probably what led to the rumors that Lady Gaga is a hermaphrodite. Eventually, the rumors became so prevalent that MTV weighed in with their speculations on the matter and Barbara Walters asked Gaga directly about her genitals and her sexual preference.[59] These rumors could be seen as simply a response to the confusion generated by bio-drag and the overall physicality of Gaga's stage performance. Lady Gaga is certainly not the first woman in the spotlight to be plagued with rumors that she has a penis. What is interesting is not the rumor but the way she has recrafted this rumor and claimed it as a moment to critique media depictions of sex and gender. Gaga's playing with this rumor served as a bridge between her early performance of bio-drag and her later presentation of a male and an asexual alter ego. Furthermore, she relates this rumor to the depiction of herself as a monster, excessive and sexual in a way not often accessed by female celebrities.

Questions about Lady Gaga's sex started circulating through the media in early 2009. Online, the rumor has taken on a few different forms—Gaga is a hermaphrodite, she is a man with a very small penis, or possibly she is a very well-endowed man. Gaga has used humor to craft her response to these speculations. For instance, on April 17, 2009, Gaga was interviewed in Britain on *Friday Night with Jonathan Ross*. In the interview she wore a couture dress, created by Singapore-British designer Ashley Isham, made entirely of red Post-it notes. When the Internet rumor that Gaga had a penis was brought up, Ross commented, "If you're well-endowed, I don't know where you're hiding it!" And Gaga responded, to great applause by the audience: "I have a really big donkey dick!"[60] In June of that same year, Gaga performed at the MuchMusic Video Awards in Toronto; the singer wore a leotard that was cut in such a way to make part of the labia visible.[61] This raised questions about whether or not her wardrobe choices were a direct response to the conversations about her genitalia. Then, on June 25, during the Glastonbury festival in the UK, someone took a video with a cell-phone camera that appeared to show the performer's penis coming out from under her dress. As pictures and video circulated on the Web, a quote attributed to Gaga started appearing on blogs that seemed to confirm what the images implied. Supposedly she had said in an interview, "It's not something I'm ashamed of, I just don't go around telling everyone.... I have both male and female genitalia, but I consider myself female. It's just a little bit of a penis and doesn't interfere much with my life."[62] By August, the quote had expanded: "The reason I haven't talked about it is that it's not a big deal to me. Like, come on. It's not like we all go around talking about our [genitalia]. I think this is a great opportunity to make other multiple-gendered people feel more comfortable with their bodies. I'm sexy, I'm hot. I have both. Big f — — ing deal."[63] The quotes were never substantiated, but there is speculation that Gaga staged the original video and circulated the quote as a publicity stunt.[64]

The "Lady Gaga has a penis!" rumor is a prime example of the typical relationship between the mainstream media and celebrity bodies. Mainstream media often treats celebrities as subjects of discourse, which removes a lot of agency involved in the relationship between the media and the mediated. These attempts to get at the "truth" of Lady Gaga's body discipline her gender choices and function as an example to others about the dangers of transgression. The conversation makes the body the objective standard for identity and allows both the mainstream media and viewers to analyze Gaga without necessarily taking her voice into account. As the rumor developed, Gaga began using interviews as a space not just to respond to the speculation but also to reshape the conversation taking place around her. In a September 2009 interview with an Australian radio show, she commented, "I think this is society's reaction to a strong woman. The idea that we equate strength with men and a penis is a symbol of male strength.... I'm not offended at all, but my vagina might be a little bit upset."[65] This was the beginning of Gaga recrafting the rumor. This continued in December 2009 in an *LA Times* interview with the performer. Lady Gaga told interviewer Ann Powers, "I'm getting the sense that you're a little bit of a feminist, like I am, which is good.... I find that men get away with saying a lot in this business, and that women get away with saying very little.... In my opinion, women need and want someone to look up to that they feel have the full sense of who they are, and says, 'I'm great.'"[66] At this point we see a consistent message coming from Gaga. Rather than argue against the rumor, she uses this as a moment to comment on the reasoning behind the rumor. As part of MAC Cosmetics's AIDS fund, Gaga appeared with Cindy Lauper in an interview, where she stated that "people think if you are strong about your sexuality, you must have a dick. [But] You can be strong about your sexuality and be a smart woman who wears lipstick and high heels and looks pretty."[67] As she puts it: "I don't make it as a defense. I make it as, OK, guys, it's been two years, and I've made a lot of music, and I know my greatness is individual. And I want every woman to be able to say that."[68]

The conversation about Gaga's anatomy is translated to a discussion of the role of women in the music industry. Instead of asking if she has a penis, many reporters started asking if she was a feminist. In an August 2009 interview, Gaga said: "Yes. Yes I am. I am a feminist. I reject wholeheartedly the way we are taught to perceive women. The beauty of women, how a woman should act or behave. Women are strong and fragile. Women are beautiful and ugly. We are soft spoken and loud, all at once. There is something mind-controlling about the way we're taught to view women."[69] In this conversation about the nature of women, there is a commentary about what that means for how woman is performed and about the backlash for performing woman inappropriately. Gaga relates that to a larger discussion about her role as a celebrity: "Perhaps we can make women's rights trendy. Strength, feminism, security, the wisdom of the woman. Let's make that trendy."[70] The comments on trendiness indicate Gaga's awareness of her role as a celebrity, and its culturally implicit duties of making things popular.

The lyrics and videos of Gaga's music often contribute to the gender ambiguity of her performance by raising questions about the singer's sexuality. Take, for instance, the single "LoveGame"; the video was released in August of 2009. The song is known for the repetition of the phrase "I want to take a ride on your disco stick." In an interview with *Rolling Stone*, Gaga explained that the term "disco stick" is "another of my very thoughtful metaphors for a cock. I was at a nightclub, and I had quite a sexual crush on somebody, and I said to them, 'I wanna ride on your disco stick'"[71] This might give the impression that this catchy dance number is typically heteronormative. However, while the song seems to be about desiring the male body, in the video Gaga carries her own disco stick. She describes it as "a giant rock-candy pleasuring tool — that lights up."[72] The song may be a sexual invitation to another, but the performance implication is clear: Gaga can pleasure herself. Throughout the video, Gaga is shown engaged in a number of sexual activities and her sexuality is often portrayed as masculine and aggressive. At one point, Gaga is shown making out with a police officer in a New York City subway. Each time the image is played in the video, the sex of the police officer changes. In the scenes at the end of the video, Gaga is dancing with a large group of male dancers. The dancers are all grabbing their crotches and gesturing in a typically sexually aggressive masculine manner. Gaga, the only female in the group, is shown grabbing her crotch in the exact same gesture. Through most of the video

Gaga is carrying her disco stick, and at one point she seems to be using the disco stick to fend off the male dancers.[73] The disco stick is part of a larger trend of Lady Gaga performing with her own phallus.

In November of 2009, Gaga released the video for her single "Bad Romance" and questions of her sexuality started to meld more with the monster metaphor. The plot for the video is based on the sex trade: Gaga has been kidnapped by a bunch of supermodels who are forcing drugs and alcohol on her to make her pliant, then selling her to the highest bidder. The video plot is a larger metaphor for the way that celebrities are sold, and the song is transformed into a metaphor for the "Bad Romance" that female celebrities have with the media. Throughout, Gaga's sexuality is combined with various monstrous elements. In the beginning of the video, Gaga and several other dancers are shown climbing out of coffins. Her coffin is labeled "Monster." She is shown dancing in a white latex suit with claws. At one point, she is naked in a shower and her back appears to have a set of spiky growths. The video features the famous 12-inch-high McQueen Alien heels, which indeed make Gaga look fittingly alien when she attempts to walk in them. All of this culminates in Gaga using a pyrotechnic bra to kill the man who purchased her — making her breasts literally weapons. As proof of her liberation from being bought and sold, Gaga says in the song she's "a free bitch." The selling of Gaga's sexual performance is combined with the images of her as a monster. While the video does not comment overtly on the rumors of Gaga as a hermaphrodite, it does continue the conversation about her sexuality as aberrant and establishes her body as othered, weaponized, and even obscene.

Lady Gaga responded directly to the hermaphrodite rumor in a January 2010 interview with Barbara Walters. Gaga was interviewed as part of a series on the most fascinating people of 2009. For the interview, she showed up in Chanel and "dressed, for the broadcast, like her eighty-year-old interlocutor, who did not seem to get the joke."[74] The performer was dressed in an almost drag version of the typical *20/20* interviewee and sitting in what could be a living room, having a heart-to-heart with Barbara Walters. This established a unique space to address the question of Gaga's sex. Before discussing such matters directly, however, Walters focused on Gaga's sexual orientation, asking Gaga questions about fantasizing about women and whether or not she had ever had sex with a woman. In this interaction, Walters is performing the typical role of mainstream media —

turning the speaker into the subject of the discussion so that they are the object being examined. After this lead-in, Walters asked Gaga directly: "You know, there also is this strange rumor that you're part man and part woman. You've heard this rumor?"[75] When Gaga acknowledged the rumor and said it was not true, Walters asked how she felt about it. She responded that "at first it was very strange and everyone sorta said, 'That's really quite a story!' But in a sense, I portray myself in a very androgynous way, and I love androgyny.... I like pushing boundaries."[76] Most noticeably, Gaga did not respond to the underlying question of her maleness or femaleness. Instead, the answer focuses on the reasoning behind the rumor and Gaga relates the speculation to her performance of gender. The response can be seen as a commentary on both the overall rumor and the interview itself. Gaga's performance of the typical Barbara Walters interviewee, juxtaposed with conversations about fantasizing about women and her feelings about androgyny, raises questions about the traditional sexual performance of celebrity.

Around the time of the Barbara Walters interview, Lady Gaga began using other media outlets to take charge of the rumor and to play with the implications of her potentially having a penis. The rumor slowly became part of her overall use of gender parody. Perhaps the most direct instances of this can be seen in the music videos for "Telephone" and "Alejandro." The music video for "Telephone" was a follow-up to the "Paparazzi" video. At the end of "Paparazzi" Gaga is arrested for poisoning her lover. This leads to the opening scene in "Telephone," where two female prison guards are dragging Gaga into a prison cell. After performing what appears to be a strip search, the first guard says, "I told you she didn't have a dick," and the second one responds, "Too bad." This exchange encourages the viewer to think of the rumor while watching the rest of the video. One of Gaga's costumes for the video is a thong made out of police evidence tape. While she is dancing in this outfit, there are close-ups of the performer's genital region and the evidence tape is so tight one can see the outline of her labia. The comment is both that her body is "evidence" of her femaleness and her gender-ambiguous body is the scene of a crime. In the video, Gaga makes out with one woman and there is a plotline that depicts a close relationship with Beyoncé Knowles's character, Honey Bee. At the end of the video, Gaga and Beyoncé, after killing off Beyoncé's lover, are shown driving off together in what looks like homage to the movie *Thelma and Louise*. Though, as David Annandale points out, "everything about the ending implies a revision of Thelma and Louise's finale. This particular sisterhood need not preserve itself by going over a cliff."[77] It has long been a trope in media depictions of homosexuality that the sexually aberrant die in the end, but this is not Gaga's fate. In fact, the final scene says "to be continued," making it clear this duo does not suffer the same punishment that befalls most women who transgress social boundaries. Gaga's sexual performance is placed next to her evidence of sex. This forces the audience to confront her as both female and sexually free. If she were to allow the rumor to continue that she was a hermaphrodite, or if she were to respond in less overt ways, then any of these performances could be written off simply as evidence of the performer's sex. When the two are placed together, the audience is asked to process the relationship between Gaga's sex and gender performance.

The music video for the song "Alejandro" also raises some interesting questions about anatomy and the performance of gender. Filmed a few months after "Telephone," much of the video looks like a gay cabaret, with constant images of attractive, half-naked men in military garb. In an extended series of scenes in the video, Gaga simulates homosexual sex with a male lover, with the positions implying that she has a penis. In these scenes Gaga and her lover are only wearing undergarments and at various points the underwear clearly outlines both Gaga's labia and her lover's penis. This creates a contrast between the visual presence of the performer's vagina and the performance of the invisible penis. One of the more haunting scenes in the video occurs when the camera pulls back and the viewer is shown a very solemn-looking young soldier watching the room full of men, and Gaga, simulating sex. The shot reminds one of Gaga's campaign against Don't Ask, Don't Tell. In an interview about the video, Gaga said the concept behind all this was about "purity of my friendships with my gay friends, and how I've been unable to find that with a straight man in my life. It's a celebration and an admiration of gay love — it confesses my envy of the courage and bravery they require to be together. In the video I'm pining for the love of my gay friends— but they just don't want me to be with them."[78] Gaga's parody of sexual performance in the video functions as another commentary on the physical limits of the body and the way those limits influence both homosexual and heterosexual relationships.

Even as Gaga is being forced to provide evidence of her body and is playing with gender norms, there is a constant sensuality to her performance. The question of her as a hermaphrodite echoes historical discussions of the physically deformed as monstrous aberrations.[79] Gaga's sexuality combines with her discussion of monstrosity: "[S]he is indeed the monster. But the monster is also sexual. The Alien is a grotesque, predatory creature, but it also sports a phallic head, drools KY Jelly, and its movements are sinuous and fluid.... The sexual/monstrous image simultaneously draws the viewer's attention to the contradiction and shows that the two forms, in fact, are not contradictory."[80] In the end, "Gaga does make the sexual monstrous, but she also makes the monstrous sexual and desirable."[81] This is not uncommon; "you will find that each monster embodies and embroiders an eroticized tale, as each body is slowly stripped, deliciously moralized in public: the revelation of one, the exhibition of another, the forced display of a third are moralized for the profit of the sentimental viewer. The obscene offered as civic tableaux for the public good."[82] The difference here is that as Gaga manipulates the media discussion of her body, the moral of the story becomes less clear. Which performance is good and which is bad? This is a question she does not clearly answer. Instead, she directs attention to the media habit of moralizing female behavior and the way it restricts celebrities and women in general. Eventually, the message evolves past conversations about women's bodies, to discuss bodies and gender performance in general.

Introducing Jo Calderone

In March of 2011, Gaga did an interview as part of the Musicians@ Google series. During the interview she was asked what it is like being a female pop star and an artist at the same time. Lady Gaga told the interviewer that the music industry had reached a point where they did not expect much from women; the conversation echoed statements she had previously made about sex being part poison for women in music. Still, as an artist she was adamantly unwilling to give up any part of herself for her performance. She told the interviewer that "me and my tits and my ass and my brain are very proud to be here today."[83] As a performer, Lady Gaga has never shied away from sex or sexuality in her work. With the release of her 2011 album, *Born this Way*, and in particular its fourth single, "Yoü+I," she took this performance to a whole new level. In the "Yoü+I" album cover art and music video, Lady Gaga featured two alter egos: Jo Calderone and Yüyi. These alter egos allow Lady Gaga to explore the transgressive nature of transgender identity within the context of the overtly mainstream genre of popular music.

Each of Germanotta's three identities—Lady Gaga, Jo Calderone, and Yüyi—highlights an extreme relationship between sex and gender performance. As discussed previously, Lady Gaga pushes the hyperfeminine performance to the point where it is questioned as drag and generates speculation about the nature of her physical sex. Jo Calderone, as will be discussed, is constructed as hypermasculine. As part of this performance, penile prosthetics are used to display extreme sex—the always erect and visible penis—in parallel with extreme masculinity. In interviews about Calderone, Gaga has used this identity to comment on the current social position of transsexuals. Her statements about Calderone are a far cry from her previous comments on the trans community; Gaga once used the slur "tranny" as a descriptor for her appearance. The Calderone alter has a sophistication that demonstrates an evolution in Gaga's conceptualization of gender. Yüyi's identity is placed somewhere between the two performances of Gaga and Calderone. As a mermaid, while Yüyi is gendered feminine, she has no physical sex. This is further emphasized by latex skin binding her breast to eliminate nipples, as markers of sexuality, while making her appear nude. In addition, the fish tail is constructed as an appendage, as opposed to a costume. It is displayed as an irremovable part of Yüyi and as an indication that she has no genitals. These three performances echo Butler's argument about the political nature of sex: One's anatomical sex is not a given; it is a politically defined category. As such, "if the very designation of sex is political, then 'sex,' that designation supposed to be most raw, proves to be always already 'cooked.'"[84] According to Butler, the constructions of sex, gender, and desire are deeply encoded into language. Put another way, "The existence of individuals who do not readily fit into the traditional, prescribed categories of man or woman and the existence of those who, like Lady Gaga, can 'try on' a different gender at will, calls into question the very presence of these categories."[85]Instead of seeking some kind of pre-sexed, pre-gendered, androgynous identity, these alter egos place categories of sex next to those of sexual desire and gender identity, to illustrate the strain created by the binaries of sex and gender. As each alter ego performs sexual desire, the social constructs of sex and gender are heightened. It is in the want of another that the alter egos reveal themselves.

JO CALDERONE

From the first introduction of Jo Calderone, the character has been presented as having an intimate relationship with Lady Gaga. The way that Calderone talks about the relationship allows him to simultaneously construct Gaga's hyperfemininity and his own hypermasculinity. Germanotta uses the sexual relationship between her two alter egos— Lady Gaga and Jo Calderone — to go from highlighting gender as a performance to highlighting the constructed nature of heterosexuality and desire. While drag can allow for new or alternative gender performances, Germanotta's competing performances of Calderone and Gaga operate largely on essentialization and standard images of masculinity and femininity. For the most part, "Jo Calderone is a character who respects the dimensions of the drag king performance with an exaggerated male form interested in stereotypically male things."[86] The essentialized male and female performances result in a very typical heterosexual relationship between Gaga and Calderone.

Calderone made his first media appearance in a September 2010 issue of the Japanese *Vogue Hommes*.[87] He was featured in a fashion editorial titled "The Elegant Mechanic." The interview described Calderone as a Sicilian-American mechanic who works in his father's shop and has a typically masculine obsession with muscle cars. Calderone's male-ness was reinforced in the interview when he implied there was a sexual relationship between him and Lady Gaga. As pictures were released from the shoot, the media immediately began outing Jo Calderone as Lady Gaga.[88] However, there was no confirmation of Calderone's identity until a year later when Gaga released "Yoü+I." In a memorandum to *V Magazine*, Gaga described Calderone as a "mischievous experiment."[89] The male alter ego was envisioned by Gaga and Nick Knight, a Haus of Gaga collaborator, as a fully developed alternate identity; she stated that the ultimate goal of the project was "to co-exist with an alternate version of myself—in the same universe."[90] The performer said that with this new identity came a permissiveness: "I felt permission through him to confess things about myself as a woman, things I would normally keep hidden. In a way, it seemed that he could get away with a lot more than I can. He talked about his feelings, wore Brooks Brothers, smoked Marlboro Lights, drank beer on stage, and talked about what I refuse to discuss publicly: my relationships."[91] Gaga has said before that for a woman in the music business sex is part poison. With her female alter ego, Germanotta had to work to control interviews and manage media depictions of her sex life. Calderone does not need the same level of management. The co-existence of these two identities allows Germanotta to explore the way gender identity limits behavior. However, more than that, by placing them in a relationship with each other she is able to highlight boundaries and perform some of the language binaries of sex.

Media and technology have played an important role in creating the sexual relationship between Gaga and Calderone. The relationship was first implied in the *Vogue Hommes* interview, which shows a use of mass media to introduce a narrative. Shortly after the photos surfaced, Jo Calderone had a Twitter account.[92] Calderone and Gaga even commented on each other on Twitter. One of Calderone's first Twitter posts, August 2010, read: "I am a man. I am a human being. I am me. And I was Born This Way." The post came almost a full year before the release of "Born This Way." The capitalization of the title implies that Gaga had plans for the album long before its release. A few weeks before Calderone appeared in the music video for "Yoü+I," he tweeted: "Your identity is my religion. Marry your identity. + never be afraid to love yourself." At that stage, media and technology was just a way for the two alter egos to publicly communicate with each other. In the music video for *Yoü+I*, Calderone's previously intimated relationship with Lady Gaga became an intimately physical relationship. The two alter egos are shown kissing and fondling one another. Various filming techniques made it possible for the alter egos to publicly display their affections. The narrative of the relationship took on new depths when Germanotta performed as Jo Calderone at the 2011 Video Music Awards. At each stage, the media has been a key component of the relationship between the two identities. It is common for mainstream media to follow the ups and downs of celebrity relationships and report all the messy details to the public. Lady Gaga, rather than making her actual relationships public, exploited this with a staged relationship for the media to report on. Because Germanotta is both the people in the relationship, there is no chance for media outlets to uncover intimate details or out various aspects of the relationship. She has total control. Using the mainstream media outlets to stage the performance turns the whole thing into a parody of the typical relationship between celebrities and the media.

Calderone's voice also allowed Germanotta an outlet through which she could publicly analyze her performance as Lady Gaga in new ways. In his opening monologue at the VMAs, Calderone says that he came to the awards as a goodwill gesture after an argument with Gaga. In the monologue, Calderone gives voice to Gaga's fears about how her role as a powerful female is perceived by her male lovers. After introducing himself, Calderone announces that Gaga has just left him for being crazy like every other guy. This is followed up with the question "But she's fucking crazy too, right? I mean she is FUCKING CRAZY. For example — she gets out of the bed, puts on the heels. She goes into the bathroom. I hear the water go on. She comes out of the bathroom, dripping wet. She still has the heels on." All of this echoes common narratives about masculine jealousy and possessiveness, coupled with feminine eccentricity. Calderone's monologue is a story of competing insecurities. This performance gets at the way insecurity interacts with desire, as he tells the audience: "When she comes, it's like she covers her face, 'cause she doesn't want me to see that. She can't stand to have one honest moment when nobody's watching." The notion of spectatorship is particularly noteworthy in this monologue. This account verifies that Gaga's extreme performance continues, even when the larger audience is not around. Furthermore, the performance is both disingenuous and impossible to turn off. Through Calderone, Germanotta seems to acknowledge that even in her relationship with herself she does not know how to stop performing. Since Calderone is Gaga, what he is describing seems to be masturbation. Calderone's monologue raised questions of authenticity and honesty that have followed Gaga throughout her career. Interestingly, the Calderone persona has the same commitment to maintaining character as Lady Gaga. Throughout the VMAs, Calderone stayed in character and acted confused when reporters asked questions that implied the performance was somehow inauthentic.

When Lady Gaga publicly discusses her relationship with Jo Calderone, she alternates between acknowledging him as a construct and embracing the narrative of the two as lovers. While Jo Calderone may describe his relationship with Gaga as rocky, she professes to be very much in love with him. This is a typical social performance of masculine nonchalance and excessive feminine emotion. In the beginning of August of 2011, Gaga tweeted a picture of Jo Calderone from her new single with the words: "You will never find what you are looking for in love, if you don't love yourself." A few weeks later, and shortly before the awards show, she told one interviewer, "He's really hot. It's so weird, because I'm usually really funny about men, but he does something to me."[93] The meta-discourse here is intriguing, as Gaga goes back and forth between constructing the dynamic as a love of herself and as a love of an alter ego. This is circulated in the same conversation as another set of discourse where Gaga talks about the sex life of Germanotta. Talking to *i-D Magazine* in Fall 2010, she refused to tell the reporter her name, saying that "when I make love, they say Gaga."[94] A year later, in a *60 Minutes* interview with Anderson Cooper, she confessed that in bed she prefers to be called Steffani. The performer said she would be really "freaked out" by a lover referring to her as Gaga. Contrast this with the VMA monologue: When Jo Calderone talks about his sex life with Lady Gaga, he refers to her exclusively as Gaga and says she can't even stop performing when she orgasms. The constant movement back and forth between multiple identities, and the acknowledgment that each of them has different sexual desires, creates a lot of ambivalence surrounding sex, gender, and desire.

Buried in all this conversation over what to call Gaga in bed or who Germanotta is when she is experiencing a moment of sexual pleasure is an interesting commentary about how celebrities publicly perform their sex lives. Early in Gaga's career, everyone wanted to know what her sexual preference was, who she was sleeping with, and what her genitals looked like. This created a need for constant discourse about who she is in bed. The moment of sex, of desire and of orgasm, is treated as the authentic moment. That is defined as the space where the media will finally discover the real Lady Gaga. The focus on sexual desire as authenticity gets at the public/private dichotomy of celebrity life that Gaga has commented on in several interviews. In 2009, she told an interviewer from *Maxim Magazine*: "My concerts are about being private in public, but I'm very protective. My apartment is my stage, and my bedroom is my stage — they're just not stages you're allowed to see. When you let a bunch of people in there, they fuck with your energy and it becomes a circus. Put in another way: Everybody wants me to show my vagina to the world all the time. And the truth is, I don't have to."[95] For a female performer, there is a very real danger to revealing too much sexuality. As Lady Gaga has noted: "I have this weird thing that if I sleep with someone they're going to take my creativity from me through my vagina."[96] The ability for Gaga to define herself happens only so long as she restricts access to her sex life. Calderone becomes a way to publicly perform sex and desire without having to openly expose her vagina. More important, it allows Lady Gaga to have a sex life without taking privacy away from Germanotta.

This language produced by Gaga has worked its way into multiple public discourses about the nature of gender identity. Given the context of the rumors about Lady Gaga as a hermaphrodite and the constant comments about her being in drag, it is not surprising that much of the discourse that has surrounded the Jo Calderone performance has focused on transgender identity. When asked about reading Jo Calderone as a transgender, Lady Gaga said:

> Reading Jo in any kind of way is a fair reading. The performance of Jo is meant to manipulate the visualization of gender in as many ways as I possibly could. And in a completely different way, sort of do that by creating what seems to be a straight man — a straight and quite relatable American man. I wanted to see how I could take someone who is so approachable and so relatable and press a much more unrelatable issue that is so hidden or so chained up. [I wanted to see] how I could put someone who is challenging all of those things in a very pop culture moment and force people to deal with it no matter how uncomfortable or exciting it may be.
>
> The album tackles all sorts of ideas about dual identity and fantasy and reality and artifice versus realism and how I believe there is no line and how can we become potentially the greatest part of ourselves by releasing our inhibitions in reference to fantasy? How can I reinvent myself, how can I remodel myself to become greater? How can I become more honest every day?[97]

There are several things worth noting in Gaga's discussion of reading Jo Calderone. The first is this notion of relatability. As discussed in the previous section, something in Gaga's performance has always read as being disingenuous. There is a constant sense that what one is seeing is a performance. It is that recognition of performance that often raises questions about the "true nature" of the performer's sex. So in a reversal of sorts, male drag becomes the attempt to be more relatable and more honest. Furthermore, prior to the introduction of Jo Calderone, Gaga had pushed the conversation about her genitalia in multiple different settings. Those performances tended to be more overtly about making people uncomfortable. This performance seems to be an attempt at creating something that on the surface is more comfortable, but it still pushes at the underlying social tensions surrounding sexuality.

One of the ways this tension seems to be dealt with publicly is to treat Jo Calderone as Gaga in drag. This reading was most apparent in Jo Calderone's interaction with Britney Spears. During the VMAs, Britney Spears received the Michael Jackson Video Vanguard Award. When Jo Calderone came onstage to present the award, the announcers introduced him as Lady Gaga. This set the scene for Calderone's introduction of Britney Spears, where he talked about growing up with a picture of Britney Spears hanging above his bed. There are several intimations in the monologue that Calderone sexually desired Britney Spears and fantasized about her when he masturbated. When he originally handed her the award, Calderone kissed Spears on the cheek. Then the two began to stare each other down as if there might be more sexual tension. At the moment when Calderone, awkwardly, went in for a more passionate kiss, Britney Spears pulled back and, while laughing, said, "I've done that already": a reference to her previous VMA performance where she kissed Madonna. Throughout this interaction there is a definite tension between Calderone's commitment to performing the male identity and those around him being unwilling to treat him as a man. He is introduced as Lady Gaga, instead of Jo, and Britney Spears treats the interaction as being a throwback to her previous kiss with a woman. In a post–VMA interview, Calderone continued to make comments about Britney Spears. This prompted a variety of reactions from the media. An ABC News story on the event posited: "If an actual man had said what Gaga said after attempting to make out with Spears, he'd probably be slapped with a restraining order."[98] According to John Sloop, "people who are articulating a transgressive position, whether on the left or on the right, whether radically inclusionary or radically exclusionary, find themselves 'disciplined.'"[99] After the VMAs, much of the disciplining of Gaga came in the media pronouncement that the performance was "weird." David Schmitt, professor of psychology, commented on the performance: "Lady Gaga isn't everyone's cup of tea even as a female. But perhaps their [the media's] reactions to Jo Calderone were also because the gender-bending was a tad too good, so good that it broke down our ability to cleanly categorize Lady Gaga as female versus male."[100] Lady Gaga makes audiences uncomfortable as both a man and a woman. Yüyi offers a third option.

YÜYI

Germanotta's mythological mermaid alter ego, Yüyi, introduces a variety of new complications and tensions into her discourse on sex and gender. With Gaga and Calderone as alter egos, there is a strong sense of heteronormativity and adherence to gender norms. Butler points out that this is often the case with gender performance. Given the overall predisposition to believe that being physically male will lead to a desire for people who are physically female, "the assumption remains that boy traits will lead to a desire for women, and girl traits will lead to a desire for men. In both cases, heterosexual desire is presumed, where presumably opposites attract."[101] Even in homosexual relationships, we are inclined to read the partnership through a heterosexual lens. There is an assumption that one person in the relationship will be the masculine one and one will be the feminine one. Yüyi lacks a physical sex, but the audience is able identify her as "she" largely through the performance of frustrated desire for a male partner.

Of all the alter egos, Yüyi has been the least vocal. She was debuted in a June 2011 concert on France's *Le Grand Journal* and made a second appearance the following month during a concert in Sydney, Australia.[102] In both performances, it seemed more like Gaga had just donned a mermaid tail as an outfit and was performing in a wheelchair. When she posted images from Sydney on her Tumblr site, the caption simply read: "Would you love me no matter what?" At that point Yüyi was less a fully developed alter ego and more an extension of the Gaga persona. Also, these early performances were read primarily in the context of Gaga's performance of handicap. As was discussed in Chapter 1, the discourse on disability has functioned largely as part of the performer's larger discussion of monstrosity. It is not until the "Yoü+I" video that Yüyi emerged fully developed and moved from being about handicap to being about sexuality.

The full Yüyi persona appears in the music video for "Yoü+I," and she is featured in a short film by the Haus of Gaga that was posted on Gaga's personal YouTube page. A few months after the video was released, Yüyi was also featured on the back cover of *Visionaire* magazine. For this alter ego, a number of prosthetics and physical modifications were used. Each of these modifications was used to highlight physical limitations of the body. Most obviously, there is a full mermaid tail, which considerably restricts movement. In concerts, the tail forced her to use a wheelchair and in the video she is shown being carried around the set. During the Haus of Gaga video one sees Yüyi attempting to get up from a chair and walk, then falling down and destroying the chair in anger. On her face, neck, and shoulders there are gills. In the music video Yüyi has trouble breathing and her lover gives her an oxygen mask. This is part of a larger theme in the video where the female lover appears to be dying and the male lover is trying to keep her alive. In the short feature, the oxygen issue becomes ironic when Yüyi is shown trying to smoke a cigarette. Her breasts are covered with latex, which allows her to appear topless while still covering her nipples. At several points in both the music video and the short, Yüyi looks as if she is attempting to free her breast from the covering. The mermaid tail, in particular, seems to make Yüyi's condition a metaphor for gender dysphoria. Most often associated with transsexuals, gender dysphoria is the intense sensation of being in the wrong body. Jay Prosser argues: "Transsexual subjects frequently articulate their bodily alienation as a discomfort with their skin or bodily encasing: being trapped in the wrong body is figured as being in the wrong, or an extra, or a second skin, and transexuality is expressed as a desire to shed or step out of this skin."[103] With Yüyi there is a constant portrayal of frustration with the limitations of the body, which can be read within the larger conversation of the video as a discussion of the frustrations of sexuality and transgender identity.

The Yüyi alter ego is a symbol of the physical boundaries that can exist in a romantic relationship. In the music video, Yüyi is shown in a watering trough, in the middle of a barn, with her lover dumping water on her, presumably to help keep her alive. Notwithstanding the odd conditions, the look on her face is one of bliss. There are several scenes where it is clearly intimated that Yüyi and her lover are attempting to have sex despite the physical impossibility. In an interview about the video, Gaga explained, "Well, that's actually part of what the metaphor is— you can't. Sometimes in love, you can't make it work. No matter what you do, there's this giant boundary between you and someone else. So that's what it's about, perceiving in your imagination that there's something magical inside of you that you can make it work."[104] The mermaid tail is a physical manifestation of the boundary that prevents two people from connecting in the way that is desired. Because these images are placed in the same context as the Jo Calderone and Lady Gaga relationship, it becomes part of a larger discourse about the boundaries of transexuality.

Yüyi's liminal state can alternatively be read as representative of some of the many relationships and gender identifications that we lack language for in modern social discourse. The confusion generated by Gaga's gender performance has often been clarified by attempting to discern her physical sex. If she is a hermaphrodite, then the difficulty of reading her gender performance makes sense. This gets at a social need to know the true sex in order to understand the true self. Yüyi has no sex. Therefore, the discernment of true self must be based entirely on performance. The audience understanding of who Yüyi is comes largely from her portrayal of need and desire. Sloop has pointed out that "because there is historically only a limited number of medical and institutional terms with which to describe one's body and one's desire, one is partially a product of preexisting publicity."[105] We lack the publicly circulating discourse necessary to understand a lot of social positions. Yüyi's liminality, her joy in desire, and her striving to push the boundaries of the body work to create not just an alternative discourse on sexuality but an often unheard celebratory discourse. As Lady Gaga said in an interview about the larger music video, "I see the trans community as a very inspiring group that on a daily basis deals with obstacles and struggles that most of us can't perceive of. I think they should be revered and honored and protected and I think it's important for me, as an artist, to push those particular boundaries because of how many of them I know and how important it is to the young community."[106] One of the more important things that Gaga can do as an artist is use these alter egos to generate alternative narratives in the larger public discourse on sexuality.

A Monster in Drag

This survey of Gaga's performance of gender reveals an evolving understanding of sex and sexuality. Before she was Lady Gaga, Germanotta worked as a burlesque dancer, and her work in this community had a big impact on her early performances as Lady Gaga. Gaga attempted to incorporate elements of burlesque into a typical pop music persona. The result was often awkward and difficult to interpret. Fortunately, the support she received from the queer community pushed her to make the burlesque and drag elements of her performance more prominent. Even as she was struggling to develop her persona, in interviews Gaga showed a strong sense of her own sexuality. She repeatedly denied reporters' attempts to fetishize her bisexuality, and she did that while still maintaining the strength of her sexuality in general. Still, some aspects of this early performance were problematic. This is demonstrated when Lady Gaga used the slur "tranny" to describe her overall look; this statement showed a certain level of ignorance about the issues facing the queer community. In Lady Gaga's struggle to develop her own gender identity as a mainstream celebrity, she had to learn to negotiate her relationship with the queer community.

Lady Gaga's early awkwardness has played a large part in the ongoing rumors that she has a penis. Typically, this type of rumor would have been an excuse for increased media scrutiny and would have forced most celebrities into a defensive or outraged position. Instead, in multiple interviews Gaga used the rumor as a way to talk about the role of feminism in popular culture and women in the music industry. In music videos, Gaga responds to the rumors using humor and parodying various narratives about the consequences of homosexuality. In these responses one starts to see a more sophisticated treatment of gender issues. This allowed Gaga to transition to the creation of new alter egos that play out gender and sexuality in some interesting ways. Monstrosity and homosexuality are often linked in public conversations. Society paints gender identity confusion as a threat to the domestic unit and, as such, a threat to the social structure as a whole. Calling this out as monstrous is a way of reinforcing civic identity.[107] Often homosexuality and transgender identity are performed in public as part of a violent spectacle — a way to trigger "erotic terror."[108] Deviant desire is tied to violence in order to communicate moral judgment. When Gaga performs with prosthetic claws and a prosthetic penis she is playing up this narrative. However, she changes the moral of the story. Typically, with monstrosity, "homosexuality signified a range of unacceptable secrecies and criminality ... lives in public that were out of control."[109] Gaga's is out of control, but the consequences are spectacular instead of dire.

The spectacle that Lady Gaga has generated through her performance of gender is not without limitations. Gaga, Calderone, and Yüyi all offer alternative narratives relating to gender, sexuality, and desire. However, these narratives still rely on a lot of heterosexual stereotypes. In all of these performances masculinity and femininity are portrayed as opposites and one is seen desiring the other. To that end, what Lady Gaga has offered is limited. Approached a different way, Lady Gaga has always said that what she is doing is a performance: She reveals everything, but what she is revealing is a construct. One is reminded of what Jo Calderone said at the VMAs about his relationship with Lady Gaga: "I want her to be real, but she says, 'Jo, I'm not real. I'm theater, and you and I? This is just rehearsal.'" By bringing new identities into the mainstream, she is opening up a space for the little monsters to generate even more narratives.

Chapter 3
The Pop Culture Monster

In her much-celebrated horror novel, *Frankenstein*, Mary Shelley tells the story of a young scientist named Dr. Victor Frankenstein. The doctor, obsessed with the natural wonders of science, attempts to construct a human body out of the pieces of multiple other bodies. The result of this experiment is a creation that blurs the line between human and monster. While the book provides very few details about how Frankenstein built his creation, Shelley does note that the doctor was obsessed with understanding the inner workings of the human body. In order to make it easier to study each of the systems, he made a monster of extreme size that stood over eight feet tall. In attempting to create something new from the enlarged parts of other previously living bodies, he made a creature that was enormous, unruly, and ultimately uncontrollable. The monster took on a life of its own and wreaked havoc wherever it went. In the end, tracking and stopping his creation became Dr. Frankenstein's all-consuming mission. The story of Lady Gaga bears many of the characteristics of Mary Shelley's nineteenth-century gothic horror novel. Stephanie Germanotta's creation, the Mother Monster of the pop music scene, pulls from decades of popular culture history to construct a modern celebrity that is a study of the inner workings of fame. Like Frankenstein's monster, Gaga often appears larger than life, and while she resembles hundreds of celebrities who came before her, something in her overly constructed appearance makes it clear that she is not your typical pop star. In bringing together a legion of references from popular music, fashion, and art, Gaga has blurred the line between celebrity and monster.

In almost every choice made by Lady Gaga—from clothing and makeup to chord progressions and concert sets—there is an intentional reference to media and cultural movements of the past. The Mother Monster makes no claims of originality. Instead, she focuses her performance on effectively repurposing and combing these familiar tropes and images in a way that gives them her own new and unique meaning. Her concerts cite a wide variety of influences—ranging from classics such as *Gone with the Wind* to more obscure shock artists like Spencer Tunick. Pulling together this many disparate images results in a strangeness that is simultaneously an imitation of the past and a glimpse of the future. For example, when Lady Gaga performed for the queen of England in 2009 she wore a Victorian-style dress, with a massive collar, made from red latex, and with a long train. The dress's collar and train made obvious references to the fashion of previous British royalty, while the twist of red latex hinted at bondage subcultures, and the oversized features gave it a modern edge. Lady Gaga's attire for this appearance managed to be strange, shocking, and wholly unoriginal. Because she regards each fashion choice as intentional, whether in reference or in construction, Gaga is able to piece together other people's ideas in a way that communicates a new message. Lady Gaga has said that even the most basic performance choices have meaning. As such, it is never as simple as simply picking a color, it becomes about interpreting the meaning behind a given shade of the color:

> If I decide to make a coat red in the show, it's not just red.... I think: is it communist red? Is it cherry cordial? Is it ruby red? Or is it apple red? Or the big red balloon red? I mean there's like so many fucking different kinds of red. And so you have to say, well, what are we trying to say in this scene? Is it a happy red? Or a sad red? Is it a lace red? Or a leather red? Or a wool red?[1]

It is Gaga's eye for detail, and awareness of the meaning captured by references hidden in even the most basic choices, that allows her to continue to appear as both a copy of the celebrity culture people are familiar with and a strange new version of stardom that continues to capture media attention. Lady Gaga brings together familiar images that often hold associations with other cultures, movements, or artists in order to create a meaning that is wholly her own. Consequently, when one single choice is packed with that much meaning and a show is made up of thousands of these choices, the end result can be so overwhelming it is difficult to process without deconstruction. Interpreting all the meanings laced throughout the 24-hour-a-day celebrity performance requires a willingness to sort through the multiple and simultaneous voices speaking in each of Gaga's performances.

Parody

In an article on political parody, Robert Hariman tells a story about how, one evening at dinner, his daughter began mimicking something he was saying.[2] Although, the mimicry was initially harmless, the daughter soon figured out that parroting her father could get her a laugh from everyone at the table. So, the performance continued. As it went on, the daughter grew progressively more accurate in mirroring her father's gestures and speech patterns. Hariman noted that while his own gestures felt natural to him, they seemed patterned in an almost mechanical way when performed by his daughter. This is what parody does—it takes behaviors that on first glance seem natural and by eliminating defining features or quirks through exaggeration and repetition allow the audience to recognize repeated behaviors and other basic elements of a performance. Bakhtin explains that parodies have a type of metalinguistic meaning; the "discourse in them has a twofold direction—it is directed both toward the referential object of speech, as in ordinary discourse, and toward another's discourse, toward someone else's speech."[3] This is to say that when someone is performing a parody there are two voices speaking at the same time. There is the voice of the person, or group of people, being imitated. Then, underneath that, there is the voice of the person doing the imitating. When Hariman's daughter performed, she was both saying the words as Hariman had said them and alluding in her repetition to an underlying commentary of "*isn't this funny?*" Individuals who fail to see the two voices in the text "begin to perceive stylization or parody in the same way ordinary speech is perceived, that is, as speech directed only at its referential object," causing one to see parody as "a poor work of art."[4] As a result, parody opens up the possibility of multiple acceptable interpretations. One might watch Hariman's daughter and think how endearing it is that a young child would show respect by trying so hard to be just like her father. A second viewer might look at the scene and think that the daughter was mocking and lacked proper deference. Because both voices are present, either interpretation is entirely valid. Lady Gaga's overarching celebrity performance shows elements of fairly sophisticated parody. How that parody is interpreted tends to be a primary identifying factor for Lady Gaga's fan base. Not everyone is willing to read the critical distance in Gaga's imitations, and there are certainly those who have written her off as nothing more than a copy of a hundred other blond pop music starlets. One biographer even termed her a "cultural thief."[5] However, the little monsters often identify themselves by their willingness to interpret the many references in Gaga's performance. For them, the Mother Monster's work is a commentary on all the celebrity voices that are invoked.

Parody is a slippery thing to interpret politically. When something is being mimicked, even in a derisive way, the repetition means that the original argument remains intact. The original source is presented multiple times, often in character, so that as it is folded upon itself certain flaws are made terribly obvious. Yet because the original argument is still visible it is possible for the source to be interpreted with its original meaning. This is what distinguishes parody from satire. Satire destroys the object of discourse, while even when a parody is expressing a critical perspective the dedication to proper imitation means that the original always survives. As Matthew Turner explains:

> Parody can be distinguished from satire precisely because it does not attempt to moralize or act as a social or artistic corrective. Further, the parodied text is not necessarily inferior to the parodying text. In order for a parody to be successful, it must follow the original text closely enough to be recognized as a parody. However, if the parody is too close to the original, it is seen merely as imitation. Thus, parody must have a certain critical ironic distance in which it recognizes and addresses any risible flaws or elements of the original.[6]

The distance Turner is talking about is subtle. It is often recognized as the difference between impersonation and parody. An impersonation will try to be as faithful to the original as possible, while a parody leaves some aspect out to make the original seem "off." It is the distance that is produced when something is removed from the performance that allows parody to be critical of a system without ever explicitly challenging that system. One should note that a primary component of Lady Gaga's parody of celebrity spectacle is her access to traditional media systems. Performing in the same format and through the same outlets as other celebrities places her performance in a context where the mimicry is more recognizable. Furthermore, Dan Harries argues that the current prevalence of parody has trained Gaga's audience to see what she is doing. In the twenty years before Gaga's rise to fame, members of society had been fed a "daily diet" of ironic and parodic television and movies; "generations of kids raised on television have developed a certain 'knack' for appreciating the ironic.... The popularization of parody makes the irony of postmodernism less threatening, less radical."[7] Given that the majority of Gaga's fans do not predate the rise of parody and irony in popular media, they are likely to have enough exposure to this type of performance to recognize and interpret what Gaga is doing.

Lady Gaga's parody, in utilizing repetition of other famous artists' work, does not necessarily challenge the celebrity system. What it does do is work to provide a new way of reading the system, and allow for a critical distance that the public uses to engage with the system while reinterpreting it. As will be discussed later in this chapter, Gaga uses the direct communication possible with social media to go around traditional media outlets and collaborate with her fan community in the development and interpretation of her performance. This relates back to the central argument of Chapter 1: Lady Gaga is not opposed to the concepts of fame and celebrity. She simply wants to rethink and redefine those terms in the context of a modern media environment. Parody allows her to do that: "Parody goes beyond mere reinforcement; it also builds on the original as it layers new meaning into the artistic work."[8] By imitating a typical celebrity lifestyle and successful media formats, Lady Gaga is able to point to the mechanisms behind these processes. As Bakhtin explains, "all public discourse externalizes a cast of characters, but only parody so radically reveals that there are actors behind the masks."[9] Lady Gaga's performance takes away much of the mystery behind celebrity and reveals what is commonly treated as an automatically assumed lifestyle to be a series of behaviors and choices. This treatment of celebrity opens up an opportunity for the audience. If fame and celebrity are formulas that can be mechanized, then Gaga's fans can mimic her in the same way Hariman's daughter mimicked him. Gaga's performance illustrates that the process of rising to celebrity can be deconstructed, codified, and most important, repeated.

Lady Gaga's performance engages with recognizable media moments to comment on the ways that celebrities trade their lives for fame. Matthew Turner has written at length about the line between imitation and parody in Gaga's performance. He notes:

> Though some critics suggest that Lady Gaga's success is due in large part to her imitation of other artists, her work goes beyond mere imitation and moves into the realm of parody. It is this self-conscious employment and

performance of parody that is at least partially responsible for her incredible success. As a self-professed performance artist, Lady Gaga becomes a nexus of parodied performances, revealing and expanding the limits and the understanding of both parody and performance.[10]

It is common in popular culture to imitate, or pay homage, to the work of others. However, Lady Gaga's choice to situate herself as a performance artist who is performing celebrity alters the reading of homage. She positions herself, in her work especially, as not innately celebrity but as performing the role. For example, in the video for the song "Paparazzi," Gaga kills her boyfriend and then calls the police to report the murder. When the police arrive, Lady Gaga is taken away in handcuffs, wearing an outfit that looks fit for a night out or a media event. At the police station, she is shown posing for a series of mug shots. Gaga has said in interviews that each of these scenes was a reference to Paris Hilton's, Nicole Richie's, and Lindsay Lohan's interactions with the police and the media attention to those interactions. In particular, when the police arrest Lady Gaga she spreads her legs while getting into the car. There is a camera flash and freeze frame, which implies that one of the members of the paparazzi has taken a picture up Lady Gaga's skirt while her legs were spread. This is an obvious reference to a scandal in September 2006 where Lohan was photographed by paparazzi getting out of a car, with her legs spread and no underwear.[11] The music video interpretation of the event is not as extreme as the original media moment. In her re-creation of the scene, all that is seen up Lady Gaga's skirt is shadows. In 2010, Paris Hilton was arrested in Las Vegas for cocaine possession. The headline on TMZ, a popular entertainment news site, when Hilton's mug shot was released proclaimed that the socialite looked "So Pretty."[12] In the "Paparazzi" video, when Lady Gaga is being photographed for her mug shot she poses in a series of provocative ways, such as putting her finger in her mouth and grabbing her breast. This is in reference to the mug shots released after Paris Hilton was arrested. Gaga is treating the mug shots as part of a photo shoot that will be released to the media. All these scenes are set against the larger narrative of the video. At the beginning of the video several newspaper headlines declare that Lady Gaga's career is dead. After she kills her boyfriend, the headlines read "She's Back!" and "We Love Her Again." These images placed together are a commentary on what the media wants from celebrities. Ann Torrusio comments on the scenes of Gaga's arrest, saying that "generally speaking, the arrest functions as a method of regulating social norms that remove undesirables from public view; however, in the video, it ironically reinforces her position in the public eye."[13] In the video, Gaga both follows the formula of the typical celebrity controversy and comments on the way these performances are staged to garner media attention.

In parody, two voices are layered into a performance and it is the distance between the two that makes it possible to see the difference between the original and the reinterpretation. Lady Gaga's work is made of layers that expand upon the meaning of celebrity and utilizes the distance to twist the original into something new. Matthew Turner has argued that while her music is uninspired, it is not the central issue in Gaga's performance of parody. If anything, the derivative nature of Gaga's music makes it easier to see the element of imitation in her work. The parody comes from the extreme spectacle of the overarching performance.[14] Take, for instance, Lady Gaga's machine-gun bra. Many have commented that this is a not-so-subtle reference to the iconic pointy bra worn by Madonna during the Blond Ambition World Tour. Gaga's interpretation of the bra goes beyond the meaning in the original image. Turner points out that "Madonna's pointed bra could be considered daring or in poor taste depending on one's point of view; Lady Gaga's can only be parody."[15] Madonna's pointy bra is original and requires original interpretation. The viewer is forced to make a decision about the nature of Madonna's performance. Because Gaga followed Madonna, her machine-gun bra will always be interpreted, at least in part, as a copy. There is no "original" reading of the garment when Gaga wears it. The viewer is forced to reconcile their view of the original with their view of the reinterpretation. However, the extreme nature of the machine gun attached to the bra means that the interpretation cannot simply stop at the recognition of the imitation. It is this step past imitation to pure spectacle that makes the parody nature of Gaga's work so clear.

Lady Gaga often parodies the overly erotic behavior of female pop stars, especially within the context of her work. While her performance of sexuality contains many of the elements one would expect to see in an erotic spectacle, these components are performed in a mechanical or awkward manner that makes it clear one is seeing an imitation. In music videos, such as "Poker Face," Lady Gaga uses her gaze to create an ironic distance from her behavior and signal the parody. Images of overly sexu-alized women staring seductively at the camera and inviting the audience to stare at them and fantasize have become a common trope in music videos and magazines. In the video for "Poker Face," Lady Gaga is por-trayed playing a game of strip poker that erupts into an erotic spectacle of group sex. During the scene, she is dressed provocatively and shown both being touched and touching others sensually. However, the look she gives the viewer removes her from the sensuality of the actions being por-trayed. Gaga is staring directly at the camera, and her face has no engage-ment with the moment. Some might relate this expression and behavior as acting counter to Erving Goffman's notion of licensed withdrawal. Goff-man argues that, in advertising, women are often depicted as emotionally removed from the scene and this "disorientation" makes them more "vul-nerable" to the actions happening around them.[16] In Goffman's interpre-tation of women's emotional distance, the emphasis is on the passivity of the female subject. In contrast, Lady Gaga may be occasionally removed in terms of emotional engagement with the sexual scenes in her videos, but she consistently appears to be anything but disoriented. Her look seems to issue a challenge to her audience. Gaga has commented on the role of gaze in her work, specifically with reference to the video for "Love-Game"; the images in that video were all of airbrushed, glamorous people and overly sexualized dancing, but "when you got close, the look in every-body's eyes was fucking honest and scary."[17] Gaga and her dancers in "LoveGame" each take the opportunity to stare the audience down. The gaze, in videos like "Poker Face" and "LoveGame," is not meant to invite the audience in but to create an abrupt disruption of the fantasy element. Gaga's facial expressions are withdrawn from the sexual scenes, and her gaze is redirected towards the audience in a way that highlights the false-ness of the scene. She moves and stares at the audience in a manner that signals her awareness of their presence. However, this is not a fetishized awareness; Lady Gaga does not appear amused at the viewer's voyeurism. Often, slight alterations and nods to the audience can be used to signal the performance of a parody.[18] With parody, "additional facial expressions that provided obviously critical commentary become critical to the recog-nition that something is not exactly right."[19] The gaze in these videos func-tions as the signal, giving them a parodic element that allows Gaga to both engage a typical media form and comment on it.

In the case of the "Poker Face" video, Lady Gaga's gaze is coupled with a mechanical style to allow her to claim agency over her body in the erotic spectacle. Robert Hariman points out in his discussion of parody that with most communication genres there are certain elements that are repeated over and over again. Eventually, these are so common that they become habit and feel natural. Parody takes the habits of the genre that appear natural and makes them look mechanical.[20] There is one particular scene, in the "Poker Face" video, in which Gaga is sitting on a couch with an obviously attractive man who is wearing nothing but boxer briefs. Much like in the group sex scene, Gaga and her players continue to shift their gaze in a way that indicates the lack of reality in what the audience is seeing. The man is staring off into space, and the look on his face is like that of a zombie, or a person who has gone catatonic. The awareness of the audience, present in Gaga's gaze, is highlighted by the male in the video who performs licensed withdrawal. He appears disconnected, from both the scene and the audience, and has a distinct vulnerability. For the viewer, the awkwardness of the moment comes from staring at someone who is both fully sexualized and mentally distant. Then, as if someone offscreen has suggested they start the scene, the man leans over to Gaga and begins mechanically kissing and touching her. The inelegance that precedes the sexual encounter signals its fakeness and gives the impression this is merely a routine or mechanized aspect of any popular music video. Rather than allowing the audience to escape into an erotic scene of two attractive people engaged in foreplay, the moment is sudden and unromantic, highlighted through its awkwardness as an imitation of sexuality. In this case, "parodic imitation works by turning an organic moment into something mechanical, and so reveals the mechanization underlying the original communicative act."[21] This method of mimicking sexuality is common to Lady Gaga's performances. As Rebecca Lush explains, "Gaga's work thus copies a sexual aesthetic, not a sexual expression."[22] The gaze gives Gaga a power over her audience. Rather than being the object for viewing, she looks back at the camera in a way that halts the audience's ability to enter the fantasy realm. Claiming her agency in the situation allows her to use sexuality in new ways; "Gaga has crafted a stage and performance identity that uses the language of sexuality not to convey ideas of sexual boundary-pushing but rather to comment on the process of artistic production."[23] The stage identity that Gaga has developed situates her performance of sex as a part of her larger commentary on the role of celebrity in popular culture.

The parody elements of these videos—such as the aforementioned double-voiced references to real-life celebrities' relationships, the constant paparazzi, and the mechanization of sexuality—work to alter the way the audience communicates in relationship to the non-parodic images Gaga presents. By layering voices in the text, "the parodied object is held up to be seen, exposed, and ridiculed, rather than discussed, amended, and enacted."[24] Instead of approaching conversations about sex, disability, and death with a level of seriousness or deference, the videos create an air of frivolity around all these topics. As such, "this flippant grammar contains a transposed version of all grammatical categories brought down to the bodily level, especially to the erotic sphere. Not only parody in its narrow sense but all other forms of grotesque realism degrade, bring down to the earth, turn their subject into flesh."[25] When these topics are leveled or brought down, both the fantasy and the political modes of communication that are typically used to address these issues are changed. Lady Gaga's use of parody ultimately complements her use of the grotesque body and gives a coherence to her overall communication style.

Not "Just Another Madonna"

Despite her constant use of parody, Lady Gaga is often defensive about the notion that she is merely imitating her predecessors. One such example was early in Lady Gaga's career; during the 2007 Lollapalooza concert she was followed and harassed by photographers and fans who mistakenly believed she was Amy Winehouse.[26] Callahan implies that Lady Gaga went blond shortly thereafter just to avoid repeating the incident. In moments like this, Gaga often becomes angry, and she expresses extreme self-protectiveness in the face of accusations that she is borrowing from other pop stars. Once she dyed her hair blond, she was no longer compared to Amy Winehouse. Now she is consistently compared to Madonna. More accurately, according to Callahan, both Madonna and Gaga resemble another eighties female vocalist—Dale Bozzio.[27] The observation by Callahan points to a common thread. Often when Gaga is accused of copying someone, it becomes clear that person was copying someone else, and that person was copying someone else, and so on. In Gaga's parody, the copying "exhibits characteristics of ironic critical awareness in her parodic imitations of others in her own performance. She becomes a nexus of parodic transformation, being parodied and parodying others. While this kind of parody is common in the modern era, Lady Gaga has taken it a step further, parodying her own self-created image in its various incarnations."[28] Gaga points to the things that she is copying and makes the whole process of imitation in popular culture more apparent.

It is questionable whether or not the celebrities being referenced find the imitation flattering or obnoxious. In spring of 2009, when Gaga was first becoming popular, it was commonplace for people to single her out as a knockoff of Madonna. Around the same time period, Gaga appeared on an episode of *Saturday Night Live* with the popular blond diva. The two performed a skit where they get in a catfight about the fact that Madonna thinks she is being copied and Gaga thinks Madonna is old. In the sketch, Madonna even asks, "What kind of name is Lady Gaga?" and Gaga responds, "The kind that is number one on the *Billboard* charts." At the time, both women seemed willing to make light of the various media comparisons between them. The *Saturday Night Live* skit was funny and did not trigger a territorial behavior in Madonna's performance probably because it did not challenge the initial roles of both performers: Madonna is the original and Gaga is played as the imitation. However, shortly thereafter a shift happened and Gaga was suddenly everywhere. What had once been a joke now appeared to be reality and the rift between the two pop stars became real. It was one thing when Madonna was able to claim the signature look and the belief was that Gaga was simply copying that look. As Gaga became more popular, she was increasingly seen as the original. Lady Gaga's celebrity status makes her parody a challenge to the legacy of other pop stars, and her ownership of her celebrity status makes her all the more threatening. Stein and Michelson explained it well in *Out Magazine* in 2009: "Madonna and other pop matriarchs should take cover. Lady Gaga may nod their way, but she won't bow."[29] While much of her work is a parody and an imitation, Lady Gaga is read by her fans as an original. Even as Gaga is pulling from past artists so liberally, fans understand themselves as copying the Mother Monster and treat her as the source of these trends. A lot of Gaga's references are more than 25 years old, and most of her fans are less than 25 years old. To her fans, this sometimes makes her work appear more original than it is.[30]

One of the more troubling moments of imitation in Lady Gaga's career came with the release of her single "Born This Way." Several reporters commented that the chord progression sounded a lot like Madonna's hit "Express Yourself." Shortly after the release of "Born This Way," Madonna was quoted in an interview describing Lady Gaga's work as "reductive."[31] Lady Gaga responded to the accusations during an interview with Peter Robinson, a reporter for the UK–based publication *NME*, saying:

> I'm not dumb enough or moronic enough to think that you are dumb or moronic enough not to see that I would have stolen a melody. If you put the songs next to each other, side by side, the only similarities are the chord progression. It's the same one that's been in disco music for the past 50 years. Just because I'm the first fucking artist in 25 years to think of putting it on Top 40 radio, it doesn't mean I'm a plagiarist, it means I'm fucking smart.[32]

Notice that Gaga did not argue that the chord progression was original. Instead, she made the claim that it was old and common. Framing the conversation this way implies that Madonna's work is also referential. Over a year later, it seemed the controversy continued. In May of 2012, when Madonna was prepping for her most recent tour, footage was released of Madonna performing a mash-up of the songs "Born This Way," "Express Yourself," and the title piece from her then new album, "She's Not Me."[33] The newest piece, "She's Not Me," is a song about Madonna being emulated by another woman. The combination of the three songs created a performance that was an obvious attack against Lady Gaga. While Gaga discussed the chord progression as being part of a larger musical history, Madonna claims it as her own artistic creation. This shows a decided contrast in how the two divas understand the nature of their craft. Just a few months later, Elton John responded to Madonna's mash-up by telling interviewers for the show *Sunday Night*, "She's [Madonna's] been so horrible to Gaga," and following this up by declaring "her [Madonna's] career's over.... And she looks like a fucking fairground stripper."[34] The vehemence in the exchange illustrates the strong feelings in the entertainment industry regarding imitation. Both performers are constantly adopting iconic looks or referencing well-known sounds, and yet the two treat the origins of their look and sound in drastically different ways.

When Lady Gaga copies something, she uses it to develop a perspective. So, it is both about homage or reference and about creating a new argument out of the original. The layering of her voice with previous voices builds something new. As early as 2009, when Gaga was asked to talk about Madonna during an interview, she said that "nobody will ever be as groundbreaking as Madonna for sex. But we can try to apply new contexts, lifestyles, music and different mediums to it."[35] There is a definite sense here that Gaga understands what she is doing as reinterpreting and altering the context of things her audience had already seen. As Rebecca Lush explains, "Gaga's use of copying, in particular, shows her perspective on fame and artistry as social constructs by building on cultural symbols and works from the past."[36] Lady Gaga might be saying what someone else has said but does not necessarily mean what they meant when the ideas were initially presented. As a result, "Gaga's strategy troubles copying by making the audience work to separate the strands of the pop culture past she has combined."[37] This can affect artists such as Madonna by making them worry that audiences will no longer attribute what they hear to broader historical influences in pop music.

A Pop Culture Librarian

There is an intentionality behind Lady Gaga's pop culture references that demonstrates a strong grasp of the history of popular music and fashion. As a columnist for *V Magazine*, Gaga has written a series of what she terms "memorandums" on a variety of pop culture topics. In her first memorandum to the magazine, Gaga defends her knowledge of the culture she is referencing and challenges her fans to be just as aware. She writes that "glam culture is ultimately rooted in obsession, and those of us who are truly devoted and loyal to the lifestyle of glamour are masters of its history. Or, to put it more elegantly, we are librarians."[38] The term "librarian" calls to mind the trope of a quiet, studious girl in cat's eye glasses, poring over card catalogs. This is maybe not an image people often associate with Lady Gaga. However, she boasts that she is a true scholar of fashion and she "can look at almost any hemline, silhouette, beadwork, or heel architecture and tell you very precisely who designed it first, what French painter they stole it from, how many designers reinvented it after them, and what cultural and musical movement parented the birth, death, and resurrection of that particular trend."[39] Gaga told Anderson Cooper, during a *60 Minutes* interview, that she is "a true academic when it comes to music and when it comes to my style, my fashion. There's nothing that I've ever put on my body that I didn't understand where it came from, the reference of it, who inspired it. There's always some sort of a story or a concept that I'm telling."[40] All this knowledge explains why Gaga feels entitled to include, in a memorandum to *V Magazine*, a challenge to her fans and critics: "As someone who references and annotates her work vigilantly, I am putting all of you on notice. I've done my homework, have you? Where are your library cards? Have they expired?"[41] Her argument is that those who accuse her of mere plagiarism do not understand just how far back her references go. As Gaga explains, most of modern fashion is stolen, ripped off, or inspired by something that came before it. The key to being more than just a thief of the ideas of the people who came before you is an awareness of the history and meaning behind the many references. While her fan base may be too young to remember the people she is copying, she is still pushing them to do their homework. Lady Gaga uses the history of the images she chooses to combine influences in a way that produces new arguments and new ideas. Being a Lady Gaga fan is not just about memorizing the Mother Monster's work like an encyclopedia. One needs a much broader scope to understand the references made and to claim expertise in Gaga. She challenges her fans and detractors to learn the past in order to keep up with her present.

Lady Gaga's inspiration comes from a broad and varied list of cultural icons, artistic movements, and media genres. Back in 2009, Gaga told a reporter from *Out Magazine*, "You're only as great as your best reference," and she has many to choose from.[42] Biographers have pointed to a wide range of influences for Lady Gaga works. There are her musical influences: Billy Joel, New Kids on the Block, Britney Spears, Boy George, The Cure, Madonna, Freddy Mercury, Reba McEntire, Wendy O. Williams, Duran Duran, and the band Kiss. Then there are her visual references, such as the commonly cited Andy Warhol. Even more important, she often notes shock artists such as Spencer Tunick, Tracey Emin, and Damien Hirst.[43] A *Vanity Fair* reporter reviewing Gaga's work added Grace Jones, Isabella Blow, Leigh Bowery, Daphne Guinness, Klaus Nomi, Led Zeppelin, Patti Smith, Carole King, Prince, John Lennon, and David Bowie to the list.[44] In a March 2009 interview with *Nylon Magazine*, Gaga mentioned the top eight people she would most like to meet: Andy Warhol, Grace Jones,

Sophia Loren, Edie Sedgwick, David Bowie, Mick Jagger, Leigh Bowery, Kaus Nomi.[45] These are just a sampling of the influences Gaga has discussed in her interviews and others have attributed to her. Obviously, some of these references have had a bigger impact than others. Donatella Versace has often been cited as having a critical influence on Gaga's physical appearance: "Isn't it obvious from the tan and the hair.... She's beautiful, Italian, with impeccable taste."[46] Also, David Bowie and Grace Jones have had more than a passing influence on Gaga's fashion choices. The lightning bolt that Lady Gaga painted on her face during performances while promoting her first album was a direct reference to David Bowie. She has said: "When I think of David Bowie, I imagine a specific shape — his hair from Ziggy Stardust. With Grace Jones, I see a shape for her. It's about creating these kinds of shapes from my own work and balancing every outfit like it's a painting. And this is who I am, a performance artist from Rivington Street."[47] A look at Lady Gaga's concerts and music videos quickly expands the list of references. Beyond the influence of specific individuals, Gaga also draws liberally from a variety of media texts. During the Monster Ball Tour, Gaga's concerts made allusions to *The Wizard of Oz, Zoolander, The Flying Nun, Wings of Desire, Mad Max Beyond Thunderdome, This Is Spinal Tap*, as well as Japanese horror films of the 1950s.[48] In the video for "Telephone," Gaga's acting, wardrobe, and cinematography pay homage to *Thelma and Louise*, Quentin Tarantino, *NCIS, Star Wars*, Japanese anime, Shania Twain, and the 1974 flick *Caged Heart —* just to name a few. All this referencing makes Lady Gaga's work a point of convergence for the current state of popular culture. When Gaga was named one of *Time Magazine's* artists of the year for 2009, Cyndi Lauper wrote that "an artist's job is to take a snapshot — be it through words or sounds, lyrics or song — that explains what it's like to be alive at that time. Lady Gaga's art captures the period we're in right now."[49] Still, some have argued that Gaga's persistent referencing is really just a form of plagiarism. The bibliography of voices present in her work makes it hard to see where Gaga's voice is truly emerging.

However, seen in another way, the constant historical referencing in Lady Gaga's work gives her overall performance a weight and a history that many female pop stars her age lack. As David Annadale explains, "the sheer number of influences turns Lady Gaga into a pop culture legion. There is no longer one stable identity ... but the entire world now explodes from this one point."[50] The referencing means that an attack on Lady Gaga can be interpreted as an attack on any of the pop icons from which she draws her influence. Anchoring her work to a greater historical time line protects Gaga's work and is critical to her longevity. As Katrin Horn argues, "Gaga is building her unique performances on quotations and pop ready-mades in order to establish a pop ancestry, which she at the same time outpaces, and a gendered identity, which she deconstructs at the very moment of its construction."[51] When most pop stars emerge into the media spotlight they have an exciting quality of newness and freshness. The historical references in Lady Gaga's work make her appear less new and more like she is part of a longer artistic history. So, audiences, rather than meeting her for the first time, are invited to interpret her against the backdrop of a history they already possess. As Ann Turrusio explains, "Gaga's performances are a barrage of radically different looks. They invite us to project onto her performance whatever meanings we want: we can choose to embrace certain allusions to different performers while dismissing others, and we can determine for ourselves if these allusions are artistic tributes to various performers of the past or ironic commentaries on the social conditions under which these former stars appeared and thrived."[52] Most audience members will not get all the references in a performance. However, even if an audience member just gets one, it becomes one shared point of meaning that connects the performance to a larger narrative. When Gaga is immediately woven into the history of popular culture there is no question that she will continue on as part of it. She is not proving herself. She is part of something that is already proven. Gaga explains that "maybe it's just that the resolution is: art gives birth to new art. There is no chicken or egg. It's molecular. Cells give birth to cells. To put it more bluntly, the Hussein Chalayan vessel I wore at the Grammys wasn't inspired by a chicken. It was stolen from an egg."[53]

A Pop Culture Frankenstein

Style — in terms of both fashion and music — is a critical component of Lady Gaga's public performance. Barry Brummett explains style as "a complex system of actions, objects, and behaviors, that is used to form messages that announce who we are, who we want to be, and who we want to be considered akin to."[54] When a person adopts a clothing style — such as punk, gothic, preppy, or sporty — that clothing choice serves to define them as a member of a community. Ultimately, "we use style to make claims about ourselves and others, to bring about desired results. When we put on a pair of jeans, we are not just clothing our nakedness, we are speaking a language formed in cloth."[55] The same can be said for musical styles. Hip-hop, jazz, classical, and country music, just to name a few, are stylistic choices that go beyond simple composition preferences to encompass communities that have their own unique language and history. Lady Gaga's choices — to root herself in popular music, embrace popular culture, and live in high fashion — all speak volumes about who she is as an artist. When Lady Gaga was first developing her persona, in early 2007, she "was still unable to divine a clear aesthetic, still working her heavy-metal-stripper look for lack of another idea. Gaga knew that she needed her look to be extreme," but early on she looked like something about out of the "fashion don't" section of a magazine.[56] Developing a clear aesthetic and style was a major component of developing Gaga's public identity and her fan base. This may help to explain the difficulty that reporters have in separating out Gaga's personality from her style choices. As discussed in the preface, reporters often conflate Gaga's clothing choices with her identity. For her part, Gaga has been both adamant that she is the same person whether she is nude or covered in Versace and, conversely, that her fashion choices make up a critical component of her sense of self. In her second memorandum to *V Magazine*, Gaga wrote that "the lines for myself have become so blurred now, I know not the difference between a moment of performance and a moment of honesty. If you were to ask me to remove my Philip Tracy hat at a party, in truth it is the emotional and physical equivalent of requesting I remove my liver."[57] Lady Gaga takes the relationship between her sense of self and her fashion choices to an extreme: "[T]alk about giving 'clutching her pearls' a new meaning! I know not the difference between the hair that grows from my head and the teal wigs that grow from my imagination. They are the same. They are both honest, and always have been."[58] For Lady Gaga, there is also a strong link between her artistic creations and her stylistic choices. She thinks of the two as part of the same artistic project: "I always have a vision — when I'm writing a song I'm always thinking about the clothes, and the way I'm going to sing.... How I move, that kind of stuff is written into the song. It's not just a song and I'm not just gonna stand on stage and sing."[59] In this sense, it becomes easier to see how the constant copying and referencing do not negate Gaga's sense of authenticity—these style choices are her identity.

Stylistically, Lady Gaga has long professed a commitment to popular culture. Given that her monster status works to define both her and her little monsters as outsiders, it might seem strange for Gaga to so adamantly align herself with the popular. Amazingly, Gaga is able to articulate her alignment with all things pop as part of her outsider status. Lady Gaga deems herself a performance artist. In artistic communities, being associated with popular culture might be seen as selling out or making fake art. Lady Gaga uses her position as a performance artist and a pop singer to position herself as rebellious. In a 2008 performance on the show *So You Think You Can Dance*, Gaga started the show wearing her LCD sunglasses, which were scrolling a message: "Pop music will never be low brow." By making art out of a style that is often looked down on as simplistic and overly commercial, Gaga is pushing at a set of social boundaries. She explains that "pop music is commercial art the way Andy Warhol's Campbell's soup cans pictures were commercial art. I don't know why everyone is against pop music. I love a good chorus—sue me. It's that fuckin simple! Who doesn't love a good chorus?"[60] In statements like this, one can hear Gaga's defiance. Her dedication to hyperemphasizing the mainstream and the cliché as stylistic choices defines her as an outsider in the midst of those who dedicate their celebrity to being in tune with trends.

Stylistic choices in language are highly revealing of an individual's identity. In Gaga's case, part of that stylistic choice involves speaking multiple languages in her work. One of the signature elements of Lady Gaga's music has been the inclusion of short interludes in foreign languages. For instance, in "Bad Romance" Lady Gaga speaks French and in "Born This Way" she speaks Italian. When Weird Al Yankovic parodied Lady Gaga's "Born This Way" with his song "Perform This Way," he mocked her habit with his own lyrics, in French, saying that she sings in French for no reason. Matthew Turner, in his analysis of the Weird Al parody, has claimed that Lady Gaga does not even speak the languages she uses in her lyrics.[61] At least in the case of her inclusion of French, this claim seems unwarranted. In the 36th Gagavision video, Gaga teaches Katie Perry how to speak French before a show they both did in Marseilles, France.[62] In addition, a *Vanity Fair* reporter, in her article about Lady Gaga, talked about showing up on the set for "Marry the Night" and hearing the performer speak fluent French.[63] So, there is some evidence that Gaga does speak French. However, there is little evidence that she actually speaks some of the other languages she includes in her work. In the opening scenes of the "Paparazzi" video, Gaga speaks Swedish, which she does not speak in real life. At the Mugler fashion show in Germany, Gaga starts out the performance by saying, "I don't speak German, but I can if you like," which is followed by a song of the same title sung at least partly in German. Later, she uses the phrasing from the fashion show as the subject line for a memorandum to *V Magazine* about escapism.[64] For Gaga, speaking a foreign language is often an artifice. One might argue that she uses it to signal her work as artistic and also that it is an appeal to her global fan base. Just like clothing choices and music style, the incorporation of foreign language also functions to signal who Gaga is as a celebrity. It communicates her desire to be understood as an international superstar. Speaking multiple languages places Gaga in multiple communities. At the same time, the acknowledgment of her voice as "faking it" and escapist pushes at the edge of the artifice of presenting popular culture as high art.

Lady Gaga's combination of multiple reference points allows her to transcend stylistic and generic boundaries. One primary example of this is the video for "Telephone." Interscope Records, Gaga's label, described this video as a "gritty, erotic, and wildly fierce, nine-minute, visually stunning, cinematic masterpiece."[65] The overarching narrative and multiple plot points were meant to transcend the genre of music video and place "Telephone" as a film. What Gaga and her creative team produced is both a music video and something slightly more. The final product draws on images of lesbian prison pornography and Quentin Tarantino–style action films. To get at these elements, when making the video, the director put out a casting call through Wicked Pictures, an adult entertainment company. Most of the extras in the prison scenes are porn actresses.[66] In addition, at the end of the video Lady Gaga and Beyoncé are seen driving away in the pussy wagon that Uma Thurman drove in *Kill Bill: Vol. 1*. These moments of imitation from other film genres reinforce the notion that this video crosses out of the music video genre.

Crossing genres and speaking to multiple stylistic choices only works to increase Lady Gaga's overall fan base. One strong example of this is the single "Yoü+I." Gaga has said of the single, "I wrote the song just to write a beautiful song and I intend to put it on the new album, yes, but it's not totally indicative of the new album sound; it's just a really big rock and roll hit. I do have these hopes that it could be a great crossover record, so I'm going to put my producer's hat on and get it to a place where I feel like it could reach the masses." In an interview with Derek Blasberg of *Harper's Bazaar*, Gaga elaborated on her desire to use the "Yoü+I" album as a whole to court a new fan base: "I was happy with the fans I've already got. But it [the album] opened this new fan base of people who love the simplicity and joyfulness of it."[67] David Annandale explains that it is the openness of her fan base that has made the Mother Monster such a success.[68] Feeling estranged or isolated from popular culture depictions of normalcy is a problem that transcends demographic markers like age, race, and religion. Gaga's narrative has a broad audience even if her music seems confined to a particular genre. The demographic crossing of her marketing techniques also demonstrates the artificiality of the generic community lines in the music business.

While Lady Gaga's musical style is classified as pop, many of her early roots are in rock 'n' roll. One of her first collaborators, Lady Starlight, a DJ and go-go dancer from Gaga's burlesque days in New York City, has commented that the mentality of rock music continues to influence Gaga's approach to celebrity, even as her style has changed: "She was in the commercial pop world, which didn't encourage risk ... but she has absolutely a rock 'n' roll mentality. So I encouraged her. If you have an idea, do it. All the way. Rock 'n' roll is supposed to stun. And appall. She wanted to shake up the industry, and I'd compare her to Bowie way before Madonna in terms of bringing alternative culture into the mainstream. She is anarcho-punk!"[69] In this short quote, one can see some of the issues placing Lady Gaga's style. Because she pulls from so many sources and translates them into a very commercial product, there is no authentic association of genre to be made. As Gaga's work has developed, she has embraced more of the crossover nature of her craft: "I have sort of created a genre of metal-dance-techno-pop music with a lot of rock anthemic choruses, because that is the music that I love. I'm actually really obsessed with Bruce Springsteen.... Lots of almost like big Def Leppard–style melodies in the choruses, but it's very hard and very edgy."[70] Having such a diverse style has really benefited Lady Gaga, as she developed a community of fans that spans many styles. Gaga admits, "I do have a bit of a rock and roll heart even though I'm a pop artist."[71] Even more than that, Lady Gaga articulates popular music as a style that has a strong potential for crossover: "I think most music is pop music.... The mark of a great song is how many genres it can embody. It's about honesty and connection-look at a song like 'I Will Always Love You.' Whitney killed it as a pop song, but it works as a country song, a gospel song, everything. If I can play a song acoustic, or just on the piano, and it still works, I know it's good."[72]

Lady Gaga's music videos often play out popular narratives of celebrity life. "Paparazzi" shows how scandal can revive a celebrity's career. "Bad Romance" likens celebrity culture to the sex trade and shows Gaga being sold to the highest bidder. The video for "Marry the Night" mixes the story of Lady Gaga's own rise to fame with a narrative and images common to popular dance films. Lady Gaga has said that "there's an art to fame. Even in the most humiliating and defaming moment of your life, you're still ready for the camera."[73] While the "Paparazzi" and "Bad Romance" videos look at larger themes of fame and humiliation, the "Marry the Night" video is about Gaga's own personal most defaming moment. The plot of the video takes the Mother Monster back to the night when she was dropped by her first record label — Island Def Jam. In the video, after going through a breakdown, Gaga shows up at a dance school. On arriving at the school, Gaga is wearing an acid-wash denim outfit — jeans, vest, and bustier top — all covered with rhinestones and studs, which the voice-over tells the viewer she applied with her BeDazzler. Her appearance in this scene provides an immediate contrast with the group of students at the school, who are all staring at her ominously, wearing more traditional black or pink leotards. The marble floors and high painted ceilings lend the overall impression that Gaga has wandered into an established institution and that she does not belong in this place. Lady Gaga's acid-wash clothes, peroxide-blond hair, and garish red lipstick quickly cast her as lower class, noncomforming, and out of place. Despite her differences in appearance, Gaga's talent and kindness quickly win over the other dancers. The dissimilitude between Lady Gaga, her classmates, and the overall environment hints at tropes of class and economic disparity. The narrative of the video is that even though Gaga may not fit in to the culture of upper-class art embodied by those surrounding her, she perseveres and her talent earns her a place among the elite. Where an audience could be drawn to the video because it uses familiar images — moments that could be referencing any one of hundreds of popular dance-themed films—what makes this moment of imitation particularly interesting and engaging is how closely it follows the actual story of Gaga's rise to stardom. Having such a classic celebrity narrative—the unlikely odd duck and underdog of below-average opportunity who reaches extraordinary success—serves to validate Lady Gaga's own claims to fame. As was discussed in previous chapters, celebrities serve as proof that anyone could possibly rise up the economic ladder and take a place among the elite. Lady Gaga's choice to perform this hero myth in a way that is simultaneously ham-fisted and claimed as genuine highlights the class struggle inherent in media depictions of celebrity culture.

Despite the obvious ways that she performs celebrity as an established star, Lady Gaga has consistently maintained that the narrative of "rags-to-riches" is authentically hers. It can be difficult to reconcile Gaga's parody of so many classic images with her claim that the performance of her story is a candid representation. The ambivalence is deepened by the fact that audiences are used to celebrities functioning more as ideas and fabricating attractive pasts in order to sympathize with audiences. Richard Dyer explains that "stars are, like characters in stories, representations of people. Thus they relate to ideas about what people are (or are supposed to be) like."[74] The spectacle of celebrity typically only acts symbolically, but Gaga moves past that, connecting the myth of the rising star to the reality of her performance. Lady Gaga is asking her fans to accept that she is actually the embodiment of that idea; as she told a reporter: "What I'd like people to know is that as fabulous as I may look in a magazine, it's who I am. This isn't a ploy for people's attention ... this is me."[75] Yet the thing that Gaga is saying is her is also a copy of many of the celebrities that came before her. What one is seeing is Gaga grafting her own story onto a much larger, lasting narrative of celebrity.

Lady Gaga's development of her celebrity narrative is subtle and has come together over a long period of time. She has approached describing her own rise to fame both metaphorically and theoretically. One main example she provided for the way that celebrities function in pop culture was the narrative of her own purple china teacup, which developed a life of its own as a European media sensation. In early 2009, Lady Gaga began carrying a purple flowered teacup with her everywhere she went. The profile of the teacup was raised in February of that year when Gaga performed dressed as her teacup at the annual BRIT Awards. A few months later, in April, she started carrying the teacup full-time, and the media started feigning interest, including one high-profile interview on *Friday Night with Jonathan Ross* where she was asked about the teacup. The media attention became even more vigilant after a night out on the town in London where Gaga left the teacup at a restaurant, threw a fit, and sent a car back the restaurant to pick it up.[76] It cost £35 to send the driver back. After the restaurant incident, a spokesman for Gaga said, "Lady Gaga does not want to reveal anything about the teacup itself, but drinking ginger tea is very good for singers."[77] In an interview with *Billboard* magazine reporter Courtney Harding, Lady Gaga finally opened up about the now famous piece of china. She told the interviewer it was all part of an "experiment": "I was talking to the members of the Haus [her creative team] about the power of image and the camera, and I wanted to say something on a real level about fame."[78] So, after some brainstorming, she came to the decision: "I drink a lot of tea, and I decided to take a purple teacup out of my china collection and take it to London and make it famous. I put it in videos and had fans pose with it and put it on TV — at one point, the teacup had a call time."[79] Lady Gaga's attempts to make a teacup famous reveal, at a very practical and spectacular level, just how mechanized celebrity culture has become. The teacup experiment is a parody performance of fame, which critiques how easy it is for something trivial to become highly visible and generate media buzz. In the years since the experiment, the teacup has continued to make appearances. It was part of the "Paparazzi" music video, and in 2012 it was sold for $75,000 at an auction raising money for ongoing tsunami disaster relief.[80]

The teacup experiment further reveals how knowledgeable Lady Gaga is about the mechanics of celebrity, and it proves that she is able to manipulate these techniques for her own success. Another example of this awareness is Gaga's performance of the celebrity tell-all interview, which holds opportunity as one of the most established and mechanized moments in media. Lady Gaga gave one of her first big celebrity interviews in the U.S. in March 2009 to Jonah Weiner, for *Maxim Magazine*. Weiner asked many of the questions a reporter would typically ask a newly minted female pop star at the time, such as "What do you think of Britney Spears?" and "Do you like to have sex with women?"[81] Later, he told Maureen Callahan that Gaga's behavior in the interview was unique; "She flirted, but in such a way, he [journalist Jonah Weiner] says, that she was almost acknowledging that the dual seductions in every interview resemble nothing so much as espionage-level attempts to extract information."[82] He said, even at this early point in her career, "she was cultivating this disarmingly coquettishness, but always in big quotation marks ... like a commentary on interviewee strategies and the journalist's interviewing tropes."[83] Gaga knew what an interview was supposed to look like, and she was playing with that image. A few years later, in an interview for *Rolling Stone*, Brian Hiatt noted that "when Gaga enters interview mode, her syntax becomes self-consciously formal, and she sits up straighter."[84] Lady Gaga recognizes the performance aspect of the celebrity interview, and she has spent years making decisions about what her performance would look like.

In the years that followed, Lady Gaga developed a unique interview style that often involved parodying the person interviewing her. Mimicking the interviewer has become a strategy for Lady Gaga in her interviews. Ann Torrusio explains:

> During her interviews, Lady Gaga affirms the instability of her identity while underscoring its performativity as well as the performativity of the interviewers' identity. Gaga's physical display of mirroring her hosts usurps the interviews, which reminds the audience of the meta-theatricality of the interviews.... Gaga's reflexive performance bears an uncanny resemblance to her interviewer as she plants herself somewhere between the interview and the interviewee; she performs for and as the interviewer, positioned in the cultural crossroads of the monster figure.[85]

Some of the more notable examples of this behavior are her interviews with Larry King, Barbara Walters, Howard Stern, and Oprah Winfrey. In her interview with Barbara Walters, Gaga wore a Channel suit, similar to the one Walters was wearing. At various points in the interview, Gaga seems to be giving answers that mimic responses given by other celebrities in previously successful Walters interviews. The mimicking was even more pronounced in Gaga's interview with Larry King. Lady Gaga came to the interview wearing King's trademark suspenders and button-up shirt. As she answered questions, her hand gestures were patterned after King's. In her at-home interview with Oprah, Lady Gaga wore a red, eighties-inspired business suit that looked like classic Oprah Winfrey. Gaga's tone of voice and cadence in her interactions with Oprah sound like homage to the techniques the talk show host has used in the past to sound empathetic and encourage guests to open up on her show. During the Howard Stern interview, Lady Gaga dressed in full leather and biker gear, to complement Stern's style. The choice might not have mattered, given that it was a radio show, but Gaga took multiple pictures posing with Stern and posted them on social media sites. What makes the overall strategy of mimicking the interviewer so apparent is how much Gaga's look changes from one interview to the next. She is not adopting the visual appearance and gestures of simply one celebrity interviewer. Gaga tackles them all. After a while the pattern becomes clear. Once the pattern is evident, the performance begins to develop the critical distance necessary to allow viewers to see Lady Gaga's interviews as parody. Lady Gaga recognizes the power of the celebrity interview. She told Neil Strauss, of *Rolling Stone*, during an interview: "If I say one thing in our interview right now, it will be all over the world the day after it hits the stands. And it would be twisted and turned."[86] Lady Gaga avoids this fate by recognize the celebrity interview as the artifice it is and treating it as part of her performance.

The narrative of the rise from obscurity to stardom is so deeply imbedded into modern culture that it has started to appear natural and at times it seems that celebrities are an inevitable result of an established mass media infrastructure. Lady Gaga's parody denaturalizes the mechanisms of stardom in order to comment on the overall structure. She grafts her personal narrative onto the rags-to-riches story that has been popularized in hundreds of films. She proves that even a teacup can become famous if it follows the right steps. She revels in and reveals the techniques behind the infamous celebrity tell-all interview. What makes these performances all the more powerful is Gaga's choice to situate them within the stylistic realms of popular culture. If Lady Gaga was a member of punk or rock 'n' roll subcultures, these performances might be dismissed as nothing more than stunts—the behavior of misanthropes who are simply trying to cause trouble. However, as she is an established member of the pop culture community, her performance takes on a uniquely destabilizing role. The Mother Monster's assault on celebrity culture is an inside job.

A New Media Monster

Lady Gaga's work draws from a host of historical references, and she has often complained that media critics read her referencing too simplistically. When *V Magazine* reporter John Norris questioned Gaga about media accusations that her work was purely derivative, she responded: "[L]ook, when I was a brunette they called me Amy Winehouse. When I was a blonde, they called me Madonna. Then they called me Christina [Aguilera], then Gwen [Stefani]. I just don't think people's reference points go back very far."[87] The media often does not look back far enough historically to recognize that Gaga's references are more than copying; she is building on trends with deep roots in celebrity culture. Matthew Turner argues that Gaga's awareness of the history and meaning behind her choices makes her homage distinct from mere copying: "Lady Gaga is hyperaware of where her artistic tradition has come from and consistently imitates the tradition's style to copy its success. However, she also copies it with some of the critical separation."[88] The simplistic readings of many media critics may recognize the initial moment of reference in Gaga's work but often fail to see its points of departure. In another interview for *V Magazine*, Gaga told interviewer Mark Jacobs that people who find her fashion outrageous just do not get the references: "I don't choose pieces based on their shock value. I really think that what I wear and what we design as a house is very beautiful and when people say it's outrageous or over-the-top, to me we just don't share the same references ... it's not my job to do something that is safe for people. I just do what I think is beautiful."[89] It is worth noting that while Gaga's performance might be described as a parody, the media that is reporting on her performance is most often not engaged in parody. So, while she may utilize a critical distance between her work and its references and thus have her performance acknowledged as parodic instead of merely imitation, traditional reporting outlets often digest Gaga's work on the same level as that of other modern pop superstars. They overlook the multi-voiced style of her performance. A close examination shows that Gaga has a knack for "telegraphing irony and wit through carefully cultivated bad taste," but that talent does not always translate in a system where the media is attempting to break things down to a 15-second sound bite.[90] Lady Gaga has used digital media in conversation with mainstream media outlets to generate opportunities for less simplistic readings and take charge of framing her work. Furthermore, the digital media allows her to develop a close relationship with her fans and influence how they read her artistic choices.

Lady Gaga continually fights for fame to be defined and understood as something that anyone can have and which does not rely on recognition from mainstream media outlets. As I argue in Chapter 1, this conception of fame places the agency with the individual and allows them to decide for themselves who they will be and how they will be understood. In many ways, it is the current media environment that makes Lady Gaga's notion of fame a reality. Media theorists have argued that the rise of digital media has created the necessary conditions for what is known as convergence culture. Henry Jenkins defines media convergence as "the flow of content across multiple media platforms, the cooperation between multiple media industries, and the migratory behavior of media audiences who will go almost anywhere in search of the kinds of entertainment experiences they want."[91] The flow of media across platforms allows seeming amateurs to create work that interacts with, and potentially even rivals, the work of large-scale media producers. Conversations between sites like Twitter and more traditional media outlets, such as CNN, make it possible for individuals to respond more directly to media critics. In new media forums, Lady Gaga does not have to fight the mainstream media message that what she does is simply a copy or an imitation. Instead, she distributes her own countermessage — through both traditional and non-traditional media sources — and maintains an active role in defining her own fame. Lady Gaga's use of new media outlets makes her parody critique of celebrity possible. In addition, it allows her to model, more effectively, her meaning of the fame.

For Gaga to override the media critiques about her work, she had to find a way to establish and maintain power over the way she is marketed and described. Her tactic, which has proven to be both successful and unprecedented in many ways, centralizes on developing a relationship directly with her fans and using user-centric digital media, which allows her to cut the mainstream media out of the communication process. Eric Garland, CEO for the media measurement company BigChampagne.com, explains the difficulty of what Gaga is doing on social networking sites: "[T]echnologies like Twitter and Facebook and MySpace have created these platforms for 'mass intimacy,' but mostly it doesn't work very well, mostly because you know that I'm not talking to you — if I wanted to talk to you, I'd call or email. When you're speaking to ten million 'friends,' you don't have that intimacy."[92] For Gaga to argue that fans have access to her notion of fame, she has to talk to them like equals and treat them like family. The technology is there to do that, but using it in this way is difficult. Speaking about Gaga, Garland says that "some artists can make that happen — like in live performances, where people in the cheap seats feel like they're having a command performance. An artist like Lady Gaga feels like she is doing that, on the Internet, in real time."[93] Lady Gaga is able to use social media in a way that makes fans feel like she is talking directly to them. Having this relationship with her fans means that she can communicate with them directly about what her work means and where she is drawing her influences. Often she does not take a defensive posture, as if she is reacting to criticism. Instead, through social media Lady Gaga engages with her audience and shares her creations as if she is part of the larger participatory culture.

New social media technologies have provided Gaga with novel ways to perform her rethinking of fame. Social media has played a key role in Gaga's own fame and her ability to perform the philosophy of "the fame." Gaga started tweeting in March of 2008, and by February of 2010 she was one of the most popular celebrities on Twitter, with 2.8 million followers. She joined Facebook in April of 2008, and by July of 2010 she was reporting 9.76 million Facebook friends.[94] At the time, that was more Facebook fans than President Obama and more Twitter followers than Britney Spears. Famecount.com has called her the single most popular person online.[95] It's no wonder in October of 2009, when Obama introduced Gaga at the Human Rights Campaign National Dinner, he stated: "It's a privilege to be here tonight to open for Lady Gaga. I've made it."[96] Throughout her career, Gaga has used these social media technologies extensively to release exclusive images, music, and information directly to fans. Biographer Maureen Callahan points out that "controlling and crafting one's myth is hardly new ... what's remarkable about Lady Gaga is that she's the first star born in and of the Internet age to master this art."[97] More important than the popularity she experiences on these platforms is the way in which Gaga actively uses them to engage with other users.

On her YouTube channel, Gaga often posts what appears to be amateur, user-generated content. At the end of June 2008, Gaga started making weekly videos called *Transmission Gagavision* and uploading them to her site.[98] Later these videos moved to YouTube. They were often black-and-white videos of Gaga on the road, hanging out with her dancers and DJs. In the very first one, Lady Gaga buys a tabloid in a drugstore and excitedly shows all her friends a picture of herself with Michelle Williams.[99] In this scene, Lady Gaga is simultaneously a member of the celebrity community, appearing in magazines with established stars, and a giddy fan, excited over images of her teen idol. The dual role she occupies in this video is indicative of the larger persona Lady Gaga has developed for herself on YouTube. Elsewhere on the site, Gaga has posted mobile phone videos of her friends and sometimes her fans while she is on the road. In response to legislation on Don't Ask, Don't Tell, Gaga has posted several videos of her sitting on a tour bus or in her dressing room, talking to viewers about her opinions and updating them on the legislation. These videos all seem to be unedited and not of particularly high quality, much like the user-generated content posted by amateurs throughout the YouTube community. Gaga has been known to add videos to less prominent YouTube users' playlists, showing an interaction with the site's general community. Traditionally, on YouTube mainstream media producers and users have co-existed, but always with a sense that the two groups were engaging in different types of behavior on the site.[100] Gaga's choices in presenting herself not only as a traditional, removed celebrity but also as a communicative, interactive part of the community on YouTube allow her to be received as a carnival-style peer performer, as opposed to a high-profile media maker trying to exploit an audience and capitalize on a new outlet.

Lady Gaga's understanding of fame translates in tangible ways into her interactions with her fans in person and online. Sites like Twitter and Facebook are designed in a manner that leads users to assume they always have an audience. People broadcast their thoughts and current status with the belief that a social media platform is connecting them to a network of viewers who are interested in knowing the information. Lady Gaga embraces this culture of social media and feeds on having a captive audience, just like many non-celebrity users. In the early Gagavision videos, Gaga makes no attempt to perform or cater to an audience, creating videos consisting of her and her backup dancers sitting around after shows or during downtime, chatting about the shows. Although the first few videos were not particularly popular — most had around 100,000 views on YouTube — the conversational nature of them soon attracted quite a fan base. The 36th video, released in March 2009, has a view count of more than 645,000, and that number continues to grow.[101] The seventh video in the

Gagavision series is made up of clips of Lady Gaga, with two friends, sitting on the sidewalk outside a Frank Lloyd Wright building in Los Angeles, talking about the fact that she is famous.[102] It all seems very grandiose, but as she says in episode 8, "it is about speaking to effect or acting to effect." Put another way, "it's vanity but in reverse."[103] It is not until episode 14 that the videos start to show Gaga promoting her music. Many Gagavision videos contain footage from a concert that Gaga did in LA in 2008.[104] The concert is on a small stage, with just Gaga, two backup dancers, and Space Cowboy, her DJ. The audience is visible and most of them are just standing in front of the stage, having a beer, and looking unimpressed. At one point Gaga dances on the edge of the stage where a large number of men are standing. The men actually back up when she gets closer to them. Clips shown in episode 9 mark a transition as Gaga is starting to get famous.[105] The concert shown in that episode has the kind of screaming crowds you would expect to now see at a show for Lady Gaga. So, when the Gagavision and YouTube videos are watched in the order they were released, a narrative of Gaga's fame emerges—from start to stardom. The "behind the scenes" story gives fans and viewers a deeper sense of Gaga's dream and how the evolution of her performance influenced her concept of fame.

On Twitter, Gaga's posts have ranged from the endearing to the abrasive. Thanksgiving Day 2010, Gaga posted a message saying that "I'm so thankful for the blessing of my fans. My family+I are thankful for u. For those lonely today, we set an extra place at our table. <3."[106] Not all of her messages are this sweet. After her video for the song "Paparazzi" was posted anonymously online a week ahead of schedule, she tweeted the angry outburst: "Stop leaking my motherfucking videos!"[107] She responds to questions from fans and retweets their comments, images, and even YouTube videos of them performing her music. In addition, Gaga uses Twitpic, a photo site that is linked to Twitter, to post random images from her day and reinforce a sense of everyday communication and access. Often the photos she posts are snapshots from her cell phone, taken in hotel rooms while she is on tour. For example, in June of 2012 she posted images of herself with a black eye and the caption "Still remiss if I should go outside with this clonker. I may be of questionable styling." These images encourage a real sense of familiarity with her fans. Sites like Twitter are social spaces that straddle the line between mainstream media and interactive media. Mainstream media outlets— like CNN or ESPN — often construct these digital media spaces as simply another broadcasting site. Gaga uses the technology the way a lot of day-to-day users would. For the Mother Monster this is less a broadcasting outlet and more a place to reach fans and get to know them. While on the road for the Born This Way Ball, Gaga posted an image of a coffee cup with Britney Spears's face on it. In the caption Gaga proclaimed herself a true fan, who would stick by Britney no matter what. Much like the video of Gaga gushing over pictures of herself with Michelle Williams, this Tweet puts her in the role an everyday user or fan of mainstream media. The sense of self she displays on the site cast it as a more intimate space and cast her as a kind of average user. The casting disrupts the image of a celebrity as someone removed from daily life.

For Lady Gaga, articulating her role as a fan, and as part of a community, is critical to the larger messages she is pushing about the fame and the fame monster. As she told Oprah during an interview in 2010, "all the things I do in terms of fame and the fame monster is meant to make it a bit easier to swallow this kind of horrific media world that we live in."[108] Mainstream media continually uses celebrities and monsters to constructive a narrative of what is right and wrong. Lady Gaga is using her message about fame and her relationship with her fans to disrupt that narrative. Brian Solis, a writer and popular technology blogger, has said that the influence she has developed and the relationship Lady Gaga has with her fans are critical to her ability to make larger political and social statements about the role of media in daily life: "It's all about how you cultivate your community.... Celebs have never shied away from causes and in many ways it's expected that they will use their celebrity to gain attention for those causes. But it's what (Gaga) does over time and how her community responds that starts the lean-over into the influence factor."[109] The message about fame translates into direct influence as Lady Gaga pushes political agendas like repealing Don't Ask, Don't Tell and social initiatives like the Born This Way Foundation. Both these causes, allowing gays to live openly in the military and working to stop bullying, get at the underlying premise of the fame. Individuals need to stop letting society tell them that some fundamental aspect of who they are is bad or shameful. Lady Gaga uses the mainstream media to get her message out to the public, but in her construction of celebrity there is an attempt to remove the mainstream media from their role as intermediary between fans and stars. With projects like Littlemonsters.com, she is envisioning a world where celebrities actually own their media outlets. On the Internet Lady Gaga occupies both the role of star and the role of fan, she communicates directly with her fans, and she articulates her work as part of a collaboration with her fan community. Gaga's whole project is premised on the argument that the monsters are not who we think they are; the real monsters are the forces in the society, such as the mainstream media, trying to make people afraid and the fear that those forces generate. By eliminating the role of those forces in mediating her communication with fans Gaga is able to craft her message of fame more clearly.

On YouTube, Gaga again walks on each side of the line between professional and amateur, acting as both a mainstream media producer and an everyday user. The movement back and forth between the two roles allows her, once again, to avoid being made an object by media framing. Her music videos are all released online before they are aired on more traditional channels. This is important for two reasons. First, it shows how she prioritizes her interactions with her fans over her interactions with the mainstream media. Second, it allows her to act as an amateur user who is sharing her creations with her online community. Amateur media producers often distribute things on YouTube with the hope they will become popular enough to attract the attention of the mainstream media. However, if their videos were syndicated exclusively through traditional mainstream media outlets, users would not have the experience of interacting simultaneously with the performer and the audience. Television as a media platform creates a clear delineation between performer and audience. On YouTube, the music videos are offered up to a crowd that is able to respond and comment directly on the performance, interacting both with other spectators and with the original poster. Paul J. Booth argues that the collectivity experienced on interactive online sites promotes carnivalesque communication, a communication that does not acknowledge traditional social boundaries.[110] Both the anonymity and the invitation for amateur media result in casual, intimate, informal, and sometimes abrasive responses. Take, for example, an exchange that took place in the comments section for the "Born This Way" music video. On August 15, 2012, teezandroid posted: "HAPPYYYYYYY BIRTHDAYYYYYYYYY QUEEN MADONNA:)" Posting this on a Lady Gaga video angered fan thonyXDifyy, who responded: "How old is Madonna D: ? like 999.999.999 years old she's living since before Christ was born." From there, the conversation took a more extreme turn, with user kram1190 responding: "disrespectful cunt! shut up! if there was no Madonna ... surely there will be no horseshit face gaga ... THE ULTIMATE MOTHER COPY OF POP! :)" Users in this exchange follow spelling and grammatical conventions loosely, and they readily use language that would be far less acceptable outside this format. Interestingly, they also take the "catfights" portrayed elsewhere in the media and translate them into one-on-one confrontations. The comments are not exclusively made by Lady Gaga fans. So, the site opens up a space for fans to interpret media but also exposes their interpretations to people outside the fan community.

Lady Gaga's biggest contribution to celebrity use of social media came with the launch of her own personal social networking site: Littlemonsters.com. The site was opened to the general public in July of 2012, and *Business Insider* described it as a mix of Pinterest and a more traditional Internet bulletin board.[111] The social networking site was designed by an Internet start-up called Backplane, which hopes to design similar sites for other celebrities. One of the main designers of the site is a Gaga fan who found the job when Lady Gaga posted on her Facebook page "Gaga Seeks Geeks."[112] The company has been backed by Lady Gaga, and Littlemonsters.com is meant to be a prototype for future celebrity social networking sites.[113] The site includes sections where fans can trade Lady Gaga–related media, including images and videos; discussion boards for sharing ideas; news and recent Gaga-related information; user profiles for developing a network of friends; and an events page where users can buy tickets to concerts. Many of the functions mirror typical social networking sites. Site members can "like" things or leave comments. In an article for *Wired Magazine*, Troy Carter, one of the masterminds behind Littlemonsters.com, points out that even before the site existed Lady Gaga was visiting some of the larger privately run fan sites to communicate with fans directly.[114] The Mother Monster has always been an active participant on social networking sites like Twitter and Facebook. Littlemonsters.com took that participation to a whole new level by moving the discussions to a site where Gaga could contribute more types of media in a single space and exercise better control over what is accessed by other users. Lady Gaga routinely posts pictures taken from her phone, thoughts while she is on tour, advance information about events, comments on fashion choices, and responses to media controversy about her behavior. Beyond all her personal posts, she "likes" comments on the site and redistributes the posts made by other site users. This site allows Lady Gaga to communicate with her fans even more directly than a site like Facebook where the rules for communication are still being created by a larger entity. Once the site was fully launched, Lady Gaga even began using her profile on more-established social networking sites to redirect users to Littlemonsters.com. Often, when Gaga post something on Littlemonsters.com, she provides links to those posts on Facebook and Twitter. As a result, the Mother Monster is engaging fans in multiple different arenas at once. The constant engagement increases fan awareness of Gaga and makes her more a part of fans' day-to-day lives. What's more, with the advent of Backplane, Gaga is attempting to market this as the new celebrity model for communicating online.

Summary and Concluding Thoughts

In July of 2010, Lady Gaga became the first person to reach 10 million friends on Facebook. To commemorate the milestone, she posted a video on YouTube thanking her fans for all their support. In the video she expresses gratitude to the little monsters for "sticking by me through *The Fame* and *The Fame Monster*."[115] Though the video is only 35 seconds long, it provides some key insights into the links between Gaga's parody performance of fame, her larger philosophy of fame, and the relationship she has with her fans. Lady Gaga's performance of celebrity challenges the argument that fame is organically derived from mainstream media forces. She uses parody to self-consciously reference and annotate her work, which makes it clear that there are mechanized patterns and behavior associated with fame. Gaga's music videos highlight the relationship between celebrities and the mainstream media. She has a history of parodying media attention by making teacups famous and mimicking noted celebrity interviewers. In all these ways, Lady Gaga uses parody to perform and problematize social constructions of fame. When media critics attempt to challenge her behavior by calling her a cultural thief, a plagiarist, or just another Madonna wannabe, she pushes back with charges that critics are not drawing from a large enough history to understand what she is really doing with her work. This is where the monster becomes a critical part of Gaga's overarching argument: "[T]he point of monster rhetoric is to show that the monster, while suddenly upon us, is not, after all, new, nor really much of a surprise."[116] Monster culture is framed as naturally old, while celebrity culture is articulated as new. The combination of the two through parody reveals that what is old in celebrity culture is the insidious patterns repeated over and over with each new starlet.

Lady Gaga's parody of fame makes it clear that in many ways it is nothing more than a mechanical process. This opens up fame as something achievable by her fans. The parody becomes an inside joke between Gaga and her community of little monsters. Still, with that said, as Judith Butler points out, "parody by itself is not subversive, and there must be a way to understand what makes certain kinds of parodic repetitions effectively disruptive, truly troubling, and which repetitions become domesticated and recirculated as instruments of cultural hegemony."[117] It is Gaga's articulation of fame as something can be accessed by her fans, and her demonstration of that through social media outlets, that moves the parody from simply revealing to actively disruptive.

Chapter 4
Selling the Monstrosity

Monsters are typically thought of as existing outside social norms and codes of conduct. They are maladapted freaks who have been rejected and spurned by the public. Either deified or vilified, monsters are constantly made separate from the rules and lives of a civilized society. Still, as has been repeatedly argued, they serve a necessary function, and because of this they may be removed from day-to-day life, but they are always present. The monster serves a crucial function in society; "in current practice the term 'monster' still registers an uneasy alliance between the abnormal as spectacle and the abnormal marked out as moral failure ... despite being dismissed as a marginal genre, as pulp, or pop, and being consigned to video back rooms ... making monsters is a necessary social hygiene, helping to keep citizens straight."[1] In the interest of making monsters both visible and harmless, contemporary society has worked to commodify them. As Edward Ingebretsen argues, in our modern culture fear is something to be consumed. Monsters are tamed so that they can be bought and sold. Take, for example, Pokémon — literally translated it means "pocket monster." The Pokémon phenomenon started with a series of video games owned by Nintendo. Since its creation, it has spawned a cartoon series, several movies, and a wildly popular set of trading cards. In their merchandized format these pocket monsters "are collectable, of course, because they are shoppable," and in their packaged-for-consumer form they are containable.[2] The marketability of monsters helps both to tame them and to increase their visibility in day-to-day life. As luck would have it, selling monstrosity not only serves the social function of keeping monsters present and visible; it is also highly profitable.

Lady Gaga has proven herself a master at marketing monstrosity. This is due in large part to her ability to capitalize and merchandize her identity.

While her discourse may push the boundaries of mainstream media structures, she has taken full advantage of economic and legal systems to maintain and control her identity. Elizabeth Kate Switaj argues that Gaga's transgressiveness should not be mistaken for operating outside the traditional economic system. To the contrary, her role as a monster only increases her monetary value: "[T]his (monstrous, white) womanhood sells and it is crafted to sell; her performance of gender, even when it seems subversive or transgressive, is thoroughly commodified."[3] If anything, Gaga's transgressiveness makes her more marketable. The Wall Street Journal has said that "Gaga's allure is that of a misfit run amok in the system." The misfit status appeals to a legion of maladjusted youths. As a result, the relationship between the Mother Monster and the system is ultimately a symbiotic one.[4] Copyright, trademark, product endorsements, and contract law have all been utilized by Gaga as tools to construct a relationship with the business side of the media industry that is profitable for both her and her collaborators. In fact, current economic practices and the laws designed to facilitate them help make Lady Gaga's public performance possible.

The booming relationship between celebrities and the business side of the media industry can be traced back to the original Hollywood star system of the 1920s. Traditionally, the scholarly focus has been on the role of stars as commodities within the system. Richard Dyer explains that "from a business point of view, there are many advantages in the star system. The star has tangible features which can be advertised and marketed — a face, a body, a pair of legs, a voice, a certain kind of personality, real or synthetic — and can be typed as the wicked villain, the honest hero, the fatal siren, the sweet young girl, the neurotic woman."[5] For celebrities — even beyond their talents as actors, singers, or models — contracts with major corporate media producers give them a monetary value associated with their very physical existence. In fact, celebrities on a large scale, not counting local celebrities, are really only possible with the right combination of economics and infrastructure. Francesco Alberoni argues that there are three basic conditions that are necessary for stars to exist: a state of law, an efficient bureaucracy, and a structured social system.[6] The existence of these factors does not ensure a celebrity culture, but without them mass media celebrity is not a tangible reality. This is in part because celebrity, at its core, is an idea and a society has to be past the point of scraping by before they start to invest ideas with monetary value. All this is to say that while Gaga's monstrosity may appear to be challenging power structures, she is reliant on the infrastructure behind that power to maintain her celebrity status and get her message out to the public. Graeme Turner refers to celebrities as "cultural workers."[7] The celebrity makes money as a commodity for a variety of endeavors that produce cultural artifacts, and the "celebrity can develop their public persona as a commercial asset" for his or her own profit.[8]

It is easy to accept that houses, cars, and clothes are all marketable goods. Still, the notion of identity as something that can be packaged, marketed, and sold is sometimes harder to grasp. However, in a capitalist society it can have a tangible monetary value. Richard Dyer points to four ways that stars become goods in the economic structure of the media industry: (1) capital — "stars represent a form of capital possessed by the studio," (2) investment — "stars were a guarantee, or a promise, against loss on investment and even of profit on it," (3) outlay — "stars were a major portion of a film's budget," and (4) the market — "stars were used to sell films, to organize the market."[9] The legal system, through mechanisms like copyright and trademark, allows celebrities to develop and protect identities as marketable products. Rosemary Coombe explains that "the law constructs and maintains fixed, stable identities authorized by the celebrity subject but ... the celebrity is authored in a multiplicity of sites of interpretive practice."[10] The legal system provides a foundation for the interactions between celebrities, media outlets, and the media industry, as the three interested parties work together to construct the celebrity identity. Law functions in celebrity culture to preserve representations of these celebrity identities in mainstream media and establish social consequences for their misuse. Rules and laws are often locations where society translates beliefs into concrete practices. According to Barry Brummett, these practices communicate ideology as "a more or less consistent system of thought, a connected set of intellectual habits and emotional reactions that structure and inform the way we perceive and respond to experience. Such a system privileges some interests and disadvantages others; ideology always entails attempts at domination and the responses of acceptance or rejection."[11] The law decides what we do and do not accept. When those practices are in place, it becomes easier to see how one person can move up the ranks of society and achieve celebrity. Within "societies characterized by mass production, consumer capitalism, and mass-media communications, the celebrity image holds both seductive power and significant economic and cultural value."[12] Lady Gaga has crafted an identity that capitalizes on these factors.

An analysis of the economic and legal aspects of the development of Lady Gaga's public persona offers several lessons about the changing nature of celebrity. Much of Lady Gaga's public performance is based on the notion that she is somehow fighting the media. Sasha Frere-Jones argues in a *New Yorker* article titled "Ladies Wild: How Not Dumb Is Gaga?" that "Stefani Joanne Angelina Germanotta would have you believe that she's not just beating the system — in her version, she's stormed the castle walls, spirited away the Dauphin, and changed the national language to semaphore."[13] However, the truth is that "Gaga is not odd, give or take some warbles and that one time during a session for AOL when she pounded on her keyboard with her high heel, but she is as smart as she repeatedly claims to be."[14] There is a corporate model to selling Gaga, and it is part of everything she does. Red One, who mixes most of her work, points out that the chanting Gaga does in songs makes her music easier for non–English speakers to pick up. This makes her popular for clubs in other countries.[15] Every part of the process has been calculated. This chapter looks at the contradiction in Gaga's performance between being a "rebel" and someone who is actively participating in celebrity as a commodity system. This contradiction raises serious questions about the authenticity of Gaga's performance. While she claims to be a monster destroying our typical media culture, she is also developing new models to make that media culture profitable in the age of the Internet and free music downloads.

The first part of the chapter will look at Gaga's performance of celebrity as commodity. She performs the trading of her body for status in some very visible ways that, while not subverting the system, definitely make it more visible. The second part of the chapter will look at the way Gaga deals with the legal aspect of celebrity. Lady Gaga's interactions with the legal system show a shift in the understanding of what it is a celebrity sells. Where typically legal systems are used to uphold the notion that celebrities make money on their art, Lady Gaga uses the legal system to demonstrate the value of her identity. For Lady Gaga, she *is* the product that she is selling.

Celebrity as Commodity

In early 2006, while Lady Gaga was making the demos for her first album, *The Fame*, she had a small studio apartment in New York's East Village.[16] One might expect that when her first album took off she would take the money and invest in a lavish home or an expensive car. Instead, that East Village apartment has turned out to be the last official home of the Mother Monster. Despite rumors that Gaga has been house hunting in 2011, as of 2012 she had no permanent address or home. She told a *Vanity Fair* reporter that the "Gypsy queen couldn't take the leap.... I'm not going to pay millions of dollars for something. I can't commit to being an adult — I'm not ready."[17] When Oprah Winfrey interviewed Gaga in March of 2012, in her Upper West Side childhood home, Oprah and Gaga's mother teased the celebrity about being 26 years old and not having a place of her own. After decades of shows like *Lifestyles of the Rich and Famous* and *MTV Cribs*, Gaga's very public choice not to own an expensive home or car is a shift from the typical celebrity performance.

Part of the appeal that celebrities have to the general public is the image they present of the average person who has risen up the ranks and achieved wealth and status. Dyer argues that "stardom is an image of the way stars live. For the most part, this generalized lifestyle is the assumed backdrop for the specific personality of the star and the details and events of her/his life. As it combines the spectacular with the everyday, the special with the ordinary."[18] The idea becomes that a star is just like you, that is, if you had a lot more money. The spectacle promotes celebrity culture as escapism and, furthermore, associates status with consumption. Celebrities reinforce capitalist culture by encouraging the everyday person to strive for material goods as symbols of success. Lady Gaga has repeatedly said that she spends all of her money on her tour and her performances. Even just making these public statements disrupts some of the fantasy of celebrity and points to the cost of being a star. It also helps to shape Gaga's public identity: "the tragic image of the artist as married to the art, forever a loser in love, intermittently sated by random sex but relying on the adulation of the audience to live, devoted to them above all."[19] Rather than having a traditional home and a family, for a home Gaga has her tour, her fans are her family, and her art is her first priority. She lives that performance 24 hours a day, 7 days a week. Her manager, Tony Carter, said in

August 2009 that Gaga is a throwback to "the days when artists were artists. She's an iconic figure, and it's not like she ever takes a day off and put on khakis and a T-shirt. She's in showbiz, and fans have been missing people like that."[20] As Gaga biographer Maureen Callahan explains, "this alterego long ago subsumed her former identity ... she is never off-duty."[21] The image of Gaga "at home" in any traditional sense would somehow imply that sometimes she is not performing publicly.

One of the major commodities of any star, but particularly female stars, is their physical body. It is common for interviewers to ask female celebrities how they maintain their figure and hear responses about just trying to avoid fried food or being dedicated to yoga. This, again, feeds the escapism: You, too, could have a million dollar body if you had more willpower and just exercised a little more. What most of these reports leave out is the strict low-calorie diets that are maintained by hiring personal chefs, and the perfectly toned bodies that can only be sustained by keeping a personal trainer on staff. Lady Gaga's responses to these questions are not as simple. Elizabeth Switaj points out that Gaga trades her body for fame, to the point that she likes to announce in interviews that she does not eat: Pop stars do not eat![22] With these answers, "Gaga does not rebel against the systems that require women to risk their health in favor of arbitrary standards of appearance; instead, she reveals and revels in their absurdity. She shows that they exist and exist to be transgressed but does not herself violate them."[23] Part of this response may be because often during her early career Gaga was described as overweight.[24] However, it is more likely attributable to her overall conversation about fame; "she is unashamed about having fame and almost never appears to be burdened by it. She allows the public to believe that fame is as wonderful as they might imagine it to be. It's refreshing."[25] Whereas many celebrities might shrug off the body maintenance that is involved in being a commodity, Lady Gaga flaunts it. She does not own a home. She does not eat. She works. This is part of her larger message of prioritizing her career over everything else: "Some women choose to follow men, and some women choose to follow their dreams.... If you're wondering which way to go, remember that your career will never wake up and tell you that it doesn't love you anymore."[26] Gaga's approach to career makes her overt body maintenance seem more masculine in its relationship to economics, given that it supports her means of living.

Gaga's well-maintained body is ideal for selling the glamour and fashion she preaches as part of the fame. Much of Lady Gaga's career has been tied up with her connection to the fashion industry. In October 2009, "Gaga posted a link to one of her own videos on fashion icon Alexander McQueen's Web site. After a single tweet by Gaga, her rabid fans streamed in and crashed the site's servers."[27] Within the next few years she had walked the runway in a Mugler fashion show, been given private access to the Versace vault, and had her dress made out of meat embalmed and showcased in the Rock and Roll Hall of Fame. It seems that Gaga never appears out of costume, "she takes care never to be photographed out of character, and really, it speaks to her work ethic. At a time when talentless civilians thrust themselves in front of TV cameras and then complain about blogs and gossip and paparazzi, here is a performer — ironically and perfectly a classmate of Paris Hilton's — who writes songs about wanting to be both pursuer of the paparazzi and pursued by them."[28] Constantly appearing in high fashion is one way that Gaga maintains the celebrity culture of escapism. Lady Gaga understands fashion and style as liberatory. Before she became a star, when she moved from her parent's house to the Village, she described her relationship to fashion this way: "I found all these shops on Eighth Street and I integrated fashion into my life in a healthy way because it made me feel powerful, ambitious and much more resilient."[29] It has also allowed her to influence the fashion of others. In December 2009, *Flare* magazine reported "Jean Paul Gaultier, Christian Lacroix, Givenchy and even Chanel were cited as channeling Gaga's recessionista-bashing hyper-glamour."[30] Gaga's image makes a larger economic statement, because it not only feeds upon the markets of the fashion industry — it also fuels them.

Much of Lady Gaga's ability to manage her overall image comes from her established online relationship with her fan community. Eric Garland, CEO of BigChampaigne.com, described Gaga as "an incredibly social animal in the new definition of social. She's sort of promiscuous. And I don't mean in the Ke$ha sense — I mean socially promiscuous online."[31] Lady Gaga does not confine herself to a single medium or limit her voice to any one outlet. She has recognized repeatedly the power of developing a multimodal message for her fan community. Maureen Callahan argues that "it was Gaga's innate understanding of creating and cultivating an online identity — and a sense of community with those who responded — that would, as much as a major label backing, catapult her to global consciousness."[32] In fact, for a big part of her early fame Gaga owes a debt of gratitude to Perez Hilton, an online blogger who became a fan early in her career. In 2010, his blog was the 192nd most trafficked site in the U.S., and he linked to every one of her videos when they were released online. Lady Gaga cultivates a fan community that drives audience traffic to her work. More interesting than her online presence is the way that Gaga translates the possibilities of each medium into a larger multimedia conversation. In 2008, after the release of "Just Dance," after shows Gaga recorded introductions for the song for different radio stations, "specifically singing out each one's call letters until, finally, she'd recorded a tailor-made single for every radio outlet in the United States."[33] Lady Gaga establishes her fan base online, and then she uses all available outlets to continually personalize her message to impact the daily lives of her little monsters.

Gaga's extreme maintenance of her life as a celebrity has also allowed her a certain freedom to define her identity. Callahan, in her examination of Gaga's past, claims that unlike many developing pop stars, Lady Gaga fully developed her persona before receiving any media attention.[34] Celebrities are given new exposure in the age of the Internet. By controlling her public identity, she has been able to mold and craft herself to fit the height of desire for a given moment. This control allows her to play with image and identity in a highly marketable way:

> Gaga's business model starts with an incongruous product. Listen to Gaga's *Poker Face* and you might imagine it's Britney Spears in a track suit. But watch the video and you'll see a work of conceptual porn. Gaga, a 23-year-old blonde with bulletproof bangs and 3-inch lashes, slinks across stages in gleaming metal bustiers, smoked latex underwear and thigh-high stiletto boots. Performing *Paparazzi* at the Video Music Awards, she ended the set dangling above the stage in gauzy white La Perla lingerie, horrifying her audience as fake blood gushed from her bosom.[35]

Lady Gaga is able to violate expectation because she allows so little of what is normal to seep into her public performance. Simon Dumenco, music industry veteran, was quoted in *Forbes* saying Lady Gaga "is directing every frame of her music and her life, imagining how clips will appear on YouTube and what people will tweet after she appears on the VMAs."[36] All of this is about the process of fame. From the beginning, the elements were all there: "[W]ho she would become — this avant-garde freak show who would work for days on end crafting the perfect dance song despite wanting to be taken seriously as a singer-songwriter — was, she saw, merely a vessel to get her to the what."[37] Gaga's persona was unprecedented, introduced to the market with no prior presentation. What Gaga wanted was celebrity, and she has proven herself adept at working the system to achieve it.

Who Owns Gaga?

Despite the popular myth that Lady Gaga has worked to generate, she was not born this way. She was born March 28, 1986, as Stefani Joanne Angelina Germanotta.[38] It was not until 20 years later, in 2006, that she would be reborn as Lady Gaga.[39] There are several stories about where the title "Lady Gaga" came from and, more important, who came up with it. The consistent element of the narrative is that her name came from the Queen song "Radio Ga Ga."[40] Before Lady Gaga signed her first record deal with Def Jam, she was working with producer Robert Fusari to develop a demo. During that time Fusari and Germanotta developed a romantic relationship, and the two worked together on a lot of her early music.[41] On Gaga's first album — The Fame — Fusari is credited as album producer and co-writer of three songs, including one of the first hits, "Paparazzi."[42] The working relationship between the two was not an act of serendipity. Fusari had been looking for a new artist to craft her career. He said that what he was looking for was an artist "that would read as traditionally male but be subversively female."[43] The producer found all that and more when Wendy Starland, an assistant, introduced him to Stefani Germanotta. Lady Gaga was created out of the collaboration that followed. One version of events is that, during a work session Fusari said to Germanotta, "You are so freaking Freddie Mercury, you're so dramatic!" and then called her Gaga as a Queen reference.[44] Another popular narrative attributes the name to a combination of Fusari and an auto-corrected text message. The producer was texting Germanotta something about "Radio Ga Ga" and it was auto-corrected to "Lady Gaga."[45] Fusari said later in an interview with the Star-Ledger: "Every day, when Stef came to the studio, instead of saying hello, I would start singing 'Radio Ga Ga,'... That was her entrance song.... It was actually a glitch.... I typed 'Radio Ga Ga' in a text and it did an autocorrect so somehow 'Radio' got changed to 'Lady.' She texted me back,

'That's it.' After that day, she was Lady Gaga. She's like, 'Don't ever call me Stefani again.'"[46] These two versions of the story have some backing, since Gaga has attributed the title to Fusari in interviews.[47] There is a third version of the story that involves Fusari and Wendy Starland, who would later leave Fusari to work for Gaga. According to Starland, while the team was developing Gaga's demo they were also working to develop the star's public identity. There were multiple conversations about the type of celebrity she would be and what that would mean for her look, her music, and her name. Starland claims that she suggested the Queen reference during a meeting with the creative team and that Germanotta added the "Lady."[48] The debate about which version of events is true might have been nothing more than the subject of an episode of VH1's *Behind the Music*, but in March 2010 Fusari sued Gaga, leaving it up to the court to determine what actually happened.

Regardless of which version of the events you believe, Lady Gaga is a creative work, and like many other creative works—movies, books, paintings—her identity has a monetary value. Richard Dyer points out that the notion of stars as manufactured, or created, is well accepted by most media consumers.[49] The general public tends to be aware of the designation of the star as a "creation" and accepts the produced nature of celebrity culture. This awareness often results in claims by reporters to find the real or authentic person behind the celebrity persona.[50] The many lawsuits that have plagued Lady Gaga's career make the manufactured nature of her identity even more apparent than with traditional celebrities. While the media industry may make a lot of money off the lives of celebrities, they do not in any legal sense own the stars' identities. Those identities are considered naturally occurring creations of the star themselves, as opposed to the celebrity status that is cultivated by the media and the media industry. According to Charles Bazerman, "to create profit from an idea, the idea has to be transformed into an ownable piece of property assigned to an individual. The procedure for this transformation must identify an idea as an invention, establish the limits of the idea ... establish the period of ownership, and designate an owner.... This transformation process consists entirely of words and symbols."[51] Once an idea has been established as a tangible thing, it can be owned and it can be profitable. Intellectual property recognizes that certain commodities are not valued based on their usefulness but on their ability to be traded.[52]

To make a profit, you need to be the one who owns the idea, but owning an idea is by no means automatic. Instead, "the individual seeking ownership of an idea must define the idea in specific symbolic form, through words and pictures, and then apply for this representation to be granted status as an invention according to the criteria of the granting body."[53] Lady Gaga is in the unique position of being one of the few celebrities to go through the legal system to establish that she created her own identity and that she owns the idea of herself.

Rob Fusari was the first to fight Lady Gaga for ownership of her identity. In April 2010, Fusari sued the star for $30.5 million — 20 percent of the profits from her first album. In the lawsuit he claimed that he acted as her agent and that he named her Lady Gaga.[54] In interviews, Fusari has taken credit for a lot more than producing some of Lady Gaga's early hits; he also claims that he chose the pop direction for her sound (originally she sounded like a cross between No Doubt and Fiona Apple) and helped to "fix" her look.[55] Early in her career, Gaga wanted to be more of a singer-songwriter, but the feeling by media executives was that she lacked "the ready-made look of an American pop star in waiting. Fusari and Starland didn't think she could pull off the girl-at-a-piano thing, because ... you have to be very pretty to do that."[56] *Billboard* magazine referred to Fusari as the "Dr. Frankenstein to Gaga's Fame Monster."[57] Much like the original Frankenstein, Fusari's creation took on a life of its own and left him behind. By her second album, *The Fame Monster*, Gaga was no longer affiliated with her first producer. When asked about the lawsuit with Fusari during a *Vanity Fair* interview, Gaga said:

> Nobody made me.... Nobody fuckin' made me who I am today. And what is so funny is that everyone that was spitting in my face and treating me like dirt and making me feel so worthless.... The price that a woman pays for people destroying you over and over again.... I'm a fuckin' lion. I'm a lion and I can't be destroyed. The things I have been through.... I would not take any of it back, because it's made me the writer that I am. But how dare [anyone] that treated you like dirt on the bottom of their shoe try to turn around and tell you that they made you? The minute that you have a glimpse of sunlight on your eyelids, they fuckin' made you that mascara.[58]

Gaga's outrage at the lawsuit resulted in a countersuit, where the performer argued that the original deal between her and her producer had been "predatory."[59] Ultimately, both suits were thrown out by the New York Supreme Court and neither party won.

The legal battle between Fusari and Gaga had many of the elements that make for riveting television: a romance gone bad, a lover scorned, and a woman's struggle to establish her sense of self. More than that, the narrative of events gets at one of the issues that constantly get raised with Gaga: authenticity. Despite persistent claims that she sleeps in wigs and lives in high heels, the media continually questions the realness of Lady Gaga. Fusari's claims that he "made" Gaga are presented as proof that there once was a time when Stefani Germanotta was not yet Gaga, fueling the public's need to see Gaga as performed. By placing this battle in the court system, Fusari sought a chance to settle the issue once and for all. While Gaga cannot be forced to answer questions about who she really is, court decisions provide definite outcomes and answers to questions. Court trials are often compelling because they include resolution about questions of right and wrong. The majority of individuals experience trials through the media, and reporters translate the vagueness of legal decisions into narratives about absolutes. Barry Brummett argues that the media takes the mechanical and technical nature of trials, attempts to turn them into stories about everyday individuals, and naturalizes these activities to give us a sense of the "real" story. We are asked to identify with the characters in the trial and use the details of the trial to understand larger social events.[60] For Brummett, "the issue in legal reporting becomes primarily who wins, which bad guys get shot down on Main Street, which good guys get to ride off in triumph."[61] Robert Hariman expands on this idea, arguing that "one reason trials continue to be the representative anecdotes of issues ... is that they of all occasions for the controversy result in a decision.... This constraint on social knowledge enacted by trials is both a blessing and a curse, for though it often forces the public to move closer to serious consideration of the decision itself, it also supplies a thoroughly artificial resolution."[62] The lawsuits between Lady Gaga and Fusari do not offer resolution on the authenticity of Gaga's identity, but the reporting on the lawsuit gives the media a chance to challenge the realness of that identity.

Negotiating Lady Gaga

Lady Gaga had a rocky introduction to the music business. In the video for "Marry the Night," she dramatizes what she has called the worst day of her life — the day Island Def Jam, her first record label, dropped her. More than a year before the release of "Marry the Night," Lady Gaga described that day in an interview with *Vanity Fair* reporter Lisa Robinson:

> All I will say is I hit rock bottom, and it was enough to send a person over the edge. My mother knew the truth about that day, and she screamed so loud on the other end of the phone, I'll never forget it. And she said, "I'm coming to get you." And I remember laying on the pullout bed in the basement in my parents' house, and I said to my mom, "Can we go see Grandma?" And we didn't even call her; the next morning we got on the plane to West Virginia, showed up at the house, and I told my [82-year-old] grandma everything. I cried. I told her I thought my life was over and I have no hope and I've worked so hard, and I knew I was good. What would I do now? And she said, "I'm gonna let you cry for a few more hours. And then after those few hours are up, you're gonna stop crying, you're gonna pick yourself up, you're gonna go back to New York, and you're gonna kick some ass."[63]

The music video for "Marry the Night" begins with this day. Lady Gaga is in a women's clinic, and the video alludes to the possibility that she has just had an abortion or a miscarriage. A friend brings her home from the hospital and, while she is recovering, she receives a phone call telling her that she has been dropped from her label. What follows is almost a minute of Gaga having a breakdown: rampaging naked through her apartment, breaking mirrors, pouring Cheerios all over her body, and dying her hair blue. When the breakdown is over, Gaga proceeds to rebuild her career. At the end of the video, she writes a note on her hand about a meeting with Interscope Records. This is the record company that would ultimately be her a home and release her album. The story Gaga told *Vanity Fair* and the narrative portrayed in the video both give the impression of an epic struggle between the performer and the music industry. And yet while it is true that Gaga had a rough start with Island Def Jam, the contract that was to follow with Interscope would blossom into what has become the model for many developing recording artists.

Creating a star like Lady Gaga requires a lot of determination, an incredible creative team, and a record company willing to put a lot of money into financing the project. In September 2006, Lady Gaga signed her first contract with Island Def Jam, reportedly for $850,000.[64] Island Def Jam cut her a mere three months later, after they heard "Disco Heaven" and "Beautiful, Dirty, Rich."[65] Gaga gained two things from her relationship with Def Jam. First, she managed to take advantage of a loophole in her contract that required them to pay her regardless of whether they released the record; and second, she walked into Interscope Records with a fully produced album.[66] With Interscope Records, where she would ultimately reach her fame, Lady Gaga signed a very different kind of contract than the one she had previously with Island Def Jam. What Gaga has with Interscope is what is known in the music industry as a 360° deal. Interscope Records gets a cut of everything she does: concerts, endorsements, everything. With the 360° model they also have more of an interest in developing all parts of her career, so they put a lot more money into projects like touring and promotion, which would generally be funded by the artist. So, both the record company and Gaga have a stake in her developing all the different parts of her public persona.[67]

The 360° deal is a fairly recent addition to the history of music contracts. Prior to this kind of contract, the record company typically signed on to produce and distribute an album and the musician was paid royalties from the album sales. Often, a contract will list costs of producing an album, promoting an album, and touring as recoupable expenses. The company will take these costs out of the royalties a band would be paid. In recent years, this led to several high-profile cases of musicians declaring bankruptcy on money they owed their record label. As the sales for albums go down, recouping costs gets increasingly difficult, and that has inspired the creation of a new kind of contract. Jeff Leeds explains:

> Like many innovations, these deals were born of desperation; after experiencing the financial havoc unleashed by years of slipping CD sales, music companies started viewing the ancillary income from artists as a potential new source of cash. After all, the thinking went, labels invest the most in the risky and expensive process of developing talent, so why shouldn't they get a bigger share of the talent's success? In return for that bigger share, labels might give artists more money up front and in many cases touring subsidies that otherwise would not be offered. More important, perhaps, artists might be allowed more time to develop the chops needed to build a long career. And the label's ability to cross market items like CDs, ring tones, V.I.P. concert packages and merchandise might make for a bigger overall pie.[68]

Starting in the 2000s, 360° deals were increasingly popular. Singer Robbie Williams signed an early version of a 360° deal in 2002.[69] One of the first major full-fledged 360° deals was negotiated by Jeff Hanson, head of Silent Majority Group, for the group Paramore in 2004. Part of what made this particular deal unique is that the group was not even a band when they were signed and Atlantic Records undertook all of their development.[70] A 360° deal encourages the record company to invest in the stages of a group's career, because they will profit from every aspect. Gaga has always billed herself as more than a pop singer — she is a performance artist. If she were working with a company that was only interested in the musical aspect of what she does it is likely there would not be enough money to make the rest of her performance possible. There is also a strong argument to be made that her music would not be as popular without the rest of her performance. In the end, the deal benefits both Interscope and Gaga.

The 360° deal makes Lady Gaga's performance a joint venture between her and her record company. This relationship is critical; "what is peculiarly noteworthy about Lady Gaga is that her fame has occurred at a time when the (popular) music industry is experiencing a commercial decline."[71] Both Gaga and Interscope have recognized that it is not just her music that is making money: "[S]he is a product of a new kind of recording contract which goes beyond just selling records to encompass everything from touring, merchandise — even her make-up deal. Though she writes her own material, she is as focused on visual theatrics, fashion, and global appeal as she is on the music."[72] Every part of what Lady Gaga does is making Interscope a profit, and for her part, she is also known for putting almost all of her personal profits back into her show. In 2010, she told a reporter from Q Magazine that, so far, "I spent every dollar on my music, my art. Every dollar. I don't wait to get budgets from the label, I do it on my own. I don't give a fuck about money. Unless it's on the stage, I don't want it in my hand."[73] The cost of her show backs this statement up. Her first world tour, The Monster Ball, cost an estimated $800,000 a week.[74] Putting together such a grand spectacle is really only possible with a 360° deal, given that neither Lady Gaga nor her record company could really afford to fund this project independently and still make a profit. In interviews, Gaga defends her work within the media system: "People frown on the major label system.... I, on the other hand, am using it to my advantage. I want to create something huge and amazing, and I want to resuscitate the music industry, bring back the true superstar, the true artist."[75] That true superstar is not just a self-reliant pop star but one who flourishes in a symbiotic relationship with the record label.

Endorsements

Celebrity culture promotes consumerism in a number of ways. Most stars lead by example — flaunting expensive clothing, vacations, and cars. Many of them go a step further with celebrity endorsements. Often the products a star endorses relate directly to their talent and can even help to define aspects of their personality. For example, it is common for athletes to endorse shoes or other forms of sportswear. Many of Lady Gaga's endorsement deals relate to the things she is most passionate about. One of Gaga's first endorsement deals was with Monster Cable in 2009 for their line of in-ear headphones called Heartbeats. For a musician, endorsing headphones seems like a logical connection. With the progression of her career, Gaga's endorsements and product lines have expanded to reveal her larger sense of herself as a performance artist. Ran Florida, chief executive officer of Creative Class Group, a think tank that advises businesses and governments, argues that slowly "she has changed the way endorsement deals work.... She's putting more of her influence, thought and creative energy into a line rather than just endorsing them."[76] A closer examination of Gaga's endorsements reveals how the star is using these to strategically expand her identity as a celebrity.

Attendees at the 2010 Consumer Electronic Show got quite a surprise when a presentation by Polaroid featured Lady Gaga. Just a few days before the event, the Mother Monster signed on as a creative director with the company and posted photos of her new Polaroid business cards on her blog. Scott Hardy, the president of Polaroid and architect of the relationship between the company and the celebrity, stressed that Gaga's position was not the typical celebrity endorsement. She would not just be a mouthpiece or a figure in advertisements: "[H]ands on is the only way to describe her involvement in the Polaroid Grey Label line.... She's a close part of the working team and we take her direction. It is a much deeper partnership than just attracting new consumers. She plays an active role in the product development process."[77] The company wanted to work with Gaga to develop a product that could bridge the instantness of the Polaroid camera with the move towards digital images and, they hoped, bring in some of her fashion sense along the way. In bringing these two things together Scott Hardy stressed a desire to capitalize on the relationship Gaga has with her fans: "[S]he's a true artist who inspires her fans and the creative community. The relationship she has with her fans is exceptionally close and she is consistently in contact with them via social networks, making her messages accessible, authentic and far reaching."[78] In 2011, this partnership produced several products as part of Polaroid's Grey Label.

The Polaroid Grey Label brought a touch of fashion to the company's already identifiable line of products. The label debuted with three main products: a camera, a mobile printer, and camera glasses. The GL20 camera glasses seemed to pull inspiration from the LCD sunglasses designed by the Haus for Gaga's early television experiences. With the glasses, the wearer could take a picture of whatever they were looking at and display that picture directly on the lenses of the glasses.[79] Florida points out that one of the interesting moves that Polaroid made was to turn the creative process into a media event. They "documented the creative process through, guess what? Polaroid shots of her and her new team of associates in Tokyo developing the new line. By lending her participation and creativity to designing the line, she immediately elevated the credibility and authenticity of the product."[80] In addition to garnering attention for Polaroid, the collaboration contributed to Gaga's credibility as well. Lady Gaga has said repeatedly that she is more than pop star, she is an artist. Creating such forward-thinking products provides tangible proof for those claims.

Not all of Gaga's product endorsements have gone so well. When it comes to the law and the media industry, sometimes even frivolous lawsuits can be dangerous. In June 2011, 1-800-LAW-FIRM filed Racketeer Influenced and Corrupt Organization charges against Gaga for misrepresenting wristbands she sold as charitable donations for Japan's earthquake relief. The suit said Gaga added shipping charges in excess of what was necessary and kept the additional funds. In addition, Gaga was accused of artificially inflating the amount of money raised to encourage more people to buy.[81] While the suit received a lot of press, it was later revealed that it was based on one client.[82] Gaga spokespeople went on the record as saying that all profit did go to disaster relief and the lawsuit was "without merit."[83] The initial suit received a lot of media attention, but when the details emerged and the case was dropped that garnered little attention. Oftentimes it is the drama of these cases that the media is after. This is the kind of media moment that is impossible for Lady Gaga to completely manage.

Lady Gaga has aligned at least one of her product endorsements with the development of the Born This Way Foundation. At the end of the summer of 2012, Lady Gaga and Office Depot announced a series of back-to-school products that would promote the efforts of the Born This Way project and send the foundation's message into schools.[84] The product line included bracelets, Post-it notes, Sharpie markers, signature gift cards, and a collector clip. Each product came in a variety of colors and with the slogans from the foundation's mission statement: "Be Brave," "Be Amazing," "Be Yourself," "Be Kind," "Be Accepting," and "Be Involved." The products were all advertised as limited edition and 25 percent of the proceeds went to support the Born This Way Foundation. As part of their partnership with the foundation, Office Depot pledged to donate at least $1 million by the end of the year.[85] At the Harvard University launch of the Born This Way Foundation, Lady Gaga said, "What I want to do is strike your nerve over and over again to get you talking so that you can be a part of this message that will change everything."[86] With this product line, she was able to both raise money for her cause and raise awareness with her target audience: high school students.

One of the major questions that has been repeatedly asked of Gaga is why she has not endorsed her own fashion line. As was previously mentioned, Gaga has worked closely with several fashion designers and has walked the runway in high-profile fashion shows. She is known for her extreme fashion choices, and she often has clothing designed to work with the larger artistic concepts of her performances. In interviews, Gaga has given two major answers to this question. Both of the answers are grounded in the performer's stance that style and fashion are individual choices:

> Fashion! Style can transform and release your internal superstar. Whether it be one pair of shoes, some vintage sunglasses, a family heirloom, or a hair color that makes you feel as electric on the outside as you do on the inside. Acknowledge that this choice is a manifestation of an internal magic and the potential of your spirit. You are fan-tas-tic. And this fantasy is part of the real and honest you. It is a lie inside, waiting to be unlocked to become true.[87]

This helps to explain her answer when asked if the Haus of Gaga is putting out a fashion line: "[N]o one gets it. It's not a commodity. It's not something that's meant to be sold."[88] Lady Gaga's fashion choices are extreme and individualized: She is not selling them to be copied. Instead, she says, "I am in no way encouraging anyone to emulate my fashion sense, but rather setting a, hopefully, liberating example for anyone to look inside and know they can become any image or projection imaginable."[89] With this attitude, Gaga's product endorsement choices make a lot of sense. Polaroid provides a product that allows Gaga's fans to be more creative and express themselves. The fashion products she has endorsed, such as the wristbands for Japan earthquake relief and the Born This Way project, have all been tied directly to charity. By avoiding a fashion line, Gaga changes the way she commodifies her identity.

Lady Gaga has also aligned herself with various companies through product placement in her music videos. In one of Gaga's videos, "Love-Game," there is minor product placement in the form of her Heartbeats headphones and a Day-Glo watch. However, one of the most extreme examples of product placement is the music video for "Telephone." For this video, the major brands Virgin Mobil and Miracle Whip and the online dating site Plenty of Fish all paid to have their products strategically placed in various scenes.[90] In addition, companies such as Wonder Bread and Diet Coke were featured prominently even though they did not pay for the visibility as advertising. The placement of the products both prominently displayed the brand and worked with the music video's overall message of consumerism. Elizabeth Switaj observed that "the camera lingers on the Virgin phone while Lady Gag is kissing, fondling, and being fondled by two prisoners in the yard, thus linking the sexualized body to product placement and economic exchange. When poison receives the same treatments accorded the more legitimate brands, it lays bare the ugliness of these exchanges, yet even this transgression does not subvert the system to an extent that would endanger Gaga's income."[91] Switaj is not the only scholar to comment on the way that poison is related to other products in the video. Rebecca Lush also argues that there is a link between the blatant product placement and the framing of the poison. The poison is positioned as just another product being consumed.[92] Furthermore, David Annandale points to the provocativeness of selling a cell phone in the midst of a parody of lesbian, prison, pulp film.[93] In this video, Gaga proves she is able to walk the line between profiting from typical marketing schemes and maintaining her rebellious outsider edge.

The release of Lady Gaga's fragrance — The Fame — marked a new chapter in her market endeavors. The Fame is one of the first major products that Gaga has launched on her own instead of in cooperation with an established corporate entity. The perfume was designed in collaboration with Steven Klein. Fragrance lines by female celebrities are relatively common. Jennifer Lopez has an entire line of fragrances, including men's and women's colognes. When Lady Gaga released her own fragrance in 2012, she tried to make it stand out from the market in a couple of ways. The first is that the perfume is black. The fragrance is called The Fame, but its appearance and description closely link it with Gaga's statements about monstrosity. In the bottle the liquid is black, and when it is sprayed it goes on clear. The back of the product box announced that the perfume was designed by that Haus of Gaga and included a cartoon Lady Gaga skull and crossbones. The whole appearance of the product and the package worked to link fame and monstrosity. These themes continue in the ads Lady Gaga created for the product. MTV called the ads S and M tinged and horrifying. In one of the ads for the perfume, Gaga is shown covered in caviar eggs and stroking an androgynous figure also covered in eggs. The black eggs give both figures the appearance of rising out of muck. In another ad, we see Lady Gaga's naked body and tiny men crawling all over her, turning her into a gold statue. The images in both ads are both horrifying and decadent. The whole of the product launch has been a perfect mixture of the themes of fame and monstrosity.

Selling monsters is nothing new in consumer culture. In fact, "monsters are ubiquitous in markets and cultural byways. From cinemas, bookstalls and newspapers they issue reprisal and reproach, although coyly they offer invitation as well into a garden of fierce delights."[94] Lady Gaga has used her interactions with consumer culture to further spread her message about monstrosity and celebrity. With her product deals, such as the partnerships with Polaroid and Office Depot, she consistently uses the endorsement as a platform for reinforcing an aspect of her message and identity. In the case of Polaroid, the message is that she is more than just a pop star, she is an artist. With Office Depot, she is able to strategically spread her message about fame and the goals of the Born This Way Foundation. Of particular interest is her use of product placement. In the music video for "Telephone," Lady Gaga was able to profit from multiple product placements. Yet she placed the products in such a way that rather than appearing to sell out to consumer culture, she looked like she was commenting on it. The Mother Monster has proven repeatedly that she can work with the system to further her own agenda and maintain the critical eye necessary for her larger goals.

Copyright and Trademark Law

In economic terms, Lady Gaga has proven to be an excellent investment. As Dirk Smillie of Forbes Magazine explains: "Lady Gaga isn't the music industry's new Madonna. She's its new business model."[95] Part of that new business model is rethinking what the record company and the artist are selling and where the profits lie. In 2000, *Newsweek* did a front-page story about an Internet start-up that was wreaking havoc on the music industry: Napster.[96] The software allowed Internet users to trade music free of charge. Soon after its release, the Recording Industry Association of America sued Napster for copyright infringement. This was followed by the band Metallica suing Napster, several universities that allowed students to use the program, and around 300,000 users who had downloaded their music.[97] David Spitz and Starling Hunter argue that ultimately Napster was "domesticated" and tamed by the music industry, artists, and the legal system.[98] With that said, although Napster was put out of business within years of its boom, it managed to change how a lot of people thought about copyright and the music industry. One of its lasting legacies was to create an antagonistic relationship between music producers and fans. The strict enforcement of copyright was often portrayed as musicians failing to appreciate consumers. The Mother Monster learned from these events. As an artist, Lady Gaga pays little attention to copyright; instead, her focus is on trademark law.

Although almost all of Gaga's music is available for free through a variety of lawful and popular Internet sources, an even split of her fans seem to be getting their music from legal and less-than-legal sources. Early in her career, Gaga embraced MySpace as a free music distribution site. In a March 2009 interview with *Nylon* magazine, Lady Gaga said she had 148,000 MySpace fans, compared to the millions she has now, the number sounds almost cute. When asked what she liked about the site, she said, "[Y]ou see a lot of crazy stuff going on at my shows and my fans post it.... MySpace is the best way to have a relationship with fans."[99] By 2010, she boasted large numbers on this and other legal free music sites: 321.5 million plays on MySpace and her song "Marry the Night" has received more than 40 million plays and counting on YouTube.[100] Gaga pursued a unique free music route with the release of her album *Born This Way*. She partnered with the company Zynga to make the music available for free in their popular Facebook game Farmville. Players could visit a neighboring farm called Gagaville and hear unreleased music from the album. In addition, Gaga partnered with promoters such as Best Buy, who gave the album away with two-year phone contracts, and Amazon, who sold the album for $0.99 as an introduction to their cloud music service.[101] These routes were less about making money on the music and more about it making it very visible very quickly.

Gaga's music also tops the charts with the less-than-legal route. Lady Gaga has never had the same proprietary relationship to her music as some other artists. Part of this is because of her attitude towards parody, discussed in the previous chapter: "It is this relationship to the audience and Gaga's hyperaware constant performance that creates the Gaga-paradox. She asserts her authenticity in the most contrived and performative moments, yet because she markets herself as a collaborator between herself and her Little Monsters, it is no surprise that she sees the use of cultural copying as an authentic and original process."[102] In March of 2011, the *Sydney Morning Herald* reported that Lady Gaga was the top artist for illegal downloads.[103] That same year, Lady Gaga was one of the top five most pirated artists in the UK.[104] Even with the free and illegal downloading of Gaga being so popular, fans are still paying for her music. In the first week after its release, *Born This Way* sold 1.1 million copies. That is the highest first week sales since 50 Cent's *The Massacre* in 2005.[105] In interviews, Lady Gaga has taken a pretty cavalier attitude towards copyright violation. She told Caitlin Moran, reporter for *The Times UK*, that she did not understand why stars cared about illegal downloads when all the money is in live performances: "[B]ecause you know how much you can earn off touring, right? Big artists can make anywhere from $40 million [£28 million] for one cycle of two years' touring. Giant artists make upwards of $100 million. Make music — then tour. It's just the way it is today."[106] This conception of where money is at in the music industry helps to explain why Gaga herself has routinely violated copyright and promoted the work of fans who violate copyright on her work. Both Gaga and her record company are aware of where a profit can be made in the music industry, and they are able to work together to develop priorities based on this understanding.

While Gaga sometimes treats the legal aspects of the music industry as flexible, laws are typically regarded as rigid in American culture. The system is often seen as making a public statement about what a society values. By distinguishing between right and wrong, a community draws boundaries and forms a collective sense of self. Robert Hariman has argued that through the public performance of the law — by law enforcement officials, courts, and various other entities who enforce the system and determine punishments— a community creates their identity.[107] The language used to write laws is supposed to be precise and definite. So, when we talk about laws there is naturally a tendency to avoid ambiguity (i.e., you do not kind of steal music and copyright is not something you violate a little bit). Law is by nature adversarial and requires rulings. As such, rulings serve to communicate to society as a whole what is publicly acceptable and "right."[108] When Gaga publicly violates the law, shows a careless attitude towards other lawbreakers, or positions herself as struggling against it, she communicates herself as someone who is operating outside of norms and social standards. In the original Napster debates, there were artists who took a hard-line stance against the technology, there were artists who said the law was broken by the people who made the technology and not the ones using it, and still there were artists who supported the technology.[109] The adversarial nature of the law gives Gaga something to struggle against. When judgment is made against her, it takes her out of the position of authority and allows her to articulate the role of average person. Fighting Napster positioned artists as people enforcing the laws and fans as people potentially breaking the laws. Artists were trying to uphold social standards, and fans were trying to tear those standards down. Lady Gaga's choice to violate copyright created a different audience-artist dynamic, and with her decision to distribute the work of others who uphold the law she naturally aligns herself with her fans.

In 2011, Lady Gaga faced two major accusations of copyright violation. The first was in July, when Lady Gaga's YouTube account was suspended after she posted footage of her recent appearance on a Japanese television show, *SMAP × SMAP*.[110] YouTube users sign a contract stating that they will only post videos to which they own the rights. Lady Gaga did not own the rights to this footage. The account was restored two days later. Despite facing these consequences, after the event, as recently as July 2012, Lady Gaga has continued to post videos of her television performances. Also in 2011, Lady Gaga faced a second round of accusations of copyright violation. In August of 2011, Rebecca Francescatti, a Chicago singer, sued Gaga for stealing parts of the song "Judas." Gaga worked with Brian Gaynor, a sound engineer, on the song in question, and Gaynor had previously worked with Francescatti on a song of the same title. According to the lawsuit, even though the styles of the two songs differed, the chorus and the melody were the same.[111] While the results of the trial were not publicized, the accusation is part of a larger narrative that Lady Gaga samples and copies the musical work of other artists. That same year, allegations surfaced that the song "Born This Way" was a copy of Madonna's hit "Express Yourself."[112] The first two incidents reflected positively on Gaga because she was portrayed as someone ignoring and fighting an out-of-date copyright system. The third was much more mixed, partly because there were no legal proceedings. In the case of Madonna, the accusations moved outside the law and the story became a feud between fans of the two blond divas. The legal system provides a forum for Gaga to make definitive statements about art and her role as an artist.

Lady Gaga's interactions with fans on Twitter and YouTube show a general disregard for other people violating copyright on her work. One prominent example is a YouTube video posted in February 2011 by Gaga fan Maria Aragon. The day after Aragon posted a video of herself singing "Born This Way," the Mother Monster tweeted a link to the video with the text "Can't stop crying watching this. This is why I make music. She is the future." Within a month the video has 17 million views and Lady Gaga invited Aragon to join her onstage and sing lead vocals for the song during a concert in Toronto.[113] This is just one example of Lady Gaga promoting fan videos. In a memorandum to *V Magazine*, Gaga praised her online fan community for their creativity:

> The public is not stupid, and as a Twitter queen, I can testify that the range of artistic and brilliant intellectuals I hear from on a daily basis is staggering and inspiring. In the year 2011, everyone is posting reviews ... the reality of today's media is that there are no echelons, and if they're not careful, the most astute and educated journalists can be reduced to gossipers, while a 14-year-old who doesn't have a high school locker yet can master social media engines and, incidentally, generate a specific, well-thought-out, debatable opinion about fashion and music that is considered by 200 million people on Twitter.[114]

Copyright law is meant to delineate between media producers and media consumers. Lady Gaga's statements about online communities show a different attitude towards the hierarchy. It is not surprising then that the performer seems to have no issue with others performing her work or fans using her music.

All this is not to say that Lady Gaga does not protect her creative work; she just has a different idea of what creative work she is selling and what needs protecting. Mike Masnick, CEO of Floor64 and founder of TechDirt, explains:

> It's clear that she's [Lady Gaga's] not using copyright as an incentive to create music at all. Instead, it appears its sole purpose for her is to act as a tool for control over the use of her image. Perhaps that's fine, but that's certainly not the official reasons for copyright, and in an age when we hear about how important copyright is to artists, it seems worth noting just how much it's been twisted for totally unintended purposes here.[115]

Indeed, what Lady Gaga is interested in is ways she can use the law to protect her identity. Rosemary Coombe argues that in a postmodern society identity has become a commodity that has both monetary and cultural value. Put another way, "the law commodifies the celebrity subject and provides the means through which the celebrity may attempt to fix the identity and meaning of her persona."[116] A fixed identity can be packaged and marketed. Legally, it is possible for Gaga to turn her name, her image, and to some extent her "self" into an idea or thing that can be bought and sold.

Where copyright law is about helping artists to claim their ideas, trademark law is about authenticating the source of a product. Ted Striphas describes trademark law as an attempt to transform a cultural artifact into a "real thing," such that other artifacts can be understood as fakes.[117] Two items labeled as Gucci purses may look and seem exactly the same where one is real and one is a fake. The fakeness is that one did not originate from the actual designer; it is a copy. Lady Gaga is adamant about stopping fake Gagas, and she has engaged in several lawsuits to protect her authentic identity. Gaga does not challenge all uses of her name, just those that might alter her public identity in an undesirable way. In addition, she is not necessarily going after organizations that profit from her name; she seems more interested in how she can control her image. In London, Lady Gaga sued an ice-cream chain over a dessert made with breast milk called Baby Gaga and she won. In the lawsuit, she accused the company, Ice-creamists LTD, of using her name in a way that is, "to many people, nausea-inducing."[118] Interestingly, there is a Web site also called Baby Gaga, for pregnant women, and Lady Gaga has done nothing to interfere with it. The choice to target one for using her name and not the other demonstrates a clear sense of branding her identity. She has gone after other Web sites. In September 2011, she filed a claim through the National Arbitration Forum trying to shut down one of her largest fan sites—LadyGaga.org. Gaga claimed that the site infringed on trademark and hurt her ability to fully control her image. The arbitrator ruled in favor of the fan site because it does not gain any kind of profit.[119] In some cases, the court has ruled in Gaga's favor. In October 2011, Lady Gaga won a lawsuit to ban animated character Lady Goo Goo. The lawsuit prevents Moshi Monsters, a company owned by Mind Candy, from promoting or marketing any songs by Lady Goo Goo. The lawsuit included documents indicating that some people were confused about the difference between Lady Gaga and Lady Goo Goo.[120] Probably Gaga's biggest trademark lawsuit has involved the use of her name as a brand. A Chicago company called Lady Gaga by Design trademarked the title and effectively blocked Gaga from selling some of her own products. In September 2011 she sued them over their trademark applications.[121] Excite, the parent company for Gaga by Design, had filed trademark applications for "Lady Gaga," "Lady Gaga Fame," and "Lady Gaga by Design."[122] The "Lady Gaga Fame" trademark was particularly important for securing the name of her first perfume before it was released.

Another big part of Lady Gaga's identity that she must work to protect is her visual image. In recent years, she has pushed photographers to give up copyright of photos taken of her. Her argument is that what they are photographing—her body—is an artistic work that she has created. Lady Gaga requires all photographers attending her concerts to sign a photo release form. As part of this form "Photographer hereby acknowledges and agrees that all rights, title and interest (including copyright) in and to the Photograph(s) shall be owned by Lady Gaga and Photographer hereby transfers and assigns any such rights to Lady Gaga."[123] Photographer Jay Westcott went public with the release form in March 2011 and complained about it specifically because of this restriction.[124] According to the government law, copyright comes into effect at the moment a creative work "is created and fixed in a tangible form that it is perceptible either directly or with the aid of a machine or device." Gaga claimed that her physical identity was fixed before the presence of photographers. The release form only allows photographers to use the photos for four months on a blog or Web site. The photos cannot be sold, used in any print publication, or included in any advertisements.[125] One of the complicating factors is that many photographers sign contracts that say whatever they shoot belongs to the editor or organization they are working for at the time. This means they are guaranteeing copyright to two different entities. The release form allows Gaga tremendous control over what images circulate through newspapers, blogs, and the general public. With that control, Gaga is able to cherry-pick her media representation to a large extent and to micromanage each aspect of marketing her identity.

Summary and Concluding Thoughts

Despite Gaga's extreme economic success, she has articulated a desire to maintain a cautious relationship with the media industry. *The Fame* and *The Fame Monster* were hugely successful projects by commercial standards. The two albums sold more than 20 million copies worldwide. After all that success, Gaga said she felt a lot of pressure with the release of *Born This Way* to move to Los Angeles and become part of the establishment. She told Derek Blasberg, a *Harper's Bazaar* reporter, that she "had all these number-one records, and I had sold all these albums, and it was sort of this turning point: Am I going to try and embrace Hollywood and assimilate to that culture?... I put my toe in that water, and it was a Kegel-exercise vaginal reaction where I clenched and had to retract immediately.... I ran furiously back to New York, to my old apartment, and I hung out with my friends, and I went to the same bars."[126] In Gaga's music her performances, and her interviews, one can certainly see a struggle to define and maintain an identity of her choosing in the face of an industry that has a lot of experience commodifying young stars. To that extent, legal and economic systems have proven to be valuable weapons in Gaga's quest to create a sense of self and control her artistic work.

Some could argue that Gaga's working within the system makes her complicit with media power structures and ultimately invalidates a lot of commentary about fame and monstrosity. David Annandale warns that one should not forget that "Gaga's carnival is for the ultimate benefit of a gigantically profitable machine. The revolution has been sponsored."[127] Still, there is another narrative that implies that Gaga is using the system;

Annandale even goes so far as to infer that she is exploiting the system.[128] When asked what would have happened if her career hadn't worked out, Gaga has said: "I would still be living next door to my friend Jennifer, playing at the clubs I've always played at. It was never not going to work out for me because I was already living my dream when I was playing music."[129] Lady Gaga would have continued to play music even if Interscope Records had never signed her, but the larger performance art piece she had developed would not be possible without their infrastructure.

So, this is the devil's bargain for young celebrities. The media industry owns many of the major outlets and mechanisms that are needed to reach a larger audience. The Internet makes a lot possible, but at some point celebrities have to make the jump to mainstream media to become stars. That jump means facing the commodification of identity. Looking at Lady Gaga's negotiation of the system, one can learn a lot of lessons for young celebrities looking to survive the media industry. Gaga's work with copyright and trademark demonstrates how artists can rethink what it is they are selling and use legal systems to protect that product. Her contract with Interscope demonstrates how an artist can access the financial backing of the media industry and work with that industry to rethink commodity. Finally, her work with product placement and endorsement shows how celebrities can be more proactive in financial endeavors. All of these facets show Gaga willingly playing the money game, but they also show her changing that game. In a memorandum to *V Magazine*, Gaga argued that this is really the best you can hope for in the music industry. She told a story about watching the movie *Moneyball* on a plane:

> By the end of the film, we discover the truth about winning from our hero. It only matters if you've changed the game. Being kicked in the teeth is par for the course for this kind of win, a win that not only pisses off the team you've beat, but every other team, their coaches, owners, and even some of the greatest baseball players of all time. You've made your own set of rules and gone so far on your own talent, no one can possibly crack the truth behind your wins. You were either lucky or were cheating. Nobody likes the game that they've won over and over again to change."[130]

Lady Gaga is playing the game in a new way, playing media in a new way, and she is winning. In the Gaga celebrity model, there is still a commodification of identity. However, the Mother Monster has found a way to maintain control over what is being sold.

Chapter 5

Killing the Monster

That's what everyone wants to know, right? "What's she gonna look like when she dies? What's she gonna look like when she's overdosed?" on whatever they think I'm overdosing on? Everybody wants to see the decay of the superstar.... They wanna see me fail, they wanna see me fall on stage, they wanna see me vomiting out of a nightclub. I mean, isn't that the age that we live in? That we wanna see people who have it all lose it all? I mean, it's dramatic.[1]—Lady Gaga in an interview with Anderson Cooper for *60 Minutes*

If the role of monsters and celebrities is to teach and enforce the moral code of a society, then perhaps the most instructive thing they do is die. Monsters, for one thing, must die but are nearly impossible to kill. As Edward Ingebretsen explains, "a monster cannot be allowed to live; as historical precedent insists, the monster must be put to death. In the movies this requires that the monster be staked, burned, dismembered, or otherwise dispatched in the final reel."[2] Often the keys to their deaths are sacred objects, magic weapons, and a special individual who is pure of heart and capable of wielding such things. Even with such an arsenal, it is a common trope of horror movies for the heroes to believe the monster is dead, only to find the body is mysteriously missing or to have the creature comes back one last time. The message seems clear: Evil is difficult to kill and never entirely gone. The narrative of celebrity death differs in that it is often swift and sudden. Beautiful young stars are depicted as "taken too soon" and "gone before their time." Their deaths are portrayed as the result of their own excess or the carelessness of others. While evil is nearly impossible to destroy, beauty is easily tainted and dies quickly. Lady Gaga in her role as both monster and celebrity seems well aware of all this: "Everybody wants to see the decay of the superstar." The Mother Monster exists somewhere between the celebrity and the monster, and as such she has repeatedly died the public death of the star and just as often risen from the grave like any good fiend.

The Mother Monster has long been obsessed with her own death. In concerts, she has depicted herself being stabbed, hung, burned, and beaten. More than one music video has ended with a portrayal of the death of Lady Gaga. In interviews, Gaga has often linked the persistent acting out of her death to her philosophy of the fame and the fame monster. The fame is about making a choice to be who you are at your absolute core and embracing the notion that the thing that makes you who are is also the thing that makes you truly spectacular. The fame monster is an amalgamation of all the things the mainstream media has taught society to fear. Lady Gaga argues that we have been lied to by the media; people are told that the thing that makes them spectacular is monstrous. The answer? Accept your monstrous self and use your own monstrosity to fight the fame monster. A critical part of media depictions of fame is death. The message of the media is that anything truly beautiful decays. Lady Gaga refuses to let the mainstream media make her afraid of her decay or her death. Instead, she demands to decide what her death will look like, so she is personally directing it over and over again. In the process, she has created a powerful critique of a society obsessed with watching stars die and poring over the details of their demise.

While Lady Gaga may be critical of the mass media's obsession with depicting celebrity death, she seems to have no problem with the notion of acting out her death for her fans. Take for instance the ballad "Princess Die," a single that Gaga has said may appear on her next album, *PopArt*, and was performed for the first time during a concert in Melbourne, Australia.[3] The song talks about Lady Gaga's expectations for how she will look when she dies and, more than that, her hope that she will die for her fans. The lyrics describe Gaga appearing as a princess in death. The narrative in "Princess Die" is that of an iconic woman who is not strong enough to live a life in the public eye. Lady Gaga imagines many possible deaths in each verse: suicide; an excess of coping mechanisms, such as booze and pills; trying too hard to fit a public image, through anorexia and poisonous beauty products; and simple loneliness, for instance getting drunk one night in her mansion and drowning in an expensive silk gown. In each of these deaths, Gaga weaves together the height of celebrity and the insidiousness of the fame monster. The various demises of the pop princess bring to mind the real death of Princess Diana and the tragic suicide of Marilyn Monroe. When Gaga performed the song a few months after its debut, in Bucharest, Romania, the lyrics were made all the more poignant by the fact that after saying of her music, "I want to share that part of my life with you," she sneezed and was visibly sick before she began the number.[4] The perceptible vulnerability of her body coupled with her desire to perform for her fans made all the stories of losing her life to a commitment to celebrity culture that much more tangible. There is a sense that she very much means it when she tells her fans that she will perform even her death for them.

The lyrics for "Princess Die" are likely a result of Gaga's own obsession with celebrity death. Chapter 3 details Gaga's fastidious study of the lives of celebrities. She has crafted much of her appearance, her performances, and her sense of self from the many figures that populate popular media and fashion history. It seems natural she would also study how their final scenes played out. Lady Gaga told Lisa Robinson, a reporter for *Vanity Fair*: "I had this incredible fascination with how people love watching celebrities fall apart, or when celebrities die; I wanted to know, what did they look when they die? Marilyn Monroe, Princess Diana, JonBenét Ramsey."[5] Lady Gaga has studied these iconic deaths and used them to spin stories of her own death. She further explained to Robinson, "I think about all the dead girls, these blonde dead icons. What did they look like when they died? So then I thought, well, maybe if I show what I look like when I die, people won't wonder. Maybe that's what I want people to think I'll look like when I die."[6] There is a sense of desperation underlying Gaga's explanation for her obsession with portraying her own death. Anyone who has studied celebrity culture knows that people are often equal parts excited to see someone rise from obscurity to fame and morbidly fascinated to see them fall off the pedestal of stardom. Gaga knows the mainstream media is anticipating her decay. In her comments to interviewers, there seems to be a hope that if she voluntarily performs her fall from grace, and her untimely demise, her audiences will not demand that she do these things for real.

This chapter explores the symbolic nature of media depictions of celebrity and monster deaths. Transformed by the media into icons, celebrities and monsters generate mythologies of good and evil. In the midst of this process, the mainstream media transmutes them into symbols of larger cultural themes. Lady Gaga has repeatedly performed her death as an appeal to this iconography. The depictions of her death are mixed in with conversations about the way celebrities trade their bodies for fame, and the expectation that female celebrities will suffer that transaction silently. Exploring the various depictions of celebrity spectacle and human frailty brings together Gaga's larger philosophy of fame, her playing with gender and drag, her use of parody and persistent referencing, and her work to control her media identity. Rather than waiting for the media to translate her death into a series of lessons and morals, Lady Gaga is taking control of the iconic moment to send her own message about the true nature of celebrity culture.

Media Depictions of Celebrity Deaths

Monsters and celebrities call on their followers to give in to the overwhelming emotional experience of something truly spectacular. They invite their admirers to lose control. Lady Gaga became aware of this aspect of celebrity culture well before she became a star. She discovered it as a fan. Gaga's love of Britney Spears started at a young age. In one of Gaga's very first interviews, she described her experience of Britney fandom to *Maxim Magazine* reporter Jonah Weiner: "I was 13 when Britney became a star. My friends and I used to go to TRL once a week just to stand outside. But even then I wasn't a superfan. I was amazed by the level of superfan that Britney created. I liked to watch and be part of the huh-huh-huh-huh!—the hyperventilating. I want to bring back the feeling I used to feel."[7] She had a similar experience a few years into her career when she met the band Kiss, and she said she was so overwhelmed by the experience that if they had started flying around the room it would not have surprised her at all.[8] As a fan, Lady Gaga is well aware of the heroic status of celebrities. And as a celebrity, she remains mindful of the overwhelming emotional influence stars have on their audiences. The Mother Monster takes her role as a media icon very seriously. In one interview, she described her connection to her fans as an umbilical cord, where both parties nourish each other.[9] In another, she told a reporter that with each new project she asks herself, in reference to her fans: "How could I possibly be better for you? That's all I keep thinking: I just want to be better for you. I want to say and sing the right things for you, and I want to make that one melody that really saves your spirit one day."[10] Lady Gaga is striving to develop a public performance that continually inspires the overwhelming emotions she saw in crowds waiting for Britney Spears and felt when she was introduced to her favorite band. While Gaga pushes to continue her rise as a celebrity, she is also very aware both that all rising things fall and that the fall has serious repercussions for fans who are emotionally attached to celebrities. The intensity of emotion that fan communities feel for celebrities is driven to new heights when the star they love passes away.

The grieving process is intensely emotional, and throughout history every culture has developed its own rituals for coping with the anguish surrounding death. Douglas Davies, in his writing on funeral rites and rituals of mourning, has pointed out the need human beings have to restore order in the face of death. In particular, "the contemporary world of the media is not content to assert life as a meaningless mess but is forever bringing experts to the screen to explain the problems of life."[11] According to Davies, even before the advent of modern media religious institutions tended to occupy the role of the expert in the world of bereavement. Death can feel chaotic; it is seemingly random and often senseless. For a modern society, some semblance of order is required to survive. Dying must be fashioned into something that makes sense. Where Davies argues that historically religion has taken the role of creating ritual and order surrounding death, David Field and Tony Walter suggest that today "it is the mass media, not medicine, that have inherited religion's mantle as the interpreter of death in contemporary modern societies."[12] Mainstream media depictions of death are a critical location for bringing order to the chaos: "[O]ne of the ways in which members of contemporary 'modern' and 'post modern' societies learn about how to understand dying, death and bereavement, and how to behave when they are confronted with these, is through media representations and interpretations of these."[13] The media crafts narratives surrounding death and uses those stories to instruct audiences on how to understand death, how to grieve, and how to die. Field and Walter point out, for example, that in the case of celebrities who do pass on of natural causes or terminal conditions accounts by the media "often provide 'scripts' for coping with dying in a (usually) quiet but 'heroic' way and in so doing offer models of 'good dying' for their readers."[14] Celebrity deaths are instructive, and they provide a place to bring order and focus to an inherently chaotic moment in life.

Celebrities are symbols of what is possible; they are used as proof that the social and economic status of a given individual is not fixed. Anyone could have qualities that cause them to suddenly rise up the social ladder and take a place among the elite. The media uses celebrities as icons—recognizable figures that embody the hope of a capitalistic society. As celebrities take on this iconic status, they lose some of their sense of humanity and are made into symbols. They become places for a society to project its ideals.[15] So, when they die, it is also the death of an ideal. Daniel J. Boorstin has referred to celebrities as "human pseudo-events."[16] Their happenings and activities take on a synthetic quality that makes mundane moments appear to have great social significance.[17] As he explains, "there was never a time when 'fame' was precisely the same thing as 'greatness.' But, until very recently, famous men and great men were pretty nearly the same group."[18] Nowadays, the line between hero and celebrity has become blurred and people become events by media designation. Society follows their comings and goings not because they have done something that makes them worthy of observation but because they have been designated as important. Where the life of a celebrity takes on an iconic status, "the death of a celebrity offers insight into the associations made and how a society attempts to stabilize such affiliations at a moment when the values embodied by the celebrity seem particularly fragile."[19] When ideals die, the media must work to tell audiences how to translate that death, all the while maintaining the values portrayed by the life of a star. Furthermore, Tim Hutchings has argued that the Internet has made the fan community experience of celebrity death all the more intense. Groups of fans online are able to mourn the celebrity, as a community, in a way that is more personal and profound than the mainstream media depictions of a star's demise.[20] As such, the media messages surrounding death are reinforced in community interactions and the role of celebrities as symbols becomes even more powerful.

Not all celebrity deaths take on the same mythic status. Researchers have found that certain celebrity deaths have captured the public eye in a profound way. Sharon Mazzarella and Timothy Matyjewicz argue that using death to turn celebrities into icons allows the media to generate a mythology around each particular celebrity.[21] In these moments, it is difficult to untangle how much of the interest in death is a product of public grieving and how much is a result of media scrutiny. Scholarly discussions of media depictions of Princess Diana's death often conclude that the media got swept up in the public outpouring of grief surrounding the funeral, but William Merrin contends that the mass media actually served as a feedback loop, ultimately amplifying public grief.[22] As he explains, "the media are not a mirror reflecting the world, nor a window upon it, nor even 'media'— standing between us and a 'reality' they mediate — but are themselves constitutive of the experience and thus the reality of the event, becoming therefore inseparable from the event."[23] The media construct the audience as engaged in an outpouring of grief and, in the process, give audience members permission to grieve. The two events are not separate; they are part of the same process. In some cases, the death of a celebrity brings more media attention than the life that preceded the demise. After the death of iconic British Shakespearean actress Ellen Terry, Lisa Kazmier commented that more people observed the actress's passing than ever saw her onstage.[24] Media attention raised her to the status of heroine and provided audience members with instructions on how to *see* the death. Upon her passing, papers described Terry as looking radiant, as if in a deep sleep, and having a peacefulness that was reminiscent of her appearance onstage more than 30 years before. Since she had left the stage many years prior, much of society had lost interest in the actress, but in her death Ellen Terry regained her beauty and her ability to captivate an audience.[25] In a study of the deaths of John Lennon, Kurt Cobain, and Jerry Garcia, researchers found that in the reports of these events journalists often represented themselves as mourning with their readers. The depiction of mourning makes the iconic personal.[26] Once the icon is connected to the personal, it can transcend its original form and take on added significance. In one prominent example, Mazzarella and Matyjewicz point out that for celebrities like Kurt Cobain media framing can turn a suicide into something symbolic of not just the celebrity's life but also the despair and depression of an entire subculture or even a whole generation.[27] The mythic figure is grafted onto the day-to-day lives of the audience and provides a critical point for communicating social values.

In death, celebrities reveal the fragility of a society's ideals, and the grieving process offers a place to both mourn the loss of something valued and rededicate a community to those values. Lady Gaga's commentary on this process has been most pronounced in the wake of the deaths of other celebrities. In August of 2011, British pop singer Amy Winehouse died of an overconsumption of alcohol.[28] The performer's drinking habit had been the subject of much media attention throughout her career. While Winehouse had recently been to rehab, coroner's reports indicated that she had relapsed and, when she died, her blood alcohol level was five times the legal limit for driving. A few weeks after Winehouse's passing, Lady Gaga appeared on the television show *The View*. Barbara Walters, one of the show's hosts, asked Gaga several questions about her reactions to the recent death, pointing out that Amy Winehouse and Lady Gaga were close to the same age and had struggled with the same kind of fame-related pressures. The Mother Monster responded that part of the issue was the way the media talks about the lives of celebrities: "You know, I just think the most unfortunate thing about it all is the way the media spins things, like: oh, here, we can learn from Amy's death. I don't feel that, you know, Amy needed to learn any lessons."[29] Instead, Gaga argued that she "felt that the lesson was for the world to be kinder to the superstar. Everyone was so hard on her and everything that I knew about her was that she was the most lovely and nice and kind woman."[30] Lady Gaga's comments here reveal the way the media turns young stars' deaths into lessons by defining them in relationship to a particular failure or success. The message is that the audience can absorb the lessons that Winehouse failed to learn. Amy Winehouse's iconic status was strongly linked to her drinking, and in this interview Gaga attempts to humanize Winehouse by discussing her in relationship to other aspects of her personality. When Walters further pushed Lady Gaga to talk about the issues plaguing young celebrities, the Mother Monster mused: "Well, it's a very lonely life. That's part of what we love about her. You can't have it both ways. You can't enjoy listening to someone sing sad songs about the blues and heartbreak and then not expect them to be truly heartbroken and expect something different out of them."[31] There is an acknowledgment there that the things that made Winehouse famous were also the things that were killing her. Lady Gaga goes on to say that "sometimes I'm very sad, just like everybody watching at home, and sometimes I'm happy."[32] Ultimately, she attributed her own ability to survive celebrity culture to her relationship with her fans, her family, and her friends. Still, Gaga also pointed out that society does not want happy starlets and performing the desired tragic roles often results in tragedy.

During the early years of Lady Gaga's career, two iconic figures in popular music passed away: Whitney Houston and Michael Jackson. Gaga's responses to these deaths are revealing of her overall relationship to celebrity culture. Whitney Houston died in February of 2012. She was found unconscious after drowning in her bathtub. Coroner's reports showed a combination of prescription drugs and marijuana in her system at the time of her death.[33] In a surprising move, the *Los Angeles Times* posted Houston's coroner's report online, in its entirety, and solicited the feedback of site visitors: "Find something newsworthy? Mention it here."[34] A few months later, Lady Gaga made an appearance on Oprah's show *Next Chapter* and talked about Houston's death. Gaga said, "I don't know that I was, like, really surprised, I think it was just more I couldn't believe that her heart wasn't beating any more. That's really sort of the feeling that I felt. I was grateful that I knew that she knew I loved her."[35] In the interview, Lady Gaga remembers being a fan of Whitney Houston from a very young age. Where Gaga discusses Winehouse as a contemporary, her description of mourning Houston takes on the perspective of a fan captivated by her idol. The impact of icons like Houston on Gaga's performance can be seen in her comments about the death of Michael Jackson. Michael Jackson's death in 2009 was the subject of considerable fan and media attention. In the hours after he died, Twitter was receiving 5,000 tweets about his demise per minute and Google had so many searches for "Michael Jackson" they thought it was an attack on the site and blocked the searches for 30 minutes.[36] More than a billion people watched Jackson's memorial service on television.[37] A year after his death, Lady Gaga spoke about the event on *Larry King Live*. She told listeners that at the time the death stunned her into silence, and after talking about Michael Jackson's death she said that "my fascination with the demise of the celebrity goes along with me watching these hugely iconic and amazing people that I have heralded and admired my whole life become destroyed, whether self-destroyed or destroyed by the media."[38] As a fan she has appeared heartbroken but unsurprised when icons are destroyed, and aware that the method of destruction is not theirs alone. One way to respond to this destruction is to recognize that public performances are for fans, not the media. Lady Gaga told *Rolling Stone* magazine that "Michael [Jackson] got burned, and he lifted that glittered glove so damn high so his fans could see him, because he was in the art of show business. That's what we do."[39] Houston's and Jackson's iconic status and tragic deaths had an impact on Gaga both as a fan and as someone who meticulously studies popular culture.

The celebrity death that seems to have shaken Gaga most profoundly was that of fashion designer Alexander McQueen. Gaga and McQueen had developed a friendship in the years before his death, and she had worn several of his more memorable designs. Of note are the alien shoes that Gaga donned for the video "Bad Romance." In February of 2010, McQueen was found hanging in his wardrobe, with a suicide note instructing his family to care for his dogs.[40] Lady Gaga was so distraught over the death, she almost canceled her performance that evening at the 2010 Brit Music Awards. Instead, she performed a jazz version of her songs "Telephone" and "Dance in the Dark." At the beginning of her performance, she altered the lyrics in the first line of "Telephone" to say "Sorry we cannot hear you, we miss you so badly"; then she paused the song to dedicate the concert to McQueen.[41] In the year before his death, Lady Gaga had performed at the MTV Video Music Awards. The show had been the subject of some controversy when Gaga stabbed herself onstage and finished her musical number dangling by a rope, seemingly dead. After the song, Lady Gaga appeared to collect her award for Best New Artist wearing a head-to-toe red-lace Alexander McQueen ensemble that completely covered her face. When Oprah interviewed Gaga in 2010, she asked her about the outfit, and Gaga said: "It was meant to be a continuation of the VMA performance. So after the princess had been murdered by the paparazzi, the red lace was meant to symbolize sort of my eternal martyrdom."[42] The performance seemed almost prophetic. In the months following McQueen's death, Lady Gaga refused to answer media questions about her reaction to the suicide. Her only public statement came a week after the suicide when she posted a photo on Twitter with no commentary. It was a snapshot of Gaga and McQueen hugging each other while she was wearing one of his headpieces.

After the death of Alexander McQueen, Lady Gaga wrote the lead single for her album *Born This Way* and she credited him as her muse.[43] As the album developed she said, "I think he planned the whole thing. Right after he died, I wrote 'Born This Way.' I think he's up in heaven with fashion strings in his hands, marionetting away."[44] Gaga even claimed to be channeling McQueen in her music: "When I heard that [the single], I knew he planned the whole damn thing. I didn't even write the f——

song. He did!"[45] This was not be the first time she had credited someone who passed on with helping her develop her music. In February 2011, when Julie Naughton and Pete Born interviewed Gaga for *Women's Wear Daily*, she spoke about her aunt Joanne Germanotta, her namesake. She told them:

> I think I actually carry two souls in my body, and that I'm living out the rest of her life and her goodness— she died a virgin, she died never having experienced all these things that we all get to love and experience in our lives. I think that I work in her image. I work in this life as part pop singer and part humanitarian, and to do great things for people because she was a good person and I don't think she had enough time to do enough good.[46]

Lady Gaga depicts her talent as being connected to the dead, whether it is famous celebrities or close family. Much in the way she draws her references from a long legacy of cultural influences, she links her spirit to the people who have passed on and who influenced her most. All of this is tied to Lady Gaga's fear of the development of her own legacy.

All of Lady Gaga's commentary on celebrity and death reveals her own anxiety of being personally ruined by her fame or destroyed before she can create her legacy. When a reporter for *Jezebel* magazine asked Gaga what her biggest fear was, she said, "That I won't be able to get all my ideas out before I die."[47] Perhaps the fear explains the frantic pace of Gaga's touring and recording. She is trying to get everything out before it is too late. She wants to create a legacy. Once she told a *Rolling Stone* reporter at the end of an interview to "use the stuff that is going to make me a legend. I want to be a legend. Is that wrong?"[48] It seems that Gaga is constantly thinking about what her work will look like when she is gone and the media is left to interpret it all without her commentary. So much of the conversation about death is really about legacy: "[T]he whole world sees the number-one records and the rise in sales and recognition, but my true legacy will be the test of time, and whether I can sustain a space in pop culture and really make stuff that will have a genuine impact."[49] Still, she recognizes that her work will move on without her. Just before the release of *Born This Way*, Lady Gaga acknowledged in an interview that her album would come out whether she was alive or not. Her creations did not need her anymore.[50] Lady Gaga has termed the creative process, the thing that may make her a legend, as her destruction. In her 43rd Gagavision video, Gaga described the Internet leak of her single "Judas" as a slow death. She felt that, in the whole process of creating and releasing the single, she was being torn limb by limb.[51] All this makes her choice to take on the role of the monster even more unfortunate. After all, "why does one make a monster? In order to watch it die of course."[52]

When a celebrity dies, the media is able to ruminate on the life they led without a response from the deceased. It is the same form of celebrity objectification that the Mother Monster has challenged elsewhere in her career. The media treats celebrities as objects and illustrations for larger discourses, and in the process stars lose their voices. In the case of Gaga, she ties fragility, fame, and death together while still being physically present. Her willingness to perform her own death prevents the media process of turning her demise into something merely symbolic. The immediacy of her body and the repeated displays of her death makes the possibility of her passing more physically real. Ever since her first album, Lady Gaga has worked to link the construct of fame with the deaths of celebrities. Miranda Purves, a reporter for *Elle Magazine*, observed of Lady Gaga's album *The Fame*: "A theme she revisits in her videos and songs is herself as somehow destroyed and resurrected."[53] In 2010, Gaga told Purves: "I feel that if I can show my demise artistically to the public, I can somehow cure my own legend. I can show you so you're not looking for it. I'm dying for you on domestic television — here's what it looks like, so no one has to wonder."[54] Lady Gaga has died many deaths onstage and in her music videos. She once told a reporter, "I do have morbid dreams. But I put them in the show. A lot of the work I do is an exorcism for my fans but also for myself."[55] Gaga recognizes in her discussions of death that the media is waiting for her to die. However, instead of passing on and allowing them to take up the role of translating the event, she returns and offers her own interpretation.

The Fragility of Fame

Celebrities and monsters may be reduced to iconic figures and symbols, but before that process they are human beings. That means they have all the frailties and limits that come with human bodies. Ingebretsen warns that "monsters are less agents of social collapse than announcers that the collapse has already occurred."[56] Both celebrities and monsters are described as heralding change and inspiring new ideas, but often they are just the symbols and vehicles for communicating an already-existing trend. Lady Gaga has expressed an awareness of the way celebrities are used by the media to communicate values and ideas. One of the themes of her performance is to alter that process by focusing on the humanity behind the fame in order to create a new message. Gaga told Brian Hiatt of *Rolling Stone*, "I know it sounds crazy, but I was thinking about the machine of the music industry.... I started to think about how I have to make the music industry bleed to remind it that it's human, it's not a machine."[57] She uses her relationship with her fans to make both her own frailty and the humanity of fame more visible.

Lady Gaga micromanages and carefully directs every aspect of her interactions with mainstream media, but with her fans there is a definite sense that she lets her guard down. It is in her concert performances and her online interactions with the community of little monsters that we get a glimpse of the most authentic Gaga. In front of her fans is the place where Gaga talks about feeling most at home: "[W]hen I'm not onstage I feel dead, and when I'm onstage, I feel alive."[58] The Mother Monster said, during an interview with Sarah Casselman of *Fashion Magazine*, that of all the changes that come with fame there was one that surprised her the most: "I wasn't prepared for how much I was going to love my fans."[59] Lady Gaga's affection for her fans has led her to think carefully about how things she says and does may influence their behaviors. She told Neil Strauss, a reporter for *Rolling Stone*, that "you have to be careful about how much you reveal to people that look up to you so much. They know who I am. They can relate to me. I've laid it all on the table. And if they're smart like you, they make the assessment, but I don't want to be a bad example."[60] Gaga hopes to be an example of what fame, or at least her conception of it, could be: "I don't want them to love me; I want them to love themselves. I have a relentless pursuit in me to give everything in me to my fans to make them feel good about themselves. And if you don't like it, well, then don't come to the party."[61] One of the places where this pursuit reveals itself most clearly is in media conversations about Lady Gaga's body. The mainstream media uses Lady Gaga's body as an object lesson for discussions about physical limits and the way women should manage their weight. Lady Gaga has used social media and her concerts as spaces to respond to these conversations while stressing the humanity and fragility of celebrities. In the process, she reinforces her message about fame by reminding her little monsters that even her body is mortal.

During the Monster Ball Tour in 2010, Lady Gaga was plagued with physical symptoms of exhaustion. She was forced to cancel shows and occasionally hospitalized for dizziness and shortness of breath.[62] One newspaper reporter even used Gaga's visits to the emergency room as an introduction to an article about how people need to slow down and take better care of themselves.[63] The article signaled attempts to turn Gaga's physical condition into something universal and symbolic. At a concert in Sweden, while performing her song "Speechless," Gaga talked to her fans about the media reports of her physical condition. She told the audience, "You know when people say, 'Lady Gaga's really tired; she needs to take a break,' I just think about all those times I sang in bars when nobody was singing my lyrics," and after singing a few more lines she added, "I'll sleep when I'm dead, OK?"[64] Rather than being a symbol of the modern malady of people running their bodies into the ground, or a failing on Gaga's part to manage her body, she uses the performance to tie her exhaustion to both her fame and her need to perform for her fans. Ultimately, she muses that it is her desire for fame, and her need to please her fans, that will ultimate kill her: "I know that I work really hard and I run myself into the ground, and I also know that alcohol will kill me one day. But I would rather not die on vacation, I'd rather die onstage with all my fans."[65] The tone of the concert is confessional, and even in the video posted online one gets the sense of Lady Gaga sharing a very personal moment with her little monsters. Often celebrity deaths are linked to personal excess, moral failings, or simply bodies reaching their natural ends. Lady Gaga is using her own vulnerability to illustrate the physical price that celebrities pay for being famous. It is not excess; it is necessity. When pushed by a reporter to talk about the frantic pace she maintains in her work, Lady Gaga said, "We're supposed to be tired.... I don't know who told everyone otherwise, but you make a record and you tour. That's how you build a career."[66] There is no attempt in Gaga's discussions of her career to downplay the physical price of fame. She articulates it not as a moral failing but as a potentially dangerous necessity.

Lady Gaga's public statements often highlight the way fame pushes bodies to their physical limits in pursuit of the spectacular. In Chapter 4, I discuss Gaga's public statements about trading her body for fame — in particular, her statements, in interviews, that she does not eat because pop stars do not eat. During the preparation for the Born This Way Ball, Lady Gaga came under media scrutiny for repeating this adage. In April of 2012 she tweeted: "Just killed back to back spin classes. Eating a salad dreaming of a cheeseburger #PopSingersDontEat #IWasBornThisWay." These statements seem to be in sharp contrast with Gaga's comments about her own struggles with eating disorders. Only a few months before the tweet, Lady Gaga had spoken at a conference called "It's Our Turn," at Brentwood High School in Los Angeles, about her own personal battles with anorexia and bulimia. After an interview session with Maria Schriver, a girl in the audience raised her hand to say that she struggled with body image issues and she wanted to know how Gaga could be so confident. Lady Gaga responded by explaining that she was not always that sure of herself:

> I used to throw up all the time in high school. So I'm not that confident.... I wanted to be a skinny little ballerina but I was a voluptuous little Italian girl whose dad had meatballs on the table every night. I used to come home and say, "Dad, why do you always give us this food? I need to be thin." And he'd say, "Eat your spaghetti." It's really hard, but ... you've got to talk to somebody about it.[67]

Ultimately, according to Lady Gaga, it was her commitment to her career that convinced her to stop making herself throw up: "It made my voice bad, so I had to stop.... The acid on your vocal cords—it's very bad. But for those of you who don't sing, you maybe don't have that excuse until it's too late. It's very dangerous."[68] The way that Lady Gaga tells this story is typical to how female celebrities often describe struggles with eating disorders. Katie J.M. Baker, a staff writer for the news site *Jezebel*, points out that it is common for female celebrities to make public statements about their eating disorders with the subtext being "that was bad, it's all in the past, they're okay now, and you'll be okay (and look awesome) someday, too."[69] Katie Couric, Kelly Clarkson, Ashlee Simpson, and pop star Brandy have all gone on the record to talk about their past struggles with dieting, anorexia, and bulimia. Perhaps what makes Gaga's statements so uncomfortable for people is the recognition that her problem is ongoing and almost necessary to maintain her career. While she described her struggle with bulimia as part of her past, Lady Gaga went on to point out that "weight is still a struggle.... Every video I'm in, every magazine cover, they stretch you — they make you perfect. It's not real life ... I'm gonna say this about girls: The dieting wars have got to stop. Everyone just knock it off. Because at the end of the day, it's affecting kids your age. And it's making girls sick."[70] There is an extreme contradiction between Gaga telling people to stop the dieting wars and publicly stating that her status means she does not get to eat. Underlying all this is the realization that part of the price of fame is battling the body to make it spectacular.

Controversy over Lady Gaga's body and weight continued when several months into her touring for the Born This Way Ball press began commenting on the possibility that she had gained 30 pounds on the road. A UK publication, *The Daily Mail*, posted pictures of Gaga's performance in the Netherlands under the headline "Looking Meatier! Lady Gaga Shows Off Her New Fuller Figure After 'Gaining 30lbs' in Her Favourite Carnivorous Creation."[71] The headline was based on speculations by a nutritionist, who had not treated Gaga in person, guessing how much weight she had gained by comparing various photos. Lady Gaga admitted in a radio interview that she had gained 25 pounds while touring.[72] In the news story, images of Gaga bulging out of her costumes were compared to photos from her tour in 2009. *The Examiner*, a popular gossip and celebrity news site, reposted these same photos with the headline "The Fat Lady Gaga Sings."[73] The controversy over Lady Gaga's weight is a prime example of the antagonistic relationship that often emerges between celebrities and the media. When Lady Gaga is public about starving herself for fame media sources criticize her as a bad influence on young girls. Alternatively, when the singer gains weight she is publicly mocked. Rather than engaging in the debate over her body with the mainstream media, Lady Gaga took to social media to talk about the issue.

Lady Gaga used Facebook and her personal social networking site, Littlemonsters.com, to reframe conversations about her body in light of her own struggles with anorexia and bulimia. In the week after the images from Gaga's concert were circulated, she posted a set of four pictures of herself, in just bra and underpants, on social media sites. On Facebook, the images were posted with the caption "Join a Body Revolution," and a link to Gaga's social networking site. When one clicks through to the images on Littlemonsters.com, they have four separate captions. The first image was a photo of Gaga straight on; she is standing against a wall and her eyes are closed. The caption reads: "Bulimia and anorexia since I was

15." The second image shows Gaga from the side, standing up, with her arms in the air and her back arched. The caption reads: "But today I join the BODY REVOLUTION." The third image is also from the side and shows Gaga standing up straight. The caption reads: "To Inspire Bravery." The final image is of Gaga from behind, in an almost pinup-style pose, and the caption reads: "and BREED some m$therf*cking COMPASSION." It is worth noting that while Gaga is wearing no makeup and has said in a personal statement on the site that the pictures were not airbrushed, her body looks curvy and fit. Unlike the images from the concert, there is no visible cellulite and the performer is not bulging out of her clothes. The images and captions create a multitude of potentially conflicting messages. Lady Gaga's illness is talked about next to images of her body looking fit. The captions imply that Gaga is revealing flaws, but the suggestive under-wear and semi-provocative clothing sexualize those flaws. Lady Gaga's face in the images is sad and vulnerable; this speaks directly to the invitation to gaze at both her illness and her body. While Gaga may look spectacular, the contradictions are reminders of the humanness of the body.

The lack of consistency in Gaga's message about her body is translated by the media as a reason to attack her but is portrayed on her social media sites as part of her overall vulnerability. Lady Gaga publicly struggles with her illness and makes defiant statements about the fact pop stars not eating. Because Gaga's body is not fixed, it is more difficult for the media to trans-late her into a definite symbol. Instead, she defies the object-oriented dis-course and maintains her humanity.

Lady Gaga's fans have responded to her call for a Body Revolution. The header for the site where Gaga originally posted the images says: "Be brave and celebrate with us your 'perceived flaws,' as society tells us. May we make our flaws famous, and thus redefine the heinous." In addition to the images of Gaga, there are images of other fans struggling with disabil-ity, illness, and weight loss issues. The site also contains comments from fans talking about how these issues encourage them to relate to their bod-ies. In the past, Gaga has told reporters that she receives lots of books from fans with pictures and stories: "You would not believe the books.... I can't in my heart throw any of them away, because it took them so much time. The stories, they break my heart." People write to tell Gaga stories of being gay and bullied, being abandoned by parents, losing weight.[74] The site makes the exchange between Gaga and her fans public. Instead of responding directly to media depictions of her weight and her body, Gaga uses the interactions with her fans to critique those depictions and humanize fame. In the end, "her success is the ultimate misfit's revenge."[75]

Summary and Concluding Thoughts

The success of Lady Gaga's critiques of fame, media, and celebrity culture is ultimately dependent on the willingness of her fans to take up these conversations. Put another way, "it is practically a cliché of trash film that no monster enters without invitation or some form of human connivance."[76] Gaga's monstrous celebrity model is only successful because of an army of little monsters who have supported her and pushed her forward. With that in mind, it would be easy to dismiss all of this as nothing more than a popular culture trend, but doing so would miss all the ways that trends become part of our code of cultural values and ideals. In a 2010 *Time Magazine* article about Gaga, Cyndi Lauper wrote: "Being around her, I felt like the dust was shaken off me. I find it comforting to sit next to somebody and not have to worry that I look like the freak. She isn't a pop act, she is a performance artist. She herself is art."[77] In talking about the long-term significance of Lady Gaga, people often make this distinction — separating her role in popular culture from her importance as an artist. The Mother Monster has talked about this paradox of the separation between the popular and art in her own work: "[T]he idea is to make things—videos, fashion, performance art — which are innately significant and insignificant, that will cause the argument: 'Is Lady Gaga valid or invalid?'"[78] Lady Gaga makes things, makes art, makes arguments that "seduce people into being interested in something that is uncomfortable."[79] In embracing popular culture, she also strategically made herself easy to write off as nothing more than a fad. The result is a constant ambiguity about how seriously anyone should take Gaga's project: Is it poignant? Or merely trivial?

Complicating the decision is the fact that, for all her conversations about humanity, fragility, fame, and death, Lady Gaga's own personal performance ultimately does not revolutionize the concepts. In the end, we see Gaga trading her body for fame in ways that are typical of young female pop stars. What may be revolutionary in all of this is the space it creates for viewers to respond to and challenge media depictions of fame. Lady Gaga has acknowledged her inability to live up to many of the ideals that she puts forward. In the end, she recognizes the "music is a lie. It is a lie. Art is a lie. You have to tell a lie that is so wonderful that your fans make it come true. That has been my motivation and my inspiration for the longest time."[80] When Lady Gaga talks about revolutionizing body image, responding to media depictions of celebrity death, and destroying the fame monster, the statements are lies when they come from her. The hope is that her fans will take up the larger vision and make it honest. After all, "it's not about being rich and famous, it's about being truthful."[81] The truth just may not show up any time soon. Gaga's real legacy will be in the way her fans take what she has created and make it their own. As she explains it: "My fans are a revolution. They are living proof that you don't have to conform to anything to change the world."[82] Why would we need a revolution? "We're in the apocalypse right now. I mean, if racism, gay-bashing, the Ku Klux Klan and all of wars and presidents that we've been through is not enough, I'm not sure what we're all waiting for. We've seen The End. It's here. It's happened. So now we must be joyful. And rebuild. And that's what I'm about."[83]

Chapter Notes

Introduction

1. Gaga quoted in Emily Herbert, *Lady Gaga: Behind the Fame* (New York: Overlook Press, 2010), 49.

2. Lizzy Goodman, *Lady Gaga: Critical Mass Fashion* (New York: St. Martin's Griffin, 2010), 10.

3. Maureen Callahan, *Poker Face: The Rise and Rise of Lady Gaga* (New York: Hyperion Books, 2010), 205.

4. "Getting to Know Lady Gaga," Oprah.com, accessed 6 June 2012, http://www.oprah.com/oprahshow/Lady-Gagas-First-Oprah-Show-Appearance/3.

5. "Getting to Know Lady Gaga."

6. Andrew C. Stone, "Our Lady of Pop," *Jezebel*, July 2011, 53–54.

7. P. David Marshall, *Celebrity and Power: Fame in Contemporary Culture* (Minneapolis: University of Minnesota Press, 1997), 5–6.

8. David Giles, *Illusions of Immortality: A Psychology of Fame and Celebrity* (London: Palgrave MacMillan, 2000), 109.

9. Giles, *Illusions of Immortality*, 109.

10. Marshall, *Celebrity and Power*, 6.

11. Richard Dyer, *Stars* (London: British Film Institute, 1979), 7.

12. Marshall, *Celebrity and Power*, 9.

13. Marshall, *Celebrity and Power*, 8.

14. Dyer, *Stars*, 8.

15. Francesco Alberoni, "L'Elite irresponsable: Théorie et recherché sociglique sur 'le divismo,'" *Ikon* 12, 40/1, 45–62, reprinted (trans. Denis McQuail) as "The Powerless Elite: Theory and Sociological Research on the Phenomenon of the Stars," in *Sociology of Mass Communication*, ed. Denis McQuail (London: Penguin, 1972), 75.

16. Rachel Abramowitz, "Janice Min Helped US Weekly Feed a Hunger for Celebrity," *Los Angeles Times*, 22 July 2009, accessed 26 August 2012, http://articles.latimes.com/2009/jul/22/entertainment/et-usweekly22.

17. One example of this can be seen here: "Star Families Are Just like Us!" *Us Magazine Online*, 11 May 2012, accessed 13 September 2012, http://www.usmagazine.com/celebrity-news/pictures/star-families-are-just-like-us-2012115.

18. Abramowitz, "Janice Min."

19. Alexander Fury, "Showstudio: Lady Gaga," *In Camera*, 21 August 2009, accessed 18 June 2012, http://showstudio.com/project/in_camera/session/lady_gaga.

20. Goodman, *Lady Gaga*, 514.

21. Callahan, *Poker Face*, 165.

22. Goodman, *Lady Gaga*, 10.

23. Herbert, *Lady Gaga*, 101.

24. Brian Hiatt, "The New York Doll," *Rolling Stone*, issue 1080 (11 June 2009): 58.

25. Herbert, *Lady Gaga*, 126.

26. Lady Gaga, "*V Magazine* Lady Gaga Memorandum No. 2," *V Magazine*, Fall Preview 2011, 8.

27. Helia Phoenix, *Just Dance: Lady Gaga* (London: Orion Paperbacks, 2010), 6–8.

28. Hiatt, "The New York Doll," 60.

29. Lisa Robinson, "In Gaga's Wake," *Vanity Fair*, January 2012, 52.

30. Quoted in Paul Lester, *Looking for Fame: The Life of a Pop Princess, Lady Gaga* (New York: Omnibus Press, 2010), 3 and 4.

31. Stone, "Our Lady of Pop," 54.

32. Herbert, *Lady Gaga*, 89.

33. *60 Minutes* (television program), 13 February 2011, produced by Tom Anderson, Andy Court, Harry A. Radliffe II, Jeff Newton and Amjad Tadros.

34. Elizabeth Kate Switaj, "Lady Gaga's

Bodies: Buying and Selling *The Fame Monster*," in *The Performance Identities of Lady Gaga: Critical Essays*, ed. Richard J. Gray II (Jefferson, NC: McFarland, 2011), 36.

35. *60 Minutes*, 13 February 2011.

36. "Lady Gaga," *Q Magazine*, April 2010, 52.

37. Andrew Murfett, "Lady Gaga," *Sydney Morning Herald*, 15 May 2009, ¶6, accessed 18 June 2012, http://www.smh.com.au/news/entertainment/music/gig-reviews/art-of-ambition/2009/05/14/1241894102332.html.

38. Laura Brown, "The Real Lady Gaga: Be It Minimal or Maximal, the Star's Iconic Look Comes Naturally," *Harper's Bazaar*, October 2011, 276.

39. Lady Gaga, "*V Magazine* Lady Gaga Memorandum No. 2," 8.

40. Brown, "The Real Lady Gaga," 276.

41. Dyer, *Stars*, 20.

42. Hiatt, "The New York Doll," 59.

43. Marshall, *Celebrity and Power*, 4.

44. Switaj, "Lady Gaga's Bodies," 34.

45. Ann Powers, "When Rock Stars Fake It," *Los Angeles Times*, 12 July 2009, ¶5, accessed 13 June 2012, http://articles.latimes.com/2009/jul/12/entertainment/ca-popthe atricality12.

46. Peter Robinson, "Freak or Fraud?" *NME*, 23 April 2011, 23.

47. Edward Ingebretsen, *At Stake: Monsters and the Rhetoric of Fear in Public Culture* (Chicago: University of Chicago Press, 2001), 10.

48. Ingebretsen, *At Stake*, 7.

49. Richard Gray II, "Surrealism, the Theatre of Cruelty and Lady Gaga," in *The Performance Identities of Lady Gaga: Critical Essays*, ed. Richard J. Gray II (Jefferson, NC: McFarland, 2011*)*, 126.

50. Ingebretsen, *At Stake*, xiv.

51. Mathieu Deflum, "The Sex of Lady Gaga," in *The Performance Identities of Lady Gaga: Critical Essays*, ed. Richard J. Gray II (Jefferson, NC: McFarland, 2011), 24.

52. Switaj, "Lady Gaga's Bodies," 39.

53. Switaj, "Lady Gaga's Bodies," 43.

54. Callahan, *Poker Face*, 83.

55. Ingebretsen, *At Stake*, 203.

56. David Annandale, "Rabelais Meets Vogue: The Construction of Carnival, Beauty and Grotesque," in *The Performance Identities of Lady Gaga: Critical Essays*, ed. Richard J. Gray II (Jefferson, NC: McFarland, 2011), 148.

57. Joshua David Stein and Noah Michelson, "The Lady Is a Vamp," *Out Magazine*, September 2009, 113.

58. Herbert, *Lady Gaga*, 91.

59. Goodman, *Lady Gaga*, 70.

60. Scott Poole, *Monsters in America: Our Historical Obsession with the Hideous and the Haunting* (Waco, TX: Baylor University Press, 2011), xiv.

61. Ingebretsen, *At Stake*, 99.

62. Ingebretsen, *At Stake*, 158.

63. Poole, *Monsters in America*, 13.

64. Heather Duerre Humann, "What a Drag: Lady Gaga, Jo Calderone, and the Politics of Representation," in *The Performance Identities of Lady Gaga: Critical Essays*, ed. Richard J. Gray II (Jefferson, NC: McFarland, 2011), 76.

65. Jonah Weiner, "Bare Naked Lady," *Maxim Magazine*, July 2009.

66. Lady Gaga, "*V Magazine* Lady Gaga Memorandum No. 2," 34.

67. Poole, *Monsters in America*, xvi.

68. Ingebretsen, *At Stake*, 19.

69. Ingebretsen, *At Stake*, 47.

70. *60 Minutes*, 13 February 2011.

71. Stein and Michelson, "The Lady Is a Vamp,"106.

72. Robinson, "Freak or Fraud?" 23.

73. Stein and Michelson, "The Lady Is a Vamp," 113.

74. Robinson, "Freak or Fraud?" 23.

75. Brown, "The Real Lady Gaga," 276.

76. Christine Spines, "Lady Gaga Wants You," *Cosmopolitan*, April 2010, 32.

77. Robinson, "Freak or Fraud?" 24.

Chapter 1

1. Edward Ingebretsen, *At Stake: Monsters and the Rhetoric of Fear in Public Culture* (Chicago: University of Chicago Press, 2001), 157.

2. Terry Richardson and Lady Gaga, *Lady Gaga* (New York: Grand Central Publishing, 2011), 1.

3. Emily Herbert, *Lady Gaga: Behind the Fame* (New York: Overlook Press, 2010), 91.

4. Laura Barton, "I've Felt Famous My Whole Life," *The Guardian*, 20 January 2009, accessed 18 July 2012, http://www.guardian.co.uk/music/2009/jan/21/lady-gaga-interview-fame.

5. Gaga quoted in Lizzy Goodman, *Lady Gaga: Critical Mass Fashion* (New York: St. Martin's Griffin, 2010), 70.

6. Mikhail Bakhtin, *Rabelais and His World* (Bloomington: Indiana University Press, 1984), 17.

7. Bakhtin, *Rabelais and His World,* 16.

8. Bakhtin, *Rabelais and His World,* 17.

9. Lady Gaga, "*V Magazine* Lady Gaga Memorandum No. 2," *V Magazine*, Fall Preview 2011, 8.

10. Richardson and Lady Gaga, *Lady Gaga*, 1.

11. Bakhtin, *Rabelais and His World*, 16.

12. Bakhtin, *Rabelais and His World*, 25.

13. Joshua David Stein and Noah Michelson, "The Lady Is a Vamp," *Out Magazine*, September 2009, 113.

14. Robert Hariman, "Political Parody and Public Culture," *Quarterly Journal of Speech* 94, no. 3 (2008): 256.

15. Bakhtin, *Rabelais and His World*, 16.

16. Bakhtin, *Rabelais and His World*, 17.

17. Herbert, *Lady Gaga*, 80.

18. Hariman, "Political Parody and Public Culture," 255.

19. Bill Palmer, "Lady Gaga: The iProng Interview," *iProng*, 5 January 2009.

20. Palmer, "Lady Gaga."

21. Goodman, *Lady Gaga*, 12.

22. Herbert, *Lady Gaga*, 190.

23. *20/20* (television program), 22 January 2010, Burbank, CA: American Broadcasting Company, produced by David Sloan, Rudy Bednar, and Howie Masters.

24. Hattie Collins, "The World Goes Gaga," *i-D Magazine*, no. 308 (Fall 2010).

25. Mark Jacobs, "Lady Gaga," *V Magazine*, July/August 2009.

26. *60 Minutes* (television program), 13 February 2011, Columbia Broadcasting System, produced by Tom Anderson, Andy Court, Harry A. Radliffe II, Jeff Newton, and Amjad Tadros.

27. *60 Minutes*, 13 February 2011.

28. Lady Gaga quoted in Jonathan Van Meer, "Our Lady of Pop," *Vogue*, March 2011, 515.

29. Van Meer, "Our Lady of Pop," 515.

30. Ann T. Torrusio, "The Fame Monster: The Monstrous Construction of Lady Gaga," in *The Performance Identities of Lady Gaga: Critical Essays*, ed. Richard J. Gray II (Jefferson, NC: McFarland, 2011), 171.

31. Van Meer, "Our Lady of Pop," 516.

32. Goodman, *Lady Gaga,* 96–99.

33. Lady Gaga, "New Fans: Little Monsters," *V Magazine*, no. 69, Spring Preview.

34. Lisa Robinson, "Lady Gaga's Culture Revolution," *Vanity Fair*, no. 601 (September 2010): 140.

35. *60 Minutes*, 13 February 2011.

36. Stein and Michelson, "The Lady Is a Vamp," 109.

37. John Norris, "Gaga Over Gaga," *V Magazine*, no. 61 (Fall 2009).

38. Chris Hedges, *Empire of Illusion: The End of Literacy and the Triumph of Spectacle* (New York: Nation Books, 2009), 20.

39. David Giles, *Illusions of Immortality: A Psychology of Fame and Celebrity* (London: Palgrave MacMillan, 2000), 6.

40. Giles, *Illusions of Immortality*, 109.

41. Lady Gaga, "*V Magazine* Lady Gaga Memorandum No. 2," 96.

42. "Lady Gaga," *Q Magazine*, April 2010, 47.

43. Alexander Fury, "Showstudio: Lady Gaga," *In Camera*, 21 August 2009, accessed 18 June 2012, http://showstudio.com/project/in_camera/session/lady_gaga.

44. "*Lady Gaga: Monster Ball*, 2.0 DVD, part 12/14: "Paparazzi/Apocalyptic Film," YouTube video clip, n.d., accessed 13 September 2012, http://www.youtube.com/watch?v=5jU3zoa0Io0.

45. David Annandale, "Rabelais Meets Vogue: The Construction of Carnival, Beauty and Grotesque," in *The Performance Identities of Lady Gaga: Critical Essays*, ed. Richard J. Gray II (Jefferson, NC: McFarland, 2011), 144.

46. *Lady Gaga: Monster Ball*, part 12/14.

47. "CNN Larry King Live: Interview with Lady Gaga" (transcript), 1 June 2010, accessed 20 June 2012, http://transcripts.cnn.com/TRANSCRIPTS/1006/01/lkl.01.html.

48. "CNN Larry King Live," 1 June 2010.

49. *60 Minutes*, 13 February 2011.

50. Lady Gaga, "*V Magazine* Lady Gaga Memorandum No. 2," 118.

51. Ingebretsen, *At Stake*, 103.

52. Scott Poole, *Monsters in America: Our Historical Obsession with the Hideous and the Haunting* (Waco, TX: Baylor University Press, 2011), 171.

53. Stein and Michelson, "The Lady Is a Vamp," 113.

54. Torrusio, "The Fame Monster," 160.

55. Jennifer O'Brien, "Gaga's Oxegasmic; Cheeky Performance Has Lady's Fans Panting for More," *The Sun*, 12 July 2009, 4.

56. Hadley Freeman, "Go Gaga," *Vogue UK*, October 2009, 310.

57. Jessica Leo, Anna Vlach, and Helene

Sobolewski, "Gaga's Gross Birthday Wish," *The Advertiser*, 1 April 2010, 31.

58. Elizabeth Kate Switaj, "Lady Gaga's Bodies: Buying and Selling *The Fame Monster*," in *The Performance Identities of Lady Gaga: Critical Essays*, ed. Richard J. Gray II (Jefferson, NC: McFarland, 2011), 47.

59. Bakhtin, *Rabelais and His World*, 19.

60. Bakhtin, *Rabelais and His World*, 24.

61. Bakhtin, *Rabelais and His World*, 25.

62. Robinson, "Lady Gaga's Culture Revolution," 330.

63. The image of Gaga on the ground, after being thrown from the balcony, is meant to reference the movie *Vertigo*. Daniel Kreps, "Lady Gaga's Sexy Cinematic 'Paparazzi' Video Hits the Web," *Rolling Stone*, 29 May 2009, http://www.rollingstone.com/music/news/13379/68416.

64. Hariman, "Political Parody and Public Culture," 251.

65. Her look in this video has been compared to Minnie Mouse, and her movements in the otherwise dark scene are campy and cartoon-like. Anna Pickard, "Lady Gaga—Paparazzi," *The Guardian*, 4 June 2009, http://www.guardian.co.uk/music/2009/jun/04/lady-gaga-paparazzi-video.

66. Herbert, *Lady Gaga*, 202.

67. Goodman, *Lady Gaga*, 103.

68. Poole, *Monsters in America*, 21.

69. Herbert, *Lady Gaga*, 174.

70. Herbert, *Lady Gaga*, 214.

71. Bakhtin, *Rabelais and His World*, 26.

72. Don Waisanen, "A Citizen's Guide to Democracy Inaction: Jon Stewart's and Stephen Colbert's Comic Rhetorical Criticism," *Southern Communication Journal* 74, no. 2 (2009): 130.

73. Goodman, *Lady Gaga*, 20.

74. Bakhtin, *Rabelais and His World*, 19.

75. "Lady Gaga—Born This Way," You Tube video clip, n.d., accessed 12 September 12 2012, http://www.youtube.com/watch?v=wV1FrqwZyKw.

76. Bakhtin, *Rabelais and His World*, 25.

77. *Lady Gaga Born This Way Ball 2012*, Best View FULL HD 24/6/12," 24 June 2012, YouTube video clip, accessed September 13, 2012, http://www.youtube.com/watch?v=gBghuudHLl4.

78. Ingebretsen, *At Stake*, 52.

79. Lady Gaga, "*V Magazine* Lady Gaga Memorandum No. 2," 35.

80. Torrusio, "The Fame Monster," 161.

81. Poole, *Monsters in America*, 24.

82. Ingebretsen, *At Stake*, 12.

83. Richardson and Lady Gaga, *Lady Gaga*, 1.

84. Ingebretsen, *At Stake*, 113.

85. Ingebretsen, *At Stake*, 85.

86. Ingebretsen, *At Stake*, 62.

87. Brian Hiatt, "Monster Goddess," *Rolling Stone*, issue 1132 (9 June 2011): 42.

88. Poole, *Monsters in America*, 18.

89. Ingebretsen, *At Stake*, 44.

90. Ingebretsen, *At Stake*, 203.

91. Ingebretsen, *At Stake*, 117.

92. "CNN Larry King Live," 1 June 2010.

93. Callahan, *Poker Face*, 4.

94. Hiatt, "The New York Doll," 58.

95. Callahan, *Poker Face*, 2.

96. Stein and Michelson, "The Lady Is a Vamp," 106.

97. Paul Booth, *Digital Fandom: New Media Studies* (New York: Peter Lange, 2010), 22.

98. Booth, *Digital Fandom*, 20.

99. Dyer, *Stars*, 18.

100. Annandale, "Rabelais Meets Vogue," 147.

101. Lady Gaga, Littlemonsters.com, 12 August 2012, accessed 19 August 2012, http://littlemonsters.com/text/50296814ae5e67f649001277.

102. Jocelyn Vena, "Lady Gaga Shoots Back at PETA after 'Turncoat' Accusation," *MTV News*, 14 August 2012, accessed 19 August 2012, http://www.mtv.com/news/articles/1691715/lady-gaga-peta-turncoat-accusation.jhtml.

103. Vena, "Lady Gaga Shoots Back at PETA after 'Turncoat' Accusation."

104. Lady Gaga, Littlemonsters.com, 14 August 2012, accessed 19 August 2012, http://littlemonsters.com/text/502c1e67f35c0c5d3d00185c.

105. Lady Gaga, Littlemonsters.com, 14 August 2012.

106. Derek Blasberg, "What's Next: Take Lady Gaga's Lead This Summer and Sharpen Your Fashion Edge with Sleek Dresses, Strong Colors, and Take-No-Prisoners Accessories," *Harper's Bazaar*, May 2011, 155.

107. Annandale, "Rabelais Meets Vogue," 147.

108. Poole, *Monsters in America*, 25.

109. Lisa Robinson, "In Lady Gaga's Wake," *Vanity Fair*, January 2012, 54.

110. Callahan, *Poker Face*, 218.

111. Marina Crook, "The Style of Lady Gaga," *ASOS*, April 2009, 47.

112. Rupert Howe, "Lady Gaga: What I've Learned," *Q Magazine*, October 2010, 87.

113. Born This Way Foundation, accessed 26 August 2012, http://bornthiswayfoundation.org/pages/our-mission/.

114. Ingebretsen, *At Stake*, 28.

115. Ingebretsen, *At Stake*,33.

116. Torrusio, "The Fame Monster,"170.

117. Lady Gaga, "*V Magazine* Lady Gaga Memorandum No. 2," 96.

Chapter 2

1. Lisa Robinson, "Lady Gaga's Culture Revolution," *Vanity Fair*, no. 601 (September 2010).

2. Celebrity.com, "Lady Gaga Looks like an Angelic Drag Queen on September's Vanity Fair UK," 10 July 30, http://www.celebitchy.com/110592/lady_gaga_looks_like_an_angelic_drag_quee n_on_the_septem bers_vanity_fair_uk/.

3. Emily Herbert, *Lady Gaga: Behind the Fame* (New York: Overlook Press, 2010), 142.

4. Caitlin Moran, "My Night with Lady Gaga," *Times UK*, 22 May 2010, 20.

5. Heather Duerre Humann, "What a Drag: Lady Gaga, Jo Calderone, and the Politics of Representation," in *The Performance Identities of Lady Gaga: Critical Essays*, ed. Richard J. Gray II (Jefferson, NC: McFarland, 2011), 76.

6. Jonah Weiner, "Bare Naked Lady," *Maxim Magazine*, July 2009.

7. Katrin Horn, "Follow the Glitter Way: Lady Gaga and Camp," in *The Performance Identities of Lady Gaga: Critical Essays*, ed. Richard J. Gray II (Jefferson, NC: McFarland, 2011), 88.

8. John M. Sloop, *Disciplining Gender* (Amherst: University of Massachusetts Press, 2004), 19.

9. Judith Butler, *Gender Trouble* (New York: Routledge, 1999), 175.

10. Maureen Callahan, *Poker Face: The Rise and Rise of Lady Gaga* (New York: Hyperion Books, 2010), 54.

11. Callahan, *Poker Face*, 53.

12. Beth Wilson, "Going Gaga," *Women's Wear Daily*, 13 August 2007, 5.

13. Callahan, *Poker Face*, 59.

14. Nandini D'Souza, "Going GaGa: Lady Gaga Shakes Things Up with Catchy Songs and Loads of Underwear," W 36, issue 10 (October 2007): 150.

15. Jessica Iredale, "Lollaland," *Women's Wear Daily*, 9 August 2007, 6; Wilson, "Going Gaga," 5.

16. Sue Devitt, "Girl on Girl," in *Queering the Popular Pitch*, eds. Sheila Whiteley and Jennifer Rycenga (New York: Routledge, 2006), 29.

17. Butler, *Gender Trouble*, 175.

18. Butler, *Gender Trouble*, 175.

19. Debra Ferreday, "Adapting Femininities: The New Burlesque," *M/C Journal* 10, no. 2 (2007), accessed 9 December 2011, http://journal.media-culture.org.au/0705/12-ferreday.php.

20. Ferreday, "Adapting Femininities."

21. Wilson, "Going Gaga," 5.

22. Callahan, *Poker Face*, 107.

23. Callahan, *Poker Face*, 59.

24. Ferreday, "Adapting Femininities."

25. Horn, "Follow the Glitter Way," 91.

26. Callahan, *Poker Face*, 115.

27. Callahan, *Poker Face*, 124.

28. Callahan, *Poker Face*, 152.

29. David Annandale, "Rabelais Meets Vogue: The Construction of Carnival, Beauty and Grotesque," in *The Performance Identities of Lady Gaga: Critical Essays*, ed. Richard J. Gray II (Jefferson, NC: McFarland, 2011), 157.

30. *eTalk* (television program), 5 June 2008, Toronto, CA: Canada TV, produced by Christien Perez.

31. Mathieu Deflum, "The Sex of Lady Gaga," in *The Performance Identities of Lady Gaga: Critical Essays*, ed. Richard J. Gray II (Jefferson, NC: McFarland, 2011), 24.

32. Matt Thomas, "Going Gaga," *Fab Magazine*, issue 362 (24 December 2008), accessed 15 December 2011, http://www.fabmagazine.com/features/362/Gaga.html.

33. Brandon Voss, "'Just Dance' Singer Lady Gaga Gives Back to the Gays," *HX Magazine*, 8 August 2008, accessed 16 December 2011, http://ladygaga.wikia.com/wiki/HX_%28magazine%29.

34. Joshua David Stein and Noah Michelson, "The Lady Is a Vamp," *Out Magazine*, September 2009, 109.

35. Stein and Michelson, "The Lady Is a Vamp," 113.

36. Stein and Michelson, "The Lady Is a Vamp," 113.

37. Thomas, "Going Gaga."

38. "Lady Gaga — Transmission Gaga-vision: Episode 36," YouTube video clip, n.d., accessed 14 September 2012, http://www.youtube.com/watch?v=sZ2nfhD4azE.

39. Noah Michelson, "Lady Gaga Discusses Activism, Outing and Reading Her Male Alter Ego, Jo Calderone, as a Transgender Man," *Huffington Post*, 3 October 2011, accessed 21 October 2011, http://www.huffingtonpost.com/2011/09/23/lady-gaga-jo-calderone-transgender_n_978063.html.

40. Michelson, "Lady Gaga Discusses Activism, Outing and Reading Her Male Alter Ego, Jo Calderone, as a Transgender Man."

41. Whitney Pastorek, "Lady Gaga: Bonus Quotes from the Dance-Pop Queen!" *Entertainment Weekly*, 9 February 2009, accessed 9 November 2010, http://popwatch.ew.com/2009/02/09/lady-gaga-inter/.

42. "Lady Gaga," *Q Magazine*, April 2010, 47.

43. Pastorek, "Lady Gaga."

44. Herbert, *Lady Gaga*, 126; Callahan, *Poker Face*, 106–107.

45. Butler, *Gender Trouble*, 172–173.

46. Moran, "My Night with Lady Gaga," 20.

47. Ann T. Torrusio, "The Fame Monster: The Monstrous Construction of Lady Gaga," in *The Performance Identities of Lady Gaga: Critical Essays*, ed. Richard J. Gray II (Jefferson, NC: McFarland, 2011), 163.

48. Torrusio, "The Fame Monster," 164.

49. Judith Butler, *Bodies That Matter* (New York: Routledge, 1993), 95.

50. Butler, *Bodies That Matter*, 95.

51. Robert Hariman, "Political Parody and Public Culture," *Quarterly Journal of Speech* 94, no. 3 (2008): 250.

52. Butler, *Gender Trouble*, 174.

53. Hermione Hoby, "So Much for Lady Gaga's Feminist Credentials," *The Guardian*, 28 February 2010, accessed 5 July 2012, http://www.guardian.co.uk/music/musicblog/2010/feb/28/lady-gaga-feminist-credentials.

54. Lizzy Goodman, *Lady Gaga: Critical Mass Fashion* (New York: St. Martin's Griffin, 2010), 111.

55. "Lady Gaga," *Q Magazine*, 47.

56. Sloop, *Disciplining Gender*, 2.

57. Edward Ingebretsen, *At Stake: Monsters and the Rhetoric of Fear in Public Culture* (Chicago: University of Chicago Press, 2001), 4.

58. Ingebretsen, *At Stake*, 3.

59. Jocelyn Vena, "Is Lady Gaga Really a Hermaphrodite? Probably Not...," MTV Newsroom, 7 August 2009, http://newsroom.mtv.com/2009/08/07/is-lady-gaga-really-a-hermaphrodite-probably-not/; *20/20*

(television program), 22 January 2010, Burbank, CA: American Broadcasting Company, produced by David Sloan, Rudy Bednar, and Howie Masters.

60. Herbert, *Lady Gaga*, 142.

61. Goodman, *Lady Gaga*, 30.

62. Free Britney, "Lady Gaga Hermaphrodite Picture Sparks Rumors," *The Hollywood Gossip*, 7 August 2009, http://www.thehollywoodgossip.com/2009/08/lady-gaga-hermaphrodite-picture-sparks-rumors/.

63. Vena, "Is Lady Gaga Really a Hermaphrodite? Probably Not..."

64. Herbert, *Lady Gaga*, 184.

65. Herbert, *Lady Gaga*, 185.

66. Ann Powers, "Lady Gaga: 'I Find That Men Get Away with Saying a Lot in This Business, and That Women Get Away with Saying Very Little,'" *Los Angeles Times*, 10 December 2009, accessed 20 October 2011, http://latimesblogs.latimes.com/music_blog/2009/12/lady-gaga-i-find-that-men-get-away-with-saying-a-lot-in-this-business-and-that-women-get-away-with-s.html.

67. Goodman, *Lady Gaga*, 32.

68. Powers, "Lady Gaga."

69. Alexander Fury, "Showstudio: Lady Gaga," *In Camera*, 21 August 2009, accessed 18 June 2012, http://showstudio.com/project/in_camera/session/lady_gaga.

70. Fury, "Showstudio."

71. Austin Scaggs, "Lady Gaga," *Rolling Stone*, no. 1072 (19 February 2009): 34.

72. Scaggs, "Lady Gaga,"34.

73. Scaggs, "Lady Gaga," 34.

74. Callahan, *Poker Face*, 201.

75. *20/20*, 22 January 2010.

76. *20/20*, 22 January 2010.

77. Annandale, "Rabelais Meets Vogue," 151.

78. Caitlin Moran, "Come Party with Lady Gaga," *The Times Online*, 23 May 2010, http://entertainment.timesonline.co.uk/tol/arts_and_entertainment/music/article71296 72.ece.

79. Scott W. Poole, *Monsters in America* (Waco, TX: Baylor University Press, 2011), 108.

80. Annandale, "Rabelais Meets Vogue," 148.

81. Annandale, "Rabelais Meets Vogue," 156.

82. Ingebretsen, *At Stake*, 3.

83. Lady Gaga quoted in Musicians@Google Interview, http://www.youtube.com/watch?v=hNa_-1d_0tA.

84. Butler, *Gender Trouble*, 48.

85. Humann, "What a Drag," 80.

86. Humann, "What a Drag," 80.

87. Michelson, "Lady Gaga Discusses Activism, Outing and Reading Her Male Alter Ego, Jo Calderone, as a Transgender Man."

88. Gemma Wheatley, "Lady G Raises Fashion Steaks," *Daily Star*, 9 September 2010, p. 28; William Van Meter, "Bold Crossings of the Gender Line," *New York Times*, 9 December 2010, E1.

89. Lady Gaga, "*V Magazine* Lady Gaga Memorandum No. 4," *V Magazine*, no. 74 (Winter 2011).

90. Lady Gaga, "*V Magazine* Lady Gaga Memorandum No. 4."

91. Lady Gaga, "*V Magazine* Lady Gaga Memorandum No. 4."

92. Amy Odell, "Lady Gaga Seems to Be Taking Her Jo Calderone Alter Ego Pretty Seriously," *New York Magazine*, 25 August 2010, accessed 12 October 2011, http://nymag.com/daily/fashion/2010/08/lady_gaga_seems_to_be_taking_h.html.

93. Gaga quoted in Kara Warner, "Lady Gaga Captures 'True Spirit' of 'Yoü And I' in Video," MTV News, 18 August 2011, accessed 12 October 2011, http://www.mtv.com/news/articles/1669342/lady-gaga-you-and-i-music-video.jhtml.

94. Hattie Collins, "The World Goes Gaga," *i-D Magazine*, no. 308 (Fall 2010).

95. Weiner, "Bare Naked Lady."

96. Robinson, "Lady Gaga's Culture Revolution," 140.

97. Michelson, "Lady Gaga Discusses Activism, Outing and Reading Her Male Alter Ego, Jo Calderone, as a Transgender Man."

98. Sheila Markar, "Lady Gaga as Jo Calderone: Brilliant or Creepy?" ABC News, 29 August 2011, accessed 21 October 2011, http://abcnews.go.com/Entertainment/lady-gaga-jo-calderone-mtv-vmas-brilliant-creepy/story?id=14405227.

99. Sloop, *Disciplining Gender*, 20.

100. David P. Schmitt, "Sexual Modularity in Sex, Gender, and Orientation," *Psychology Today*, 15 September 2011, accessed 12 October 2011, http://www.psychologytoday.com/blog/sexual-personalities/201109/sexual-modularity-in-sex-gender-and-orientation.

101. Judith Butler, *Undoing Gender* (New York: Routledge, 2004), 79.

102. Jocelyn Vena, "Lady Gaga's 'Yoü And I' Personas: Who Are Yuyi And Jo Calderone?" MTV News, 18 August 2011, accessed 5 May 2012, http://www.mtv.com/news/articles/1669240/lady-gaga-you-and-i-yuyi-jo-calderone.jhtml.

103. Jay Prosser, *Second Skins: The Body Narrative of Transexuality* (New York: Columbia University Press, 1998), 68.

104. Warner, "Lady Gaga Captures 'True Spirit' of 'Yoü and I' in Video."

105. Sloop, *Disciplining Gender*, 21.

106. Michelson, "Lady Gaga Discusses Activism, Outing and Reading Her Male Alter Ego, Jo Calderone, as a Transgender Man."

107. Ingebretsen, *At Stake*, 75–77.

108. Ingebretsen, *At Stake*, 82.

109. Ingebretsen, *At Stake*, 80.

Chapter 3

1. Laura Barton, "I've Felt Famous My Whole Life," *The Guardian*, 20 January 2009, accessed 18 July 2012, http://www.guardian.co.uk/music/2009/jan/21/lady-gaga-interview-fame.

2. Robert Hariman, "Political Parody and Public Culture," *Quarterly Journal of Speech* 94, no. 3 (2008): 247.

3. Mikhail Bakhtin, *Problems of Dostoevsky's Poetics*, trans. C. Emerson (1929; repr., Minneapolis: University of Minnesota Press, 1984), 185.

4. Bakhtin, *Problems of Dostoevsky's Poetics*, 185.

5. Maureen Callahan, *Poker Face: The Rise and Rise of Lady Gaga* (New York: Hyperion Books, 2010), 200.

6. Matthew Turner, "Performing Pop: Lady Gaga, 'Weird Al' Yankovic and Parodied Performance," in *The Performance Identities of Lady Gaga: Critical Essays*, ed. Richard J. Gray II (Jefferson, NC: McFarland, 2011), 193.

7. Dan Harries, *Film Parodies* (London: British Film Institute, 2000), 22.

8. Turner, "Performing Pop,"193.

9. Hariman, "Political Parody and Public Culture," 256.

10. Turner, "Performing Pop," 188.

11. Maureen O'Connor, "An Annotated History of Lindsay Lohan Nudity," *Gawker*, 13 December 2011, accessed 27 August 2012, http://gawker.com/5867141/an-annotated-history-of-lindsay-lohan-nudity.

12. TMZ, "Paris Hilton Mug Shot — So Pretty," 28 August 2010, accessed 27 August 2012, http://www.tmz.com/2010/08/28/paris-hilton-mug-shot-arrested-cocaine-photo/.

13. Ann T. Torrusio, "The Fame Monster: The Monstrous Construction of Lady Gaga," in *The Performance Identities of Lady Gaga: Critical Essays*, ed. Richard J. Gray II (Jefferson, NC: McFarland, 2011), 168.

14. Turner, "Performing Pop,"192.

15. Turner, "Performing Pop," 200.

16. Erving Goffman, *Gendered Advertisements* (New York: Harper, 1976), 57.

17. Emily Herbert, *Lady Gaga: Behind the Fame* (New York: Overlook Press, 2010), 191.

18. Don Waisanen, "A Citizen's Guide to Democracy Inaction: Jon Stewart's and Stephen Colbert's Comic Rhetorical Criticism," *Southern Communication Journal* 74, no. 2 (2009): 125.

19. Hariman, "Political Parody and Public Culture," 249.

20. Hariman, "Political Parody and Public Culture," 4.

21. Hariman, "Political Parody and Public Culture," 250.

22. Rebecca Lush, "The Appropriation of the Madonna Aesthetic," in *The Performance Identities of Lady Gaga: Critical Essays*, ed. Richard J. Gray II (Jefferson, NC: McFarland, 2011), 178.

23. Lush, "The Appropriation of the Madonna Aesthetic," 179.

24. Hariman, "Political Parody and Public Culture," 255.

25. Mikhail Bakhtin, *Rabelais and His World* (Bloomington: Indiana University Press, 1984), 20.

26. Callahan, *Poker Face*, 59.

27. Callahan, *Poker Face*, 47.

28. Turner, "Performing Pop," 202.

29. Joshua David Stein and Noah Michelson, "The Lady Is a Vamp," *Out Magazine*, September 2009, 113.

30. Lush, "The Appropriation of the Madonna Aesthetic," 175.

31. John Mitchell, "Madonna Targets Lady Gaga with 'Express Yourself' and 'Born This Way' Mashup," *MTV.com*, 29 May 2012, accessed 6 August 2012, http://www.mtv.com/news/articles/1685970/madonna-lady-gaga-mash-up.jhtml.

32. Peter Robinson, "Freak or Fraud?" *NME*, 23 April 2011, 22.

33. Mitchell, "Madonna Targets Lady Gaga with 'Express Yourself' and 'Born This Way' Mashup."

34. Ethan Sacks, "Elton John Rekindles Feud with Madonna after Her Lady Gaga Slam," *New York Daily News*, 6 August 2012, accessed 6 August 2012, http://www.nydailynews.com/entertainment/gossip/elton-john-rekindles-duel-madonna-lady-gaga-slam-article-1.1129986.

35. Max Abadian, "World Gone Gaga," *Flare*, December 2009, 113.

36. Lush, "The Appropriation of the Madonna Aesthetic," 174.

37. Lush, "The Appropriation of the Madonna Aesthetic," 175.

38. Lady Gaga, "*V Magazine* Lady Gaga Memorandum No. 1," *V Magazine*, May 2011, 34.

39. Lady Gaga, "*V Maagazine* Lady Gaga Memorandum No. 1," 34.

40. *60 Minutes* (television program), 13 February 2011, Columbia Broadcasting System, produced by Tom Anderson, Andy Court, Harry A. Radliffe II, Jeff Newton, and Amjad Tadros.

41. Lady Gaga, "*V Magazine* Lady Gaga Memorandum No. 1," 34.

42. Stein and Michelson, "The Lady Is a Vamp," 113.

43. Lizzy Goodman, *Lady Gaga: Critical Mass Fashion* (New York: St. Martin's Griffin, 2010), 8–9; Herbert, *Lady Gaga*, 25 and 34; Mario Tarradell, "Gaga Splashy, but Little More," *Dallas Morning News*, 24 July 2010, E01; Callahan, *Poker Face*, 4 and 6; Brian Hiatt, "Monster Goddess," *Rolling Stone*, issue 1132 (9 June 2011): 42.

44. Lisa Robinson, "Lady Gaga's Culture Revolution," *Vanity Fair*, no. 601 (September 2010), 136.

45. "Lady Gaga," *Nylon Magazine*, March 2009, 32.

46. Marina Crook, "The Style of Lady Gaga," *ASOS*, April 2009, 53.

47. Crook, "The Style of Lady Gaga," 51–52.

48. Callahan, *Poker Face*, 6.

49. Cyndi Lauper, "Artists: Lady Gaga," *Time Magazine*, 10 May 2010, 40.

50. David Annandale, "Rabelais Meets Vogue: The Construction of Carnival, Beauty and Grotesque," in *The Performance Identities of Lady Gaga: Critical Essays*, ed. Richard J. Gray II (Jefferson, NC: McFarland, 2011), 148.

51. Katrin Horn, "Follow the Glitter Way:

Lady Gaga and Camp," in *The Performance Identities of Lady Gaga: Critical Essays*, ed. Richard J. Gray II (Jefferson, NC: McFarland, 2011), 89.

52. Torrusio, "The Fame Monster," 166.

53. Lady Gaga, "*V Magazine* Lady Gaga Memorandum No. 1," 34.

54. Barry Brummett, *A Rhetoric of Style* (Carbondale: Southern Illinois University Press, 2008), xi.

55. Brummett, *A Rhetoric of Style*, xi.

56. Callahan, *Poker Face*, 108.

57. Lady Gaga, "*V Magazine* Lady Gaga Memorandum No. 9," 8.

58. Lady Gaga, "*V Magazine* Lady Gaga Memorandum No. 9," 8.

59. Barton, "I've Felt Famous My Whole life."

60. Rupert Howe, "Lady Gaga: What I've Learned," *Q Magazine*, October 2010, 87.

61. Turner, "Performing Pop," 199.

62. "Lady Gaga — Transmission Gaga-vision: Episode 36," YouTube video clip, n.d., accessed 14 September 2012, http://www.youtube.com/watch?v=sZ2nfhD4azE.

63. Lisa Robinson, "In Gaga's Wake," *Vanity Fair*, January 2012, 54.

64. Lady Gaga, "*V Magazine* Lady Gaga Memorandum No. 9," 8.

65. Paul Lester, *Looking for Fame: The Life of a Pop Princess, Lady Gaga* (New York: Omnibus Press, 2010), 5.

66. Callahan, *Poker Face*, 210.

67. Derek Blasberg, "What's Next: Take Lady Gaga's Lead This Summer and Sharpen Your Fashion Edge with Sleek Dresses, Strong Colors, and Take-No-Prisoners Accessories," Harper's Bazaar, May 2011, 155.

68. Annandale, "Rabelais Meets Vogue," 153.

69. "Lady Gaga," *Q Magazine*, April 2010, 47.

70. "Musicians@Google Presents: Google Goes Gaga," YouTube video clip, n.d., accessed 25 September 2012, http://www.youtube.com/watch?v=hNa_-1d_0tA.

71. Crook, "The Style of Lady Gaga,"53.

72. Cortney Harding, "Lady Gaga: The Billboard Cover Story," *Billboard.com*, 7 August 2009, ¶4, accessed 12 June 2012, http://www.billboard.com/features/lady-gaga-the-billboard-cover-story-1004001347.story?page=2#/features/lady-gaga-the-billboard-cover-story-1004001347.story?page=2.

73. Stein and Michelson, "The Lady Is a Vamp," 113.

74. Richard Dyer, *Stars* (London: British Film Institute, 1979), 20.

75. Crook, "The Style of Lady Gaga,"53.

76. Callahan, *Poker Face*, 166–167.

77. Gordon Smart, "Lady Gaga Is Tea Potty," *The Sun*, 20 April 2009, http://www.thesun.co.uk/sol/homepage/showbiz/bizarre/article2384472.ece.

78. Harding, "Lady Gaga."

79. Harding, "Lady Gaga."

80. Deborah Arthurs, "They Must Be (Lady) Gaga! Singer's Teacup Sells for £47k at Auction ... but It Was for an Excellent Cause," *Daily Mail*, 7 May 2012, accessed 9 August 2012, http://www.dailymail.co.uk/femail/article-2140730/Lady-Gaga-teacup-sells-47k-auction-raise-money-tsunami-artist-victims.html.

81. Jonah Weiner, "Bare Naked Lady," *Maxim Magazine*, July 2009.

82. Callahan, *Poker Face*, 169.

83. Callahan, *Poker Face*, 168.

84. Hiatt, "Monster Goddess," 44.

85. Torrusio, "The Fame Monster," 167.

86. Neil Strauss, "The Broken Heart and Violent Fantasies of Lady Gaga," *Rolling Stone*, issue 1108 (8 July 2010): 68.

87. John Norris, "Gaga Over Gaga," *V Magazine*, no. 61 (Fall 2009).

88. Turner, "Performing Pop," 199.

89. Mark Jacobs, "Lady Gaga," *V Magazine*, July/August 2009.

90. Callahan, *Poker Face*, 62.

91. Henry Jenkins, *Convergence Culture: Where Old and New Media Collide* (New York: New York University Press, 2006), 2.

92. Callahan, *Poker Face*, 118.

93. Callahan, *Poker Face*, 118.

94. Andrew Hampp, "Gaga, Oooh La La: Why the Lady is the Ultimate Social Climber," *Advertising Age*, 22 February 2010, 42, and "Lady Gaga Nears 10 Million Facebook fans," *Washington Post*, 3 July 2010, C08.

95. Famecount tracks statistics for Facebook, Twitter, and YouTube. On 9 December 2010, Famecount reported that Lady Gaga had over 24 million Facebook fans, over 7 million Twitter followers, and 377,616 YouTube subscribers. Across all networks and all categories, she was the most popular user. Data accessed 9 December 2010 from http://www.famecount.com/all-platforms.

96. Herbert, *Lady Gaga*, 204.

97. Callahan, *Poker Face*, 12.

98. Callahan, *Poker Face*, 134.

99. "Lady Gaga — Transmission Gaga-vi-

sion: Episode 1," YouTube video clip, n.d., accessed 21 September 2012, http://www.you tube.com/watch?v=5-cx55NpKu4

100. Jean Burgess & Joshua Green, *You Tube* (Malden, MA: Polity Press, 2009), 35–37.

101. "Lady Gaga — Transmission Gagavision: Episode 36," YouTube video clip, accessed 21 September 2012, http://www.you tube.com/watch?v=sZ2nfhD4azE&feature =plcp.

102. "Lady Gaga — Transmission Gagavision: Episode 7," YouTube video clip, n.d., accessed 21 September 2012, http://www.you tube.com/watch?v=yjsltK0TK-E&feature =plcp.

103. "Lady Gaga — Transmission Gagavision: Episode 8," YouTube video clip, n.d., accessed 21 September 2012, http://www.you tube.com/watch?v=ow3lC0z3ECA&feature =plcp.

104. "Lady Gaga — Transmission Gagavison: Episode 14," YouTube video clip, n.d., accessed 21 September 2012, http://www.you tube.com/watch?v=pukI6s7TmrQ&feature =plcp.

105. "Lady Gaga — Transmission Gagavision Episode 9," YouTube video clip, n.d., accessed 21 September 2012, http://www.you tube.com/watch?v=ToRuQ065k7s&feature =plcp.

106. Lady Gaga, posted to Twitter 25 November 2010, accessed 16 December 2010.

107. Daniel Kreps, "Lady Gaga's Sexy Cinematic 'Paparazzi' Video Hits the Web," *Rolling Stone*, 29 May 2009, http://www.roll ingstone.com/music/news/13379/68416; Herbert, *Lady Gaga*, 21.

108. "Getting to Know Lady Gaga," Oprah. com., accessed 6 June 2012, http://www. oprah.com/oprahshow/Lady-Gagas-First-Oprah-Show-Appearance/3.

109. Lisa Respers France, "Gaga's Monster Influence," *CNN Entertainment*, 20 January 2011, accessed 18 July 2012, http://www.cnn. com/2011/SHOWBIZ/celebrity.news.gos sip/01/20/lady.gaga.career/

110. Paul J. Booth, *Digital Fandom: New Media Studies* (New York: Peter Lange, 2010), 65–67.

111. Julie Bort, "First Look: Lady Gaga Opens Her Own Social Network to the Public," *Business Insider*, 9 July 2012, accessed 20 September 2012, http://www.businessinsider. com/first-looks-lady-gaga-opens-her-own-social-network-to-the-public-2012-7?op=1.

112. Neal Pollack, "How Lady Gaga's Manager Reinvented the Celebrity Game with Social Media," *Wired.co.UK*, 21 May 2012, accessed 10 September 2012, http://www.wired. co.uk/magazine/archive/2012/06/features/ troy-carter?page=2.

113. Boonsri Dickinson, "Lady Gaga–Backed Startup Raises Over $4 Million from Top VC Firms," *Business Insider*, 16 February 2012, accessed 10 September 2012, http:// www.businessinsider.com/lady-gaga-backed-startup-raises-over-4-million-from-top-vc-firms-2012-2#ixzz20Arz39qN.

114. Pollack, "How Lady Gaga's Manager Reinvented the Celebrity Game with Social Media."

115. "Lady Gaga Thanks All Her Little Monsters on Facebook!" YouTube, n.d., accessed 21 September 2012, http://www.you tube.com/watch?v=Bu7NqI0hP9M&feature =plcp.

116. Edward Ingebretsen, *At Stake: Monsters and the Rhetoric of Fear in Public Culture* (Chicago: University of Chicago Press, 2001), 57.

117. Judith Butler, *Gender Trouble* (New York: Routledge, 1999), 176–177.

Chapter 4

1. Edward Ingebretsen, *At Stake: Monsters and the Rhetoric of Fear in Public Culture* (Chicago: University of Chicago Press, 2001), 27.

2. Ingebretsen, *At Stake*, 23.

3. Elizabeth Kate Switaj, "Lady Gaga's Bodies: Buying and Selling *The Fame Monster*," in *The Performance Identities of Lady Gaga: Critical Essays*, ed. Richard J. Gray II (Jefferson, NC: McFarland, 2011), 43.

4. John Jurgensen, "Lady Gaga's Lessons for the Music Business," *Wall Street Journal Online*, 29 January 2010, http://on line.wsj.com/article/SB10001424052748 704094304575029621644867154.html para 14.

5. Hortense Powdermaker, *Hollywood: The Dream Factory* (Boston: Little, Brown, 1950), 228.

6. Francesco Alberoni, "L'Elite irresponsable: Théorie et recherché sociolgique sur '*le divismo*,'" *Ikon* 12, 40/1, 45–62, reprinted (trans. Denis McQuail) as "The Powerless Elite: Theory and Sociological Research on the Phenomenon of the Stars," in *Sociology*

of Mass Communication, ed. Denis McQuail (London: Penguin, 1972), 75.

7. Graeme Turner, *Understanding Celebrity* (Thousand Oaks, CA: Sage Publications, 2009), 34.

8. Turner, *Understanding Celebrity,* 35.

9. Richard Dyer, *Stars* (London: British Film Institute, 1979), 11.

10. Rosemary Coombe, *The Cultural Life of Intellectual Properties: Authorship, Appropriation, and the Law* (Durham, NC: Duke University Press, 1998), 88.

11. Barry Brummett, "Mediating the Laws: Popular Trials and Mass Media," in *Popular Trials: Rhetoric, Mass Media, and the Law,* ed. Robert Hariman (Tuscaloosa: University of Alabama Press, 1990), 180.

12. Coombe, *The Cultural Life of Intellectual Properties,* 89.

13. Sasha Frere-Jones, "Ladies Wild: How Not Dumb Is Gaga?" *The New Yorker,* 27 April 2009, http://www.newyorker.com/arts/critics/musical/2009/04/27/090427crmu_music_frerejones?printable=true.

14. Frere-Jones, "Ladies Wild."

15. Jurgensen, "Lady Gaga's Lessons for the Music Business," para. 19.

16. Helia Phoenix, *Just Dance: Lady Gaga* (London: Orion Paperbacks, 2010), 28; Maureen Callahan, *Poker Face: The Rise and Rise of Lady Gaga* (New York: Hyperion Books, 2010), 42.

17. Lisa Robinson, "In Gaga's Wake," *Vanity Fair,* January 2012, 54.

18. Dyer, *Stars,* 35.

19. Maureen Callahan, *Poker Face: The Rise and Rise of Lady Gaga* (New York: Hyperion Books, 2010), 84.

20. Cortney Harding, "Lady Gaga: The Billboard Cover Story," *Billboard.com,* 7 August 2009, ¶3, accessed 12 June 2012, http://www.billboard.com/features/lady-gaga-the-billboard-cover-story-1004001347.story?page=2#/features/lady-gaga-the-billboard-cover-story-1004001347.story?page=2.

21. Callahan, *Poker Face,* 87.

22. Switaj, "Lady Gaga's Bodies," 42.

23. Switaj, "Lady Gaga's Bodies," 37.

24. Callahan, *Poker Face,* 32.

25. Callahan, *Poker Face,* 205.

26. Christine Spines, "Lady Gaga Wants You," *Cosmopolitan,* April 2010, 34.

27. Dirk Smillie, "The Business of Lady Gaga," *Forbes.com,* accessed 25 November 2009, http://www.forbes.com/2009/11/25/lady-gaga-music-business-entertainment-marketing.html.

28. Callahan, *Poker Face,* 205.

29. Max Abadian, "World Gone Gaga," *Flare,* December 2009, 113.

30. Abadian, "World Gone Gaga," 113.

31. Callahan, *Poker Face,* 70.

32. Callahan, *Poker Face,* 70.

33. Callahan, *Poker Face,* 139.

34. Callahan, *Poker Face,* 81.

35. Smillie, "The Business of Lady Gaga."

36. Smillie, "The Business of Lady Gaga."

37. Callahan, *Poker Face,* 103.

38. Paula Johanson, *Lady Gaga: A Biography* (Santa Barbara, CA: Greenwood Press, 2012), front matter.

39. Phoenix, *Just Dance,* 31.

40. Phoenix, *Just Dance,* 33; Johanson, *Lady Gaga,* 38; Callahan, *Poker Face,* 45.

41. Callahan, *Poker Face,* 48.

42. Craig Marks, "The Billboard Q&A," *Billboard* 122, no. 8 (2010): 16.

43. Callahan, *Poker Face,* 31.

44. Phoenix, *Just Dance,* 33.

45. Johanson, *Lady Gaga,* 38.

46. Lisa Rose, "Lady Gaga's Outrageous Persona Born in Parsippany, New Jersey," *Star-Ledger,* 21 January 2010, accessed 17 July 2012, http://www.nj.com/entertainment/music/index.ssf/2010/01/lady_gaga_her_outrageous_perso.html.

47. Johanson, *Lady Gaga,* 38.

48. Callahan, *Poker Face,* 45.

49. Dyer, *Stars,* 38–39.

50. Dyer, *Stars,* 20.

51. Charles Bazerman, *The Language of Edison's Light* (Cambridge, MA: MIT Press, 2002), 90.

52. Ted Striphas, "Harry Potter and the Simulacrum: Contested Copies in an Age of Intellectual Property," *Critical Studies In Media Communication* 26, no. 4 (October 2009): 297.

53. Bazerman, *The Language of Edison's Light,* 90.

54. Simon Vozick-Levinson, "Lady Gaga's Fame Bites Her Back," *Entertainment Weekly,* no. 1096 (2010): 10.

55. Marks, "The Billboard Q&A," 16–17.

56. Callahan, *Poker Face,* 38.

57. Marks, "The Billboard Q&A," 16.

58. Lisa Robinson, "Lady Gaga's Culture Revolution," *Vanity Fair,* no. 601 (September 2010): 139–140.

59. "Gaga's Lawyer Hits Back at Lawsuit," *World Entertainment News Network,* 20 March 2010.

60. Brummett, "Mediating the Laws,"188.

61. Brummett, "Mediating the Laws," 188.

62. Robert Hariman, "Performing the Laws: Popular Trials and Social Knowledge," in *Popular Trials: Rhetoric, Mass Media, and the Law*, ed. Robert Hariman (Tuscaloosa: University of Alabama Press, 1990), 27.

63. Robinson, "Lady Gaga's Culture Revolution,"137.

64. Callahan, *Poker Face*, 73.

65. Callahan, *Poker Face*, 92.

66. Callahan, *Poker Face*, 100.

67. Jurgensen, "Lady Gaga's Lessons for the Music Business," para. 12.

68. Jeff Leeds, "The New Deal: Band as Brand," *New York Times*, 11 November 2007, accessed 7 May 2012, http://www.nytimes.com/2007/11/11/arts/music/11leed.html?pagewanted=all.

69. Leeds, "The New Deal."

70. Jan Blumentrath, "Interview with Jeff Hanson," *HitQuarters.com*, 20 September 2010, accessed 7 May 2012, http://www.hitquarters.com/index.php3?page=intrview/opar/intrview_JeffHanson_Interview_Part2.html para 2–3.

71. Mathieu Deflum, "The Sex of Lady Gaga," in *The Performance Identities of Lady Gaga: Critical Essays*, ed. Richard J. Gray II (Jefferson, NC: McFarland, 2011), 20.

72. Jurgensen, "Lady Gaga's Lessons for the Music Business," para. 5.

73. Rupert Howe, "Lady Gaga: What I've Learned," *Q Magazine*, October 2010, 87.

74. Callahan, *Poker Face*, 154.

75. Callahan, *Poker Face*, 154–155.

76. Lisa Respers France, "Gaga's Monster Influence," *CNN Entertainment*, 20 January 2011, accessed 18 July 2012, http://www.cnn.com/2011/SHOWBIZ/celebrity.news.gossip/01/20/lady.gaga.career/.

77. France, "Gaga's Monster Influence."

78. France, "Gaga's Monster Influence."

79. Polaroid Press, "Polaroid and Lady Gaga Announce Grey Label," *Polaroid.com*, 6 January 2011, accessed 24 August 2012, http://polaroid.com/en/press/2011/1/6/polaroid-and-lady-gaga-announce-grey-label.

80. France, "Gaga's Monster Influence."

81. 1-800-LAW-FIRM. 0006, "1-800-LAW-FIRM Announces Class Action Lawsuit against Lady Gaga," *Business Wire (English) Regional Business News*, 24 June 2011, 6, EBSCO host, accessed 6 May 2012.

82. "Lady Gaga Lawsuit Claims She Stole Money Meant for Japan Earthquake Victims: New Comments from Lawyer," *International Business Times Regional Business News*, 27 June 2011, 6, EBSCO host, accessed 6 May 2012.

83. 2011. "Gaga Lawsuit 'without Merit,'" *Townsville Bulletin*, 30 June 2011, 25, EBSCO host, accessed 6 May 2012.

84. Office Depot, "Office Deport Partners with Lady Gaga's Born This Way Foundation to Create a Braver, Kinder School Year, *Officedepot.com*, accessed 26 August 2012, http://www.officedepot.com/special Links.do?file=/promo/pages/0710_btw.jsp&template=blank&cm_re=Home-_-Spot9-_-W32BTWFMINI.

85. Office Depot, "Office Depot Partners with Lady Gaga's Born This Way Foundation to Create a Braver, Kinder School Year."

86. Office Depot, "Office Depot Partners with Lady Gaga's Born This Way Foundation to Create a Braver, Kinder School Year."

87. Lady Gaga, "*V Magazine* Lady Gaga Memorandum No. 2," *V Magazine*, Fall Preview 2011, 8.

88. France, "Gaga's Monster Image."

89. Lady Gaga, "*V Magazine* Lady Gaga Memorandum No. 2," 35.

90. Callahan, *Poker Face*, 212.

91. Switaj, "Lady Gaga's Bodies," 45.

92. Rebecca Lush, "The Appropriation of the Madonna Aesthetic," in *The Performance Identities of Lady Gaga: Critical Essays*, ed. Richard J. Gray II (Jefferson, NC: McFarland, 2011), 186.

93. David Annandale, "Rabelais Meets Vogue: The Construction of Carnival, Beauty and Grotesque," in *The Performance Identities of Lady Gaga: Critical Essays*, ed. Richard J. Gray II (Jefferson, NC: McFarland, 2011), 150.

94. Ingebretsen, *At Stake*, xiii.

95. Smillie, "The Business of Lady Gaga."

96. Steven Levy, Brad Stone, N'Gai Croal, Jennifer Tanaka, Arian Campo-Flores, Jamie Reno, Andrew Murr, and Pat Wingert, "The Noisy War Over Napster," *Newsweek* 135, no. 23 (2000): 46.

97. Levy, "The Noisy War Over Napster," 46.

98. David Spitz and Starling Hunter, "Contested Codes: The Social Construction of Napster," *Information Society* 21, no. 3 (2005): 169.

99. "Lady Gaga," *Nylon*, March 2009, 32.

100. Jurgensen, "Lady Gaga's Lessons for the Music Business," para. 8.

101. Bill Werde, "Editor's Note: Why Billboard Isn't Revising Chart Policies for Lady Gaga's Amazon Deal," *Billboard*, 26 May 2011, accessed 17 July 2012, http://www.billboard.biz/bbbiz/industry/retail/why-billboard-isn-t-revising-chart-policies-1005205422.story.

102. Lush, "The Appropriation of the Madonna Aesthetic," 187.

103. "List: Top Illegal Downloads," *Sydney Morning Herald*, 6 March 2011, accessed 17 May 2012 from http://www.smh.com.au/technology/technology-news/list-the-top-illegal-downloads-20110306-1bj85.html.

104. Emma Barnett, "London Tops Britain's Illegal Download Chart," *The Telegraph*, 9 February 2012.

105. Steve Jones, "Gaga's 'Born' Delivers Record Sales; It's the Most in Years, but Is It a Fluke?" *Life*, 2 June 2011, 1D.

106. Caitlin Moran, "My Night with Lady Gaga," *Times UK*, 22 May 2010, 20.

107. Hariman, "Performing the Laws," 25.

108. Hariman, "Performing the Laws," 26.

109. Levy, "The War Over Napster," 46.

110. "Gaga Violation," *Northern Territory News*, 2011 July 16, 34.

111. "Lady Gaga Song 'Judas' — Plagiarism or from God?" *International Business Times*, 6 August 2011.

112. Peter Robinson, "Freak or Fraud?" *NME*, 23 April 2011, 22.

113. "Fil-Canadian Maria Aragon takes the stage with Lady Gaga," Manila Bulletin, 4 March 2011.

114. Lady Gaga, "*V Magazine* Lady Gaga Memorandum, No. 3," *V Magazine* (Fall 2011): 119.

115. Mike Masnick, "For Lady Gaga, Copyright Not About Music, but Her Image," *Techdirt.com*, 9 March 2011, accessed 17 May 2012, http://www.techdirt.com/articles/20110308/14234413404/lady-gaga-copyright-not-about-music-her-image.shtml.

116. Coombe, *The Cultural Life of Intellectual Properties*, 89.

117. Striphas, "Harry Potter and the Simulacrum," 297.

118. "Lady Gaga Nurses Grudge Over Ice Cream," *Toronto Star*, 7 March 2011, A2.

119. Justin Fenner, "What Happens When Lady Gaga Takes One of Her Own Fansites to Court?" *Styleite.com*, 24 September 2011, accessed 7 May 2012, http://www.styleite.com/media/lady-gaga-sues-fansite/.

120. "Lady Gaga Wins Lawsuit Against Animated Lady Goo Goo," *International Business Times Regional Business News*, 16 October 2011, 10, EBSCO host, accessed 6 May 2012.

121. Jose Martinez, "Lady Gaga in Trademark Suit Over Company's 'Lady Gaga for Design' Product Line," *NYDailyNews.com*, 11 September 2011, accessed 7 May 2012, http://articles.nydailynews.com/2011-09-29/gossip/30240061_1_stefani-germanotta-pokerface-singer-lady-gaga.

122. Julia Rubin, "Lady Gaga Sues Excite Worldwide Over Trademark Application," *Styleite.com*, 29 September 2011, accessed 7 May 2011, http://www.styleite.com/media/lady-gaga-excite-worldwide/.

123. Michael Zhang, "This is Lady Gaga's Photo Release Form," *PetaPixel.com*, 1 February 2012, accessed 17 May 2012, http://www.petapixel.com/2012/02/01/this-is-lady-gagas-photo-release-form/.

124. Andrew Beaujon and Jay Westcott, "Dear Photographers, Lady Gaga Wants the Copyright on Your Work," *TBD.com*, 3 March 2011, accessed 17 May 2012, http://www.tbd.com/articles/2011/03/dear-photographers-lady-gaga-wants-the-copyright-on-your-work-55567.html.

125. Zhang, "This is Lady Gaga's Photo Release Form."

126. Derek Blasberg, "What's Next: Take Lady Gaga's Lead This Summer and Sharpen Your Fashion Edge with Sleek Dresses, Strong Colors, and Take-No-Prisoners Accessories," Harper's Bazaar, May 2011, 155.

127. Annandale, "Rabelais Meets Vogue," 152.

128. Annandale, "Rabelais Meets Vogue," 154.

129. Blasberg, "What's Next," 155.

130. Lady Gaga, "*V Magazine* Lady Gaga Memorandum No. 6," *V Magazine*, March 2012, 97.

Chapter 5

1. *60 Minutes* (television program), 13 February 2011, Columbia Broadcasting System, produced by Tom Anderson, Andy Court, Harry A. Radliffe II, Jeff Newton, and Amjad Tadros.

2. Edward Ingebretsen, *At Stake: Monsters and the Rhetoric of Fear in Public Culture* (Chicago: University of Chicago Press, 2001), 8.

3. "Lady Gaga — Princess Die (the Born

This Way Ball Tour Melbourne)," YouTube video clip, n.d., accessed 25 September 2012, http://www.youtube.com/watch?v=PHy-BiSSgC0.

4. "Lady Gaga — Princess Die (Live in Bucharest, Romania, 16.08.2012)," YouTube video clip, n.d., accessed 25 September 2012, http://www.youtube.com/watch?v=3ntcZg5PA2c.

5. Lisa Robinson, "Lady Gaga's Culture Revolution," *Vanity Fair*, no. 601 (September 2010): 330.

6. Robinson, "Lady Gaga's Culture Revolution," 330.

7. Jonah Weiner, "Bare Naked Lady," *Maxim Magazine*, July 2009.

8. Brian Hiatt, "Monster Goddess," *Rolling Stone*, issue 1132 (2011 June 9): 42.

9. Hiatt, "Monster Goddess," 42.

10. Robinson, "Lady Gaga's Culture Revolution," 137.

11. Douglas Davies, *Death, Ritual, and Belief: The Rhetoric of Funerary Rites* (New York: Continuum, 1997), 22.

12. David Field and Tony Walter, "Death and the Media," *Morality* 8 (2003): 1, available online at http://www.tandf.co.uk/journals/archive/deathandthemedia.pdf.

13. Field and Walter, "Death and the Media."

14. Field and Walter, "Death and the Media."

15. William Merrin, "Crash, Bang, Wallop! What a Picture! The Death of Diana and the Media," *Mortality* 4, no. 1 (1999): 45.

16. Daniel J. Boorstin, *The Image: A Guide to Pseudo-Events in America* (New York: Random House Digital, 1987), 45.

17. Boorstin, *The Image*, 5.

18. Boorstin, *The Image*, 46

19. Lisa Kazmier, "Her Final Performance: British Culture, Mourning and the Memorialization of Ellen Terry," *Mortality* 6, no. 2 (2001): 168.

20. Tim Hutchings, "Wiring Death: Dying, Grieving and Remembering on the Internet," in *Emotions, Identity, and Death: Mortality across Disciplines*, eds. Douglas J. Davies and Chang-Wok Park (Burlington, VT: Ashgate Publishing, 2012), 46.

21. Sharon Mazzarella and Timothy Matyjewicz, "'The Day the Music Died'— Again: Newspaper Coverage of the Deaths of Popular Musicians," in *Pop Music and the Press*, ed. Steve Jones (Philadelphia: Temple University Press, 2002), 220.

22. Merrin, "Crash, Bang, Wallop!" 42.

23. Merrin, "Crash, Bang, Wallop!" 42.

24. Kazmier, "Her Final Performance," 169.

25. Kazmier, "Her Final Performance," 170.

26. Mazzarella and Matyjewicz, "The Day the Music Died," 225.

27. Mazzarella and Matyjewicz, "The Day the Music Died," 221.

28. Caroline Davies, "Amy Winehouse Inquest Records Verdict of Misadventure," *The Guardian*, 26 October 2011, accessed 26 May 2012, http://www.guardian.co.uk/music/2011/oct/26/amy-winehouse-verdict-misadventure.

29. "Lady Gaga on *The View*— 8/1/11— Live Show + Amy Winehouse," YouTube video clip, n.d., accessed 29 September 2012, http://www.youtube.com/watch?v=RC3MTiyncXw.

30. "Lady Gaga on *The View*— 8/1/11— Live Show + Amy Winehouse."

31. "Lady Gaga on *The View*— 8/1/11— Live Show + Amy Winehouse."

32. "Lady Gaga on *The View*— 8/1/11— Live Show + Amy Winehouse."

33. Andrew Blankstein, "Whitney Houston: Final Coroner's Report," *Los Angeles Times*, 4 April 2012, accessed May 25 2012, http://documents.latimes.com/whitney-houston-coroners-report-final/.

34. Blankstein, "Whitney Houston: Final Coroner's Report."

35. "How Whitney Houston Influenced Lady Gaga — Oprah's Next Chapter," You Tube video clip, n.d., accessed 25 May 2012, http://www.youtube.com/watch?v=d6ugnb3hldg.

36. Linnie Rawlinson and Nick Hunt, "Jackson Dies, Almost Takes Internet with Him," *CNN.com*, 26 June 2009, accessed 20 June 2012, http://www.cnn.com/2009/TECH/06/26/michael.jackson.internet/index.html.

37. Nick Allen, "Michael Jackson Memorial Service: The Biggest Celebrity Send Off of All Time," *The Telegraph*, 7 July 2009, accessed 20 June 2012, http://www.telegraph.co.uk/culture/music/michael-jackson/5771156/Michael-Jackson-memorial-service-the-biggest-celebrity-send-off-of-all-time.html.

38. "CNN Larry King Live: Interview with Lady Gaga" (transcript), 1 June 2010, accessed 20 June 2012, http://transcripts.cnn.com/TRANSCRIPTS/1006/01/lkl.01.html.

39. Neil Strauss, "The Broken Heart and

Violent Fantasies of Lady Gaga," *Rolling Stone*, issue 1108 (8 July 2010): 73.

40. Brian Kates, "Alexander McQueen Hanged Self in Wardrobe, Left Suicide Note: Coroner," *New York Daily News*, 17 February 2010, accessed 20 June 2012, http://www.ny dailynews.com/entertainment/gossip/alexan der-mcqueen-hanged-wardrobe-left-sui cide-note-coroner-article-1.169828#ixzz27 t9JfUX3.

41. "Lady Gaga—Brit Awards 2010 Performance HQ.avi," YouTube video clip, n.d., accessed 29 September 2012, https://www. youtube.com/watch?v=Xp7EJFpnxXA.

42. "Getting to Know Lady Gaga," Oprah. com, accessed 6 June 2012, http://www. oprah.com/oprahshow/Lady-Gagas-First-Oprah-Show-Appearance/3.

43. Derek Blasberg, "What's Next: Take Lady Gaga's Lead This Summer and Sharpen Your Fashion Edge with Sleek Dresses, Strong Colors, and Take-No-Prisoners Accessories," *Harper's Bazaar*, May 2011, 155.

44. Blasberg, "What's Next," 155.

45. Blasberg, "What's Next," 155.

46. Julie Naughton and Pete Born, "Lady Gaga on What Drives Her," *Women's Wear Daily*, 18 February 2011, accessed 25 June 2012, http://www.wwd.com/eye/people/lady-gaga-on-what-drives-her-3504137.

47. Andrew C. Stone, "Our Lady of Pop," *Jezebel*, July 2011, 54.

48. Strauss, "The Broken Heart and Violent Fantasies of Lady Gaga," 73.

49. Brian Hiatt, "The New York Doll," *Rolling Stone*, issue 1080 (11 June 2009): 61.

50. Hiatt, "Monster Goddess," 45.

51. "Lady Gaga—Gagavision no. 43," You Tube video clip, n.d., accessed 29 September 2012, https://www.youtube.com/watch?v=O6Gs6d1-Sew.

52. Ingebretsen, *At Stake*, 153.

53. Miranda Purves, "Gaga: New York Doll," *Elle Magazine*, January 2010, p. 147.

54. Purves, "Gaga," 147.

55. Strauss, "The Broken Heart and Violent Fantasies of Lady Gaga," 72.

56. Ingebretsen, *At Stake*, 203.

57. Hiatt, "Monster Goddess," 42.

58. Hiatt, "Monster Goddess," 47.

59. Sarah Casselman, "Mother Monster," *Fashion Magazine*, August 2011, 87.

60. Strauss, "The Broken Heart and Violent Fantasies of Lady Gaga," 71.

61. Robinson, "Lady Gaga's Culture Revolution," 140.

62. Peta Bee, "Exhausted? Too Much Work, Poor Diet and Too Little Sleep Can Lead to an Extreme and Even Critical State," *The Sunday Times*, 13 February 2011, 42.

63. Bee, "Exhausted?" 42.

64. "Lady GaGa—Speechless Live @ the Monster Ball," YouTube video clip, n.d., accessed 27 September 2012, http://www.you tube.com/watch?v=Vek6znZEWY4.

65. "Lady GaGa—Speechless Live @ the Monster Ball."

66. Strauss, "The Broken Heart and Violent Fantasies of Lady Gaga," 68.

67. "Lady Gaga Reveals Struggles with Bulimia," *New York Post*, 9 February 2012, accessed 27 May 2012, http://www.nypost. com/p/pagesix/lady_gaga_reveals_strug gle_with_fG0CjOdQNcSvMwtBOCbgSI#ixz zllyt4AliT.

68. "Lady Gaga Reveals Struggles with Bulimia."

69. Katie J. M. Baker, "When the World Is Your Therapist: Lady Gaga's Eating Disorder Is a Double-Edged Sword," *Jezebel*, 26 September 2012, accessed 27 September 2012, http://jezebel.com/5946532/when-the-world-is-your-therapist-lady-gagas-eating-disorder-is-a-double+edged-sword?tag=eat ing-disorders.

70. "Lady Gaga Reveals Struggles with Bulimia."

71. "Looking Meatier! Lady Gaga Shows Off Her New Fuller Figure after 'Gaining 30lbs' in Her Favourite Carnivorous Creation," *Daily Mail Online*, 19 September 2012, accessed 27 September 2012, http://www.dai lymail.co.uk/tvshowbiz/article-2205629/ Lady-Gaga-shows-new-fuller-figure-gain ing-30lbs-favourite-carnivorous-creation. html?videoPlayerURL=http%3A%2F%2Fc. brightcove.com%2Fservices%2Fviewer%2Ff ederated_f9%3Fis Vid%3D1%26isUI%3D1% 26publisherID%3D1418450360%26player ID%3D72484359001%26domain%3Dem bed%26videoId%3D&hasBCVideo=true&B CVideoID=1848469503001.

72. Joyce Chen, "Lady Gaga Embraces Fuller Figure after 25-Pound Weight Gain," *New York Daily News*, 16 September 2012, accessed 17 September 2012, http://www.ny dailynews.com/entertainment/gossip/lady-gaga-embraces-fuller-figure-25-pound-weight-gain-i-feel-bad-a-article-1.1165856# ixzz27hkEX3tl.

73. Tom Rose, "The Fat Lady Gaga Sings," *The Examiner*, 19 September 2012, accessed

27 September 2012, http://www.examiner.com/article/the-fat-lady-gaga-sings.

74. Robinson, "Lady Gaga's Culture Revolution," 140.

75. Strauss, "The Broken Heart and Violent Fantasies of Lady Gaga," 68.

76. Ingebretsen, *At Stake*, 12.

77. Cyndi Lauper, "Artists: Lady Gaga," *Time Magazine*, 10 May 2010, 40.

78. Emily Herbert, *Lady Gaga: Behind the Fame* (New York: Overlook Press, 2010), 88.

79. Strauss, "The Broken Heart and Violent Fantasies of Lady Gaga," 71.

80. Strauss, "The Broken Heart and Violent Fantasies of Lady Gaga," 71.

81. Marina Crook, "The Style of Lady Gaga," *ASOS*, April 2009, 52.

82. Hiatt, "Monster Goddess," 46.

83. Rupert Howe, "Lady Gaga: What I've Learned," *Q Magazine*, October 2010, 87.

Bibliography

Abadian, Max. "World Gone Gaga." *Flare*, December 2009.

Abramowitz, Rachel. "Janice Min helped US Weekly Feed a Hunger for Celebrity." *Los Angeles Times*, 22 July 2009. Accessed 26 August 2012. http://articles.latimes.com/2009/jul/22/entertainment/et-usweekly22.

Alberoni, Francesco. "L'Elite irresponsable: Théorie et recherché sociolgique sur 'le divismo.'" *Ikon* 12, 40/1, 45–62. Reprinted as "The Powerless Elite: Theory and Sociological Research on the Phenomenon of the Stars," translated by Denis McQuail, in *Sociology of Mass Communication*, ed. Denis McQuail. London: Penguin, 1972.

Allen, Nick. "Michael Jackson Memorial Service: The Biggest Celebrity Send Off of All Time." *The Telegraph*, 7 July 2009. Accessed 20 June 2012. http://www.telegraph.co.uk/culture/music/michael-jackson/5771156/Michael-Jackson-memorial-service-the-biggest-celebrity-send-off-of-all-time.html.

Annandale, David. "Rabelais Meets Vogue: The Construction of Carnival, Beauty and Grotesque." In *The Performance Identities of Lady Gaga: Critical Essays*, ed. Richard J. Gray II. Jefferson, NC: McFarland, 2011.

Arthurs, Deborah. "They Must Be (Lady) Gaga! Singer's Teacup Sells for £47k at Auction ... but It Was for an Excellent Cause." *Daily Mail*, 7 May 2012, retrieved 7 August 2012 from http://www.dailymail.co.uk/femail/article-2140730/Lady-Gaga-teacup-sells-47k-auction-raise-money-tsunami-artist-victims.html.

Baker, Katie J. M. "When the World Is Your Therapist: Lady Gaga's Eating Disorder Is a Double-Edged Sword." *Jezebel*, 26 September 2012. Accessed 27 September 2012. http://jezebel.com/5946532/when-the-world-is-your-therapist-lady-gagas-eating-disorder-is-a-double+edged-sword?tag=eating-disorders.

Bakhtin, Mikhail. *Problems of Dostoevsky's Poetics*. Translated by C. Emerson. Minneapolis: University of Minnesota Press, 1984. Originally published 1929.

_____. *Rabelais and His World*. Bloomington: Indiana University Press, 1984.

Barnett, Emma. "London Tops Britain's Illegal Download Chart." *The Telegraph*, 9 February 2012.

Barton, Laura. "I've Felt Famous My Whole life." *The Guardian*, 20 January 2009. Accessed 18 July 2012. http://www.guardian.co.uk/music/2009/jan/21/lady-gaga-interview-fame.

Bazerman, Charles. *The Language of Edison's Light*. Cambridge, MA: MIT Press, 2002.

Beaujon, Andrew, and Jay Westcott. "Dear Photographers, Lady Gaga Wants the Copyright on Your Work." TBD.com, 3 March 2011. Accessed 17 May 2012. http://www.tbd.com/articles/2011/03/dear-photographers-lady-gaga-wants-the-copyright-on-your-work-55567.html.

Bee, Peta. "Exhausted? Too Much Work, Poor Diet and Too Little Sleep Can Lead to an Extreme and Even Critical State." *The Sunday Times*, 13 February 2011, 42.

Blankstein, Andrew. "Whitney Houston: Final Coroner's Report." *Los Angeles Times*, 4 April 2012. Accessed 25 May 2012. http://documents.latimes.com/whitney-houston-coroners-report-final/.

Blasberg, Derek. "What's Next: Take Lady Gaga's Lead This Summer and Sharpen Your Fashion

Edge with Sleek Dresses, Strong Colors, and Take-No-Prisoners Accessories." *Harper's Bazaar*, May 2011.

Blumentrath, Jan. "Interview with Jeff Hanson." HitQuarters.com, 20 September 2010. Accessed 7 May 2012. http://www.hitquarters.com/index.php3?page=intrview/opar/intrview_Jeff Hanson_Interview_Part2.html.

Boorstin, Daniel J. *The Image: A Guide to Pseudo-Events in America*. New York: Random House Digital, 1987.

Booth, Paul J. *Digital Fandom: New Media Studies*. New York: Peter Lange, 2010.

Born This Way Foundation. Accessed 26 August 2012. http://bornthiswayfoundation.org/pages/our-mission/.

Bort, Julie. "First Look: Lady Gaga Opens Her Own Social Network to the Public." *Business Insider*, 9 July 2012. Accessed 20 September 2012. http://www.businessinsider.com/first-looks-lady-gaga-opens-her-own-social-network-to-the-public-2012-7?op=1.

Brown, Laura. "The Real Lady Gaga: Be It Minimal or Maximal, the Star's Iconic Look Comes Naturally." *Harper's Bazaar*, October 2011.

Brummett, Barry. *A Rhetoric of Style*. Carbondale: Southern Illinois University Press, 2008.

Burgess, Jean, and Joshua Green. *YouTube*. Malden, MA: Polity Press, 2009.

Butler, Judith. *Bodies That Matter*. New York: Routledge, 1993.

_____. *Gender Trouble*. New York: Routledge, 1999.

_____. *Undoing Gender*. New York: Routledge, 2004.

Callahan, Maureen. *Poker Face: The Rise and Rise of Lady Gaga*. New York: Hyperion Books, 2010.

Celebitchy.com. "Lady Gaga Looks Like an Angelic Drag Queen on September's *Vanity Fair UK*." 30 July 2010. http://www.celebitchy.com/110592/lady_gaga_looks_like_an_angelic_drag_queen_on_the_septembers_vanity_fair_uk/.

Chen, Joyce. "Lady Gaga Embraces Fuller Figure After 25-Pound Weight Gain." *New York Daily News*, 16 September 2012. Accessed 17 September 2012. http://www.nydailynews.com/entertainment/gossip/lady-gaga-embraces-fuller-figure-25-pound-weight-gain-i-feel-bad-a-article-1.1165856#ixzz27hkEX3tl.

"CNN Larry King Live: Interview with Lady Gaga," 1 June 2010. Accessed 20 June 2012. http://transcripts.cnn.com/TRANSCRIPTS/1006/01/lkl.01.html.

Collins, Hattie. "The World Goes Gaga." *i-D Magazine*, no. 308 (Fall 2010).

Coombe, Rosemary. *The Cultural Life of Intellectual Properties: Authorship, Appropriation, and the Law*. Durham, NC: Duke University Press, 1998.

Crook, Marina. "The Style of Lady Gaga." *ASOS*, April 2009.

D'Souza, Nandini. "Going GaGa: Lady Gaga Shakes Things Up with Catchy Songs and Loads of Underwear." *W* 36 (October 2007).

Davies, Caroline. "Amy Winehouse Inquest Records Verdict of Misadventure." *The Guardian*, 26 October 2011. Accessed 26 May 2012. http://www.guardian.co.uk/music/2011/oct/26/amy-winehouse-verdict-misadventure.

Davies, Douglas. *Death, Ritual, and Belief: The Rhetoric of Funerary Rites*. New York: Continuum, 1997.

Deflum, Mathieu. "The Sex of Lady Gaga." In *The Performance Identities of Lady Gaga: Critical Essays*, ed. Richard J. Gray II. Jefferson, NC: McFarland, 2011.

Devitt, Sue. "Girl on Girl." In *Queering the Popular Pitch*, eds. Sheila Whiteley and Jennifer Rycenga. New York: Routledge, 2006.

Dickinson, Boonsri. "Lady Gaga–Backed Startup Raises Over $4 Million from Top VC Firms." *Business Insider*, 16 February 2012. Accessed 10 September 2012. http://www.businessinsider.com/lady-gaga-backed-startup-raises-over-4-million-from-top-vc-firms-2012-2#ixzz20Arz39qN.

Dyer, Richard. *Stars*. London: British Film Institute, 1979.

eTalk (television program), 5 June 2008. Toronto, CA: Canada T. Produced by Christien Perez.

Famecount, 9 December 2010. Accessed 9 December 2010. http://www.famecount.com/all-platforms.

Fenner, Justin. "What Happens When Lady Gaga Takes One of Her Own Fansites to Court?" Styleite.com., 24 September 2011. Accessed 7 May 2012. http://www.styleite.com/media/lady-gaga-sues-fansite/.

Ferreday, Debra. "Adapting Femininities: The New Burlesque." *M/C Journal* 10, no. 210 (2007). Accessed 9 December 2011. http://journal.media-culture.org.au/0705/12-ferreday.php.

Field, David, and Tony Walter. "Death and the Media." *Morality* 8 (2003). Available online at http://www.tandf.co.uk/journals/archive/deathandthemedia.pdf.

"Fil-Canadian Maria Aragon Takes the Stage with Lady Gaga." *Manila Bulletin*, 4 March 2011.

France, Lisa Respers. "Gaga's Monster Influence." *CNN Entertainment*, 20 January 2011. Accessed 20 June 2012. http://www.cnn.com/2011/SHOWBIZ/celebrity.news.gossip/01/20/lady.gaga.career/.

Free, Britney. "Lady Gaga Hermaphrodite Picture Sparks Rumors." *The Hollywood Gossip*, 7 August 2009. http://www.thehollywoodgossip.com/2009/08/lady-gaga-hermaphrodite-picture-sparks-rumors/.

Freeman, Hadley. "Go Gaga." *Vogue UK*, October 2009.

Frere-Jones, Sasha. "Ladies Wild: How Not Dumb Is Gaga?" *The New Yorker*, 27 April 2009. http://www.newyorker.com/arts/critics/musical/2009/04/27/090427crmu_music_frerejones?printable=true.

Fury, Alexander. "Showstudio: Lady Gaga." *In Camera*, 21 August 2009. Accessed 18 June 2012. http://showstudio.com/project/in_camera/session/lady_gaga.

"Gaga Lawsuit 'without Merit.'" *Townsville Bulletin*, EBSCO host, 30 June 2011. Accessed May 6, 2012.

"Gaga Violation." *Northern Territory News*, 16 July 2011.

"Gaga's Lawyer Hits Back at Lawsuit." *World Entertainment News Network*, 20 March 2010.

"Getting to Know Lady Gaga." Oprah.com. Accessed 6 June 2012. http://www.oprah.com/oprahshow/Lady-Gagas-First-Oprah-Show-Appearance/3.

Giles, David. *Illusions of Immortality: A Psychology of Fame and Celebrity*. London: Palgrave MacMillan, 2000.

Goffman, Erving. *Gendered Advertisements*. New York: Harper, 1976.

Goodman, Lizzy. *Lady Gaga: Critical Mass Fashion*. New York: St. Martin's Griffin, 2010.

Gray, Richard, II. "Surrealism, the Theatre of Cruelty and Lady Gaga." In *The Performance Identities of Lady Gaga: Critical Essays*, ed. Richard J. Gray II. Jefferson, NC: McFarland, 2011.

Hampp, Andrew. "Gaga, Oooh La La: Why the Lady Is the Ultimate Social Climber." *Advertising Age*, 22 February 2010.

_____. "Lady Gaga Nears 10 Million Facebook Fans." *Washington Post*, 3 July 2010.

Harding, Cortney. "Lady Gaga: The Billboard Cover Story." Billboard.com, 7 August 2009. Accessed 12 June 2012. http://www.billboard.com/features/lady-gaga-the-billboard-cover-story-1004001347.story?page=2#/features/lady-gaga-the-billboard-cover-story-1004001347.story?page=2.

Hariman, Robert. "Performing the Laws: Popular Trials and Social Knowledge." In *Popular Trials: Rhetoric, Mass Media, and the Law*, ed. Robert Hariman. Tuscaloosa: University of Alabama Press, 1990.

_____. "Political Parody and Public Culture." *Quarterly Journal of Speech* 94, no. 3 (2008).

Hedges, Chris. *Empire of Illusion: The End of Literacy and the Triumph of Spectacle*. New York: Nation Books, 2009.

Herbert, Emily. *Lady Gaga: Behind the Fame*. New York: Overlook Press, 2010.

Hiatt, Brian "Monster Goddess." *Rolling Stone*, issue 1132 (9 June 2011).

_____. "The New York Doll." *Rolling Stone*, issue 1080 (11 June 2009).

Hoby, Hermione. "So Much for Lady Gaga's Feminist Credentials." *The Guardian*, 28 February 2010. Accessed 5 July 2012. http://www.guardian.co.uk/music/musicblog/2010/feb/28/lady-gaga-feminist-credentials.

Horn, Katrin. "Follow the Glitter Way: Lady Gaga and Camp." In *The Performance Identities of Lady Gaga: Critical Essays*, ed. Richard J. Gray II. Jefferson, NC: McFarland, 2011.

"How Whitney Houston Influenced Lady Gaga — Oprah's Next Chapter." YouTube video clip. N.d. Accessed 25 May 2012. http://www.youtube.com/watch?v=d6ugnb3hldg.

Howe, Rupert. "Lady Gaga: What I've Learned." *Q Magazine*, October 2010.

Humann, Heather Duerre. "What a Drag: Lady Gaga, Jo Calderone, and the Politics of Representation." In *The Performance Identities of Lady Gaga: Critical* Essays, ed. Richard J. Gray II. Jefferson, NC: McFarland, 2011.

Hutchings, Tim. "Wiring Death: Dying, Grieving and Remembering on the Internet." In *Emotions, Identity, and Death: Mortality Across Disciplines*, eds. Douglas J. Davies and Chang-Wok Park. Burlington, VT: Ashgate Publishing, 2012.

Ingebretsen, Edward. *At Stake: Monsters and the Rhetoric of Fear in Public Culture.* Chicago: University of Chicago Press, 2001.

Iredale, Jessica. "Lollaland." *Women's Wear Daily*, 9 August 2007.

Jacobs, Mark. "Lady Gaga." *V Magazine*, July/August 2009.

Jenkins, Henry. *Convergence Culture: Where Old and New Media Collide.* New York: New York University Press, 2006.

Johanson, Paula. *Lady Gaga: A Biography.* Santa Barbara, CA: Greenwood Press, 2012.

Jones, Steve. "Gaga's 'Born' Delivers Record Sales; It's the Most in Years, but Is It a Fluke?" *Life*, 2 June 2011.

Jurgensen, John. "Lady Gaga's Lessons for the Music Business." *Wall Street Journal Online*, 29 January 2010. http://online.wsj.com/article/SB10001424052748704094304575029621644 867154.html.

Kates, Brian. "Alexander McQueen Hanged Self in Wardrobe, Left Suicide Note: Coroner." *New York Daily News*, 17 February 2010. Accessed 20 June 2012. http://www.nydaily news.com/entertainment/gossip/alexander-mcqueen-hanged-wardrobe-left-suicide-note-coroner-article-1.169828#ixzz27t9JfUX3.

Kazmier, Lisa. "Her Final Performance: British Culture, Mourning and the Memorialization of Ellen Terry." *Mortality* 6, no. 2 (2001).

Kreps, Daniel. "Lady Gaga's Sexy Cinematic 'Paparazzi' Video Hits the Web." *Rolling Stone*, 29 May 2009. http://www.rollingstone.com/music/news/13379/68416.

Lady Gaga. Littlemonsters.com, 12 August 2012. Accessed 19 August 2012. http://littlemon sters.com/text/50296814ae5e67f649001277.

_____. "*V Magazine* Lady Gaga Memorandum No. 1." *V Magazine*, May 2011.

_____. "*V Magazine* Lady Gaga Memorandum No. 2." *V Magazine*, Fall Preview 2011.

_____. "*V Magazine* Lady Gaga Memorandum No. 3." *V Magazine*, Fall 2011.

_____. "*V Magazine* Lady Gaga Memorandum No. 4." *V Magazine*, no. 74 (Winter 2011).

_____. "*V Magazine* Lady Gaga Memorandum No. 6." *V Magazine*, March 2012.

"Lady Gaga — Born This Way." YouTube video clip. N.d. Accessed 12 September 2012. http://www.youtube.com/watch?v=wV1FrqwZyKw.

Lady Gaga Born This Way Ball. 2012 Best View FULL HD 24/612. YouTube video clip. Accessed 13 September 2012. http://www.youtube.com/watch?v=BghuudHL14.

"Lady Gaga — Brit Awards 2010 Performance HQ.avi." YouTube video clip. N.d. Accessed 29 September 2012. http://www.youtube.com/watch?v=Xp7EJFpnxXA.

"Lady Gaga — Gagavision No. 43." YouTube video clip. N.d. Accessed 29 September 2012. http://www.youtube.com/watch?v=06G6d1Sew.

Lady Gaga: Monster Ball. 2.0 DVD. Part 12/14: "Apocalyptic Film/Paparazzi." YouTube video clip. N.d. Accessed 13 September 2012. http://www.youtube.com/watch?v=5jU3zoa0Io0.

"Lady Gaga Nurses Grudge Over Ice Cream." *Toronto Star*, 7 March 2011.

"Lady Gaga on *The View*— 8/1/11— Live Show + Amy Winehouse." YouTube video clip. N.d. Accessed 29 September 2012. http://www.youtube.com/watch?v=3ntcZg5PA2c.

"Lady Gaga — Princess Die (the Born This Way Ball Tour Melbourne)." YouTube video clip. N.d. Accessed 25 September 2012. YouTube. http://www.youtube.com/watch?v=PHy-BiSSgC0.

"Lady Gaga Reveals Struggle with Bulimia." *New York Post*, 9 February 2012. Accessed 27 May 2012. http://www.nypost.com/p/pagesix/lady_gaga_reveals_ struggle_with_ fG0CjOd QNcSvMwtBOCbgSi#ixzz1lyt4AIit.

"Lady Gaga — Speechless Live @ the Monster Ball." YouTube video clip. N.d. Accessed 27 September 2012. http://www.youtube.com/watch?v=Vek6znZEWY4.

"Lady Gaga Thanks All Her Monsters on Facebook!" N.d. Accessed 21 September 2012. http://www.youtube.com/watch?v=Bu7NqI0hP9M&feature=plcp.

"Lady Gaga — Transmission Gaga-vision: Episode 1." YouTube video clip. Accessed 21 September 2012. http://www.youtube.com/watch?v=5-cx55NpKu4.

"Lady Gaga — Transmission Gaga-vision: Episode 7." YouTube video clip. Accessed 21 September 2012. http://www.youtube.com/watch?v=yjsltK0TK-E&feature=plcp.

"Lady Gaga — Transmission Gaga-vision: Episode 8." YouTube video clip. N.d. Accessed 21 September 2012. http://www.youtube.com/watch?v=ow3lC0z3ECA&feature=plcp.

"Lady Gaga — Transmission Gaga-vision: Episode 9." YouTube video clip. N.d.Accessed 21 September 2012. http://www.youtube.com/watch?v=ToRuQ065k7s&feature=plcp.

"Lady Gaga — Transmission Gaga-vioson: Episode 14." YouTube video clip. N.d. Accessed 21 September 2012. http://www.youtube.com/watch?v=pukI6s7TmrQ&feature=plcp.

"Lady Gaga — Transmission Gaga-vision: Episode 36." YouTube video clip. N.d. Accessed 14 September 2012. http://www.youtube.com/watch?v=sZ2nfhD4azE.

"Lady Gaga Wins Lawsuit Against Animated Lady Goo Goo." *International Business Times Regional Business News*, 16 October 2011, EBSCO host. Accessed 6 May 2012.

Lauper, Cyndi. "Artists: Lady Gaga." *Time Magazine*. May 10, 2010.

Leeds, Jeff. "The New Deal: Band as Brand." *New York Times*, 11 November 2007. Accessed 7 May 2012. http://www.nytimes.com/2007/11/11/arts/music/11leed.html?pagewanted=all.

Leo, Jessica, Anna Vlach, and Helene Sobolewski. "Gaga's Gross Birthday Wish." *The Advertiser*, 1 April 2010.

Lester, Paul. *Looking for Fame: The Life of a Pop Princess, Lady Gaga*. New York: Omnibus Press, 2010.

Levy, Steven, Brad Stone, N'Gai Croal, Jennifer Tanaka, Arian Campo-Flores, Jamie Reno, Andrew Murr, and Pat Wingert. "The Noisy War Over Napster." *Newsweek* 35, no. 23 (2000).

"List: Top Illegal Downloads." *Sydney Morning Herald*, 6 March 2011. Accessed 17 May 2012. http://www.smh.com.au/technology/technology-news/list-the-top-illegal-downloads-20110306-1bj85.html.

"Looking Meatier! Lady Gaga Shows Off Her New Fuller Figure After 'Gaining 30lbs' in Her Favourite Carnivorous Creation." *Daily Mail Online*, 19 September 2012. Accessed 27 September 2012. http://www.dailymail.co.uk/tvshowbiz/article-2205629/Lady-Gaga-shows-new-fuller-figure-gaining-30lbs-favourite-carnivorous-creation.html?videoPlayer URL=http%3A%2F%2Fc.brightcove.com%2Fservices%2Fviewer%2Ffederated_f9%3FisVid%3D1%26isUI%3D1%26publisherID%3D1418450360%26playerID %3D72484359001%26domain%3Dembed%26videoId%3D&hasBCVideo=true &BCVideoID=1848469503001.

Lush, Rebecca. "The Appropriation of the Madonna Aesthetic." In *The Performance Identities of Lady Gaga: Critical Essays*, ed. Richard J. Gray II (Jefferson, NC: McFarland, 2011).

Markar, Sheila. "Lady Gaga as Jo Calderone: Brilliant or Creepy?" ABC News, 29 August 2011. Accessed 21 October 2011. http://abcnews.go.com/Entertainment/lady-gaga-jo-calderone-mtv-vmas-brilliant-creepy/story?id=14405227.

Marks, Craig. "The Billboard Q&A." *Billboard*, 27 February 2010.

Marshall, P. David. *Celebrity and Power: Fame in Contemporary Culture*. Minneapolis: University of Minnesota Press.

Martinez, Jose. "Lady Gaga in Trademark Suit Over Company's 'Lady Gaga for Design' Product Line." NYDailyNews.com, 11 September 2011. Accessed 7 May 2012. http://articles.nydailynews.com/2011-09-29/gossip/30240061_1_stefani-germanotta-poker-face-singer-lady-gaga.

Masnick, Mike. "For Lady Gaga, Copyright Not About Music, but Her Image." Techdirt.com, 9 March 2011. Accessed 17 May 2012. http://www.techdirt.com/articles/20110308/142344 13404/lady-gaga-copyright-not-about-music-her-image.shtml.

Mazzarella, Sharon, and Timothy Matyjewicz. "'The Day the Music Died' — Again: Newspaper Coverage of the Deaths of Popular Musicians." In *Pop Music and the Press*, ed. Steve Jones. Philadelphia: Temple University Press, 2002.

Merrin, William. "Crash, Bang, Wallop! What a Picture! The Death of Diana and the Media." *Mortality* 4, no. 1 (1999).

Michelson, Noah. "Lady Gaga Discusses Activism, Outing and Reading Her Male Alter Ego, Jo Calderone, as a Transgender Man." *Huffington Post*, 3 October 2011. Accessed 3 October 2011. http://www.huffingtonpost.com/2011/09/23/lady-gaga-jo-calderone-transgender_n_978063.html.

Mitchell, John. "Madonna Targets Lady Gaga with 'Express Yourself' and 'Born This Way' Mashup." MTV.com, 29 May 2012. Accessed 6 August 2012. http://www.mtv.com/news/articles/1685970/madonna-lady-gaga-mash-up.jhtml.

Moran, Caitlin. "Come Party with Lady Gaga." *The Times Online*, 23 May 2010.

_____. "My Night with Lady Gaga." *Times UK*, 22 May 2010. http://entertainment.times online.co.uk/tol/arts_and_entertainment/music/article7129672.ece.

Murfett, Andrew. "Lady Gaga." *Sydney Morning Herald*, 15 May 2009. Accessed 18 June 2012. http://www.smh.com.au/news/entertainment/music/gig-reviews/art-of-ambition/2009/05/14/1241894102332.html.

"Musicians@Google Interview." YouTube video clip. N.d. Accessed 30 September 2012. http://www.youtube.com/watch?v=hNa_-1d_0tA.

Naughton, Julie, and Pete Born. "Lady Gaga on What Drives Her." *Women's Wear Daily*, 18 February 2011. Accessed 25 June 2012. http://www.wwd.com/eye/people/lady-gaga-on-what-drives-her-3504137.

O'Brien, Jennifer. "Gaga's Oxegasmic; Cheeky Performance Has Lady's Fans Panting for More." *The Sun*, 12 July 2009.

O'Connor, Maureen. "An Annotated History of Lindsay Lohan Nudity." *Gawker*, 12 December 2011. Accessed 27 August 2012. http://gawker.com/5867141/an-annotated-history-of-lindsay-lohan-nudity.

Odell, Amy. "Lady Gaga Seems to Be Taking Her Jo Calderone Alter Ego Pretty Seriously." *New York Magazine*, 25 August 2010. Accessed 12 October 2011. http://nymag.com/daily/fashion/2010/08/lady_gaga_seems_to_be_taking_h.html.

Office Depot. Accessed 26 August 2012. http://www.officedepot.com/specialLinks.do?file=/promo/pages/0710_btw.jsp&template=blank&cm_re=Home-_-Spot9-_-W32BTWFMINI.

1-800-LAW-FIRM. "1-800-LAW-FIRM Announces Class Action Lawsuit Against Lady Gaga." *Business Wire (English) Regional Business News*, EBSCO host, 24 June 2011. Accessed 6 May 2012.

Palmer, Bill. "Lady Gaga: The iProng Interview." *iProng*, 5 January 2009.

Pastorek, Whitney. "Lady Gaga: Bonus Quotes from the Dance-Pop Queen!" *Entertainment Weekly*, 9 February 2009. Accessed 9 November 2010. http://popwatch.ew.com/2009/02/09/lady-gaga-inter/.

Phoenix, Helia. *Just Dance: Lady Gaga*. London: Orion Paperbacks, 2010.

Pickard, Anna. "Lady Gaga — Paparazzi." *The Guardian*, 4 June 2009. http://www.guardian.co.uk/music/2009/jun/04/lady-gaga-paparazzi-video.

Polaroid Press. "Polaroid and Lady Gaga Announce Grey Label." Polaroid.com, 6 January 2011. Accessed 24 August 2012. http://polaroid.com/en/press/2011/1/6/polaroid-and-lady-gaga-announce-grey-label.

Pollack, Neal. "How Lady Gaga's Manager Reinvented the Celebrity Game with Social Media." Wired.co.UK, 21 May 2012. Accessed 10 September 2012. http://www.wired.co.uk/magazine/archive/2012/06/features/troy-carter?page=2.

Poole, Scott. *Monsters in America: Our Historical Obsession with the Hideous and the Haunting*. Waco, TX: Baylor University Press, 2011.

Powdermaker, Hortense. *Hollywood: The Dream Factory*. Boston: Little, Brown, 1950.

Powers, Ann. "Lady Gaga: 'I Find That Men Get Away with Saying a Lot in This Business, and That Women Get Away with Saying Very Little.'" *Los Angeles Times*, 10 December 2009. Accessed 20 October 2011. http://latimesblogs.latimes.com/music_blog/2009/12/lady-gaga-i-find-that-men-get-away-with-saying-a-lot-in-this-business-and-that-women-get-away-with-s.html.

_____. "When Rock Stars Fake It." *Los Angeles Times*, 12 July 2009. Accessed 13 June 2012. http://articles.latimes.com/2009/jul/12/entertainment/ca-poptheatricality12.

Prosser, Jay. *Second Skins: The Body Narrative of Transexuality*. New York: Columbia University Press, 1998.

Rawlinson, Linnie, and Nick Hunt. "Jackson Dies, Almost Takes Internet with Him." CNN.com, 26 June 2009. Accessed 20 June 2012. http://www.cnn.com/2009/TECH/06/26/michael.jackson.internet/index.html.

Richardson, Terry, and Lady Gaga. *Lady Gaga*. New York: Grand Central Publishing, 2011.

Robinson, Lisa. "In Gaga's Wake." *Vanity Fair*, January 2012.
_____. "Lady Gaga's Culture Revolution." *Vanity Fair*, September 2010.
Robinson, Peter. "Freak or Fraud?" *NME*, 23 April 2011.
Rose, Lisa. "Lady Gaga's Outrageous Persona Born in Parsippany, New Jersey." *Star-Ledger*, 21 January 2010. Accessed 17 July 2012. http://www.nj.com/entertainment/music/index. ssf/2010/01/lady_gaga_her_outrageous_perso.html.
Rose, Tom. "The Fat Lady Gaga Sings." *The Examiner*, 19 September 2012. Accessed 27 September 2012. http://www.examiner.com/article/the-fat-lady-gaga-sings.
Rubin, Julia. "Lady Gaga Sues Excite Worldwide Over Trademark Application." Styleite.com, 29 September 2011. Accessed 7 May 2011. http://www.styleite.com/media/lady-gaga-excite-worldwide/.
Sacks, Ethan. "Elton John Rekindles Feud with Madonna After Her Lady Gaga Slam." *New York Daily News*, 6 August 2012. http://www.nydailynews.com/entertainment/gossip/elton-john-rekindles-duel-madonna-lady-gaga-slam-article-1.1129986.
Scaggs, Austin. "Lady Gaga." *Rolling Stone*, no. 1072 (19 February 2009).
Schmitt, David P. "Sexual Modularity in Sex, Gender, and Orientation." *Psychology Today*, 15 September 2011. Accessed 12 October 2011. http://www.psychologytoday.com/blog/sexual-personalities/201109/sexual-modularity-in-sex-gender-and-orientation.
60 Minutes (television program), 13 February 2011. Produced by Tom Anderson, Andy Court, Harry A. Radcliffe II, Jeff Newton, and Amjad Tadros.
Sloop, John M. *Disciplining Gender*. Amherst: University of Massachusetts Press, 2004.
Smart, Gordon. "Lady Gaga Is Tea Potty." *The Sun*, 20 April 2009. http://www.thesun.co.uk/sol/homepage/showbiz/bizarre/article2384472.ece.
Smillie, Dirk. "The Business of Lady Gaga." Forbes.com., 25 November 2009. http://www.forbes.com/2009/11/25/lady-gaga-music-business-entertainment-marketing.html.
Spines, Christine. "Lady Gaga Wants You." *Cosmopolitan*, April 2010.
Spitz, David, and Starling Hunter. "Contested Codes: The Social Construction of Napster." *Information Society* 21.
"Star Families Are Just Like Us!" *Us Magazine Online*, 11 May 2012. Accessed 13 September 2012. http://www.usmagazine.com/celebrity-news/pictures/star-families-are-just-like-us-2012115.
Stein, Joshua David, and Noah Michelson. "The Lady Is a Vamp." *Out Magazine*, September 2009.
Stone, Andrew C. "Our Lady of Pop." *Jezebel*, July 2011.
Strauss, Neil. "The Broken Heart and Violent Fantasies of Lady Gaga." *Rolling Stone*, issue 1108 (8 July 2010).
Striphas, Ted. "Harry Potter and the Simulacrum: Contested Copies in an Age of Intellectual Property." *Critical Studies in Media Communication* 26, no. 4 (October 2009).
Switaj, Elizabeth Kate. "Lady Gaga's Bodies: Buying and Selling *The Fame Monster*." In *The Performance Identities of Lady Gaga: Critical Essays*, ed. Richard J. Gray II. Jefferson, NC: McFarland, 2011.
Thomas, Matt. "Going Gaga." *Fab Magazine*, 24 December 2008. Accessed 15 December 2011. http://www.fabmagazine.com/features/362/Gaga.html.
TMZ. "Paris Hilton Mug Shot—So Pretty." 28 August 2010. Accessed 27 August 2012. http://www.tmz.com/2010/08/28/paris-hilton-mug-shot-arrested-cocaine-photo/.
Torrusio, Ann T. "The Fame Monster: The Monstrous Construction of Lady Gaga." In *The Performance Identities of Lady Gaga: Critical Essays*, ed. Richard J. Gray II. Jefferson, NC: McFarland, 2011.
Turner, Graeme. *Understanding Celebrity*. Thousand Oaks, CA: Sage Publications, 2009.
20/20 (television program), 22 January 2010. Burbank, CA: American Broadcasting Company. Produced by David Sloan, Rudy Bednar, and Howie Masters.
Van Meer, Jonathan. "Our Lady of Pop." *Vogue*, March 2011.
Van Meter, William. "Bold Crossings of the Gender Line." *New York Times*, 9 December 2010.
Vena, Jocelyn. "Lady Gaga Shoots Back at PETA After 'Turncoat' Accusation." *MTV News*, 14 August 2012. Accessed 19 August 2012. http://www.mtv.com/news/articles/1691715/lady-gaga-peta-turncoat-accusation.jhtml.

_____. "Lady Gaga's 'Yoü And I' Personas: Who Are Yuyi and Jo Calderone?" *MTV News*, 18 August 2011. Accessed 5 May 5 2012. http://www.mtv.com/news/articles/1669240/lady-gaga-you-and-i-yuyi-jo-calderone.jhtml.

Voss, Brandon. "'Just Dance' Singer Lady Gaga Gives Back to the Gays." *HX Magazine*, 8 August 2008. Accessed 16 December 2011. http://ladygaga.wikia.com/wiki/HX_%28magazine%29.

Vozick-Levinson. "Lady Gaga's Fame Bites Her Back." *Entertainment Weekly*, no. 1096 (2 April 2010). MasterFILE Premier, EBSCO host. Accessed 6 May 2012.

Waisanen, Don. "A Citizen's Guide to Democracy Inaction: Jon Stewart's and Stephen Colbert's Comic Rhetorical Criticism." *Southern Communication Journal* 74, no. 2 (2009).

Warner, Kara. "Lady Gaga Captures 'True Spirit' of 'Yoü and I' in Video." MTV.com, 18 August 2011. Accessed 12 October 2011. http://www.mtv.com/news/articles/1669342/lady-gaga-you-and-i-music-video.jhtml.

Weiner, Jonah. "Bare Naked Lady." *Maxim Magazine*, July 2009.

Werde, Bill. "Editor's Note: Why Billboard Isn't Revising Chart Policies for Lady Gaga's Amazon Deal." *Billboard*, 26 May 2011. Accessed 17 July 2012. http://www.billboard.biz/bb biz/industry/retail/why-billboard-isn-t-revising-chart-policies-1005205422.story.

Wheatley, Gemma. "Lady G Raises Fashion Steaks." *Daily Star*, 9 September 2010.

Wilson, Beth. "Going Gaga." *Women's Wear Daily*, 13 August 2007.

Zhang, Michael. "This Is Lady Gaga's Photo Release Form." PetaPixel.com, 12 February 2012. Accessed 17 May 2012. http://www.petapixel.com/2012/02/01/this-is-lady-gagas-photo-release-form/.

Index